Guidelines for College Teaching of Music Theory

Second Edition

John D. White

With an additional chapter
by William E. Lake

The Scarecrow Press, Inc.
Lanham, Maryland, and London
2002

SCARECROW PRESS, INC.

Published in the United States of America
by Scarecrow Press, Inc.
4720 Boston Way, Lanham, Maryland 20706
www.scarecrowpress.com

4 Pleydell Gardens, Folkestone
Kent CT20 2DN, England

British Library Cataloguing-in-Publication Information Available

Library of Congress Cataloging-in-Publication Data

White, John David, 1931–
    Guidelines for college teaching of music theory / John D. White ; with an additional chapter by William E. Lake.—2nd ed.
        p.   cm.
    Includes bibliographical references (p.   ) and index.
    ISBN 0-8108-4129-0 (alk. paper)
    1. Music—instruction and study.   I. Lake, William.   II. Title.
MT1 .W448 2002
781'071'1—dc21   2001049046

∞ ™ The paper used in this publication meets the minimum requirements of American National Standard for Information Sciences—Permanence of Paper for Printed Library Materials, ANSI/NISO Z39.48-1992. Manufactured in the United States of America.

CONTENTS

PREFACE TO THE
FIRST EDITION (1981)

The teaching of music theory has experienced a metamorphosis during the past twenty-five years as the world of college music has become increasingly cognizant that freshman and sophomore theory courses are concerned not only with theoretical concepts but in large part with musical craft. The rethinking of old methods has generated an integrative approach to musicianship; and the belief has been reaffirmed that the theory teacher bears a prime responsibility for the imparting of musicianship skills to freshman and sophomore music majors. My subject, then, is the learning and teaching of musical craft and theoretical concepts in the lower-division theory courses. The increasing concern of music faculties and administrators with teaching quality has been paralleled by growing attention to teaching and learning in the arts and sciences manifest by much written and spoken controversy on college-level teaching in general. Graduate courses in college teaching have sprung up in all disciplines; and graduate courses in the pedagogy of theory have become increasingly popular.

This book, in part the result of these trends, is intended to serve as a text for pedagogy of theory courses and as a handbook for teachers of music theory. The book contains some art, some science, and some folklore; but it is based primarily on my experience over twenty-five years of teaching in a variety of settings ranging from small liberal arts colleges and developing state institutions to established comprehensive universities. The many music students of varying talents with whom I have worked over the years helped by their example to demonstrate how musicians learn their art. And along with this broad perspective came the benefit of having worked with a number of fine theory-teaching colleagues of unique musical and pedagogical skills. Thus, to a large extent the book reflects current theory-teaching practices in the United States, but I have also discussed more idealistic models.

In these days when theorists are becoming increasingly occupied with research it is not unusual to find performers teaching freshman and sophomore theory, particularly in smaller music departments. These early theory courses do in fact deal with those aspects of musical craft that are in the domain of all thoroughly accomplished musicians. Composers of course have always distinguished themselves as teachers of theory; and every theory teacher should have compositional skill. But the performer's musical perspectives are also essential to a complete musical craft. Perhaps the ideal theory teacher is a unique combination of theorist, composer, performer, and historian; for the integration of these musical disciplines is a major objective of the lower-division theory courses.

This may suggest that I am a proponent of the "comprehensive musicianship" approach that waxed and waned during the decade of the seventies. Indeed I am sympathetic to the integration of music literature, theory, history, and performance that this movement purported to achieve. Its fundamental problem, however, is that it attempted to gather all of these disciplines under one umbrella with theoretical studies at the center. This failed to gain wide acceptance because it tended to erode the identity of the individual disciplines, an identity that is essential to their well-being. The area of music history, for example, thrives on its own integrity and autonomy. Its academic integration preexisted under the aegis of department, school, or college. To integrate it further goes too far in the direction of generalism. The duplication and encroachment that inevitably exists between two such allied areas as music history and theory can result in mutual support and reinforcement without the formal alliance mandated by the comprehensive-musicianship approach.

Although I recognize that no one can learn to teach solely from a book, it is my hope that theory teachers will find this volume useful in developing their own unique teaching styles and that graduate students will also profit from it. Little attempt has been made to prescribe the content or sequence of material in the lower-division theory courses. Those who read this book will have their own ideas on that subject, which in any case will vary from one teaching situation to another depending upon the goals of the students, the objectives of the faculty, and the nature of the school. I have of course used specific concepts and skills to demonstrate approaches to teaching;

but where I have discussed course content I have tried to select what appear to be universally accepted elements of our craft.

If there is one historical model for my teaching, it is that of Socrates. Then, too, the writings of Jean Piaget and his interpreters have been useful in the articulation of a teaching philosophy, and Piagetian theories of learning are often compatible with the writings of Plato. If I have presented anything that is new, I have also drawn abundantly on a treasury of human experience that extends deeply into our past.

J.D.W.
University of Florida, 1980

PREFACE TO THE
SECOND EDITION (2001)

Much water has passed under the bridge since the first edition of *Guidelines* came out in 1981. For one thing, music theorists of the late twentieth century began to devote substantially more attention to the nature and quality of the teaching of music theory. Some manifestations of this were the establishment in 1987 of the *Journal of Music Theory Pedagogy* and the fact that the Society for Music Theory began the practice of including a session on music theory pedagogy at its annual conferences. But there have been other substantive changes as well, and among these is the movement to transcend the canon of Western music, to include musics of other cultures as well as popular or vernacular musics in the study of our art in colleges and universities. In the music theory classroom this has resulted in some expansion of musical boundaries, yet the art music of Western culture continues to be the mainstay of musical higher learning, and this is as it should be.

Obviously, another major change has been the phenomenal expansion of computer technology, music software, and new electronic technologies for use in the theory classroom. It is for that reason that this second edition includes an additional chapter entitled "Technology for Teaching and Learning" by William E. Lake, a young theorist who is highly knowledgeable in the field. One of the points he makes is that while the new technologies are highly seductive, the substance of music theory remains unchanged. He believes that new technologies can improve the quality of musical learning both inside and outside of the classroom, and he presents much good advice as to how to bring this to full realization. One of his caveats, however, is "Don't embrace technology for its own sake." Elsewhere he says, "Technology is merely a tool, not an end in itself." Thus, while musicians of all kinds have been deeply affected by new technologies, music is still music and it is still created, played and sung by live human beings, even when assisted by computers.

Writing about music in this new century tempts one to take a retrospective look at the twentieth century when so many distinguished musicians and scholars excelled in the creation, performance, and teaching of our art. Thus, there is more history of music theory in this new edition than in the old. While writing this book I was asked to contribute a chapter to a volume of essays entitled *Reflections on American Music: The Twentieth Century and the New Millennium* sponsored by the College Music Society (Pendragon Press, 2000). That chapter, entitled "Music Theory and Pedagogy Before and After the Millennium," led me to speculate upon both the past and the future of music theory, and I have drawn upon some of that reflection in this volume.

As an academic who has lived through and experienced some of the most turbulent times in the history of American higher learning, I felt it important for me to report upon the striking changes in colleges and universities during the late twentieth century, for my association with higher learning began in 1949 and has not yet ended. These sections, "The Evolving Academy" and "Evaluating Faculty," are found at the beginning of chapter 8, in which I make some emphatic value judgments about the current state of American higher learning, of student–faculty relations, grade inflation, and the use of student–faculty evaluations—all of which are interrelated. I thought long and hard about this section and decided that it would be irresponsible of me to avoid these issues. Since these comments may be controversial, I trust that they will be received in the spirit in which they are offered—to benefit higher learning in our country.

I hope that this volume will serve a useful purpose in the world of musical higher learning.

John D. White
Evergreen, Colorado

ONE

Perspective

The teacher of music theory must recognize that for musicians of any kind the single all-important activity is music making. Serious music students, whether they are children or college-level music majors, are eternally excited with the idea of performance. Among performance majors, this may be seen as a striving to achieve excellence upon their instruments or voices. Beginning composers with interests in improvisation or new performance modes will wish to hear and perform that which they have created. And for budding musicologists or theorists the hearing or playing of music from various origins is essential to their understanding of structural or historical concepts.

This fascination with the live sounds of music is generated by the overriding desire of musicians to hear music, to write music, and most of all to play music. While this is made apparent in our college and university music departments by an abundance of performing ensembles, faculties of which the majority are performance teachers, and heavy performance requirements for music majors, it should be manifest also in the nature and quality of the music theory courses.

RELEVANCE

The lower-division theory courses should be meaningful to all music majors, regardless of their areas of concentration. Whether preparing to be a performer, a composer, a conductor, a musicologist, a theorist, a music educator, or a music therapist, the student must acquire the skills offered in the lower-division theory courses. Often described as musicianship skills, they fall traditionally into a

1

handful of categories: sight-singing, ear-training, keyboard harmony, part writing (or some elementary form of composition), and
music structure or analysis. It is the task of the teacher of music theory to impart effectively the skills and concepts of these areas with
appropriate materials in ways that clarify their relevance to performance and the literature of music, to teach theory in such a way
as to demonstrate, as George Santayana put it, that "music is a playing upon instruments, not a discussion of them." It was not always
so. The American theory course of fifty years ago dealt primarily
with homophonic chord progressions, which the student learned to
write in a manner that ignored historical styles, usually in four parts
with little attention to voice-leading. Sight-singing (or solfeggio)
was often taught separately using a movable do system, and ear-
training and keyboard, as such, often were not taught at all.

Ultimately the degree of musical relevance that the teacher can
bring to the theory course may depend in large part upon one's own
innate musicality. This does not mean that any fine musician can be
a fine theory teacher, nor does it mean that a good theory teacher
must be a currently active performer or composer (though this can
help). But theory teachers should be able to think like composers,
and skillful music making should be a demonstrably meaningful
aspect of their lives whether or not they are currently active makers
of music. Let us now briefly consider the history of music theory
pedagogy in the United States.

LOOKING BACK

From our perspective in the new millennium it is easy to see a number of trends in music theory teaching in the past century. When I
graduated from high school in 1949, my mentor, a fine pianist–
composer named Orvis Ross, inscribed to me a copy of Goetschius's
The Structure of Music (Theodore Presser, 1934), a book that I still
pick up occasionally—mildewed and worn though it is. Although
Percy Goetschius (1853–1943) represented the most conservative
ideas of American music theory of the early twentieth century, he
was, nevertheless, the only well-known American music theorist of
his generation. That was partly because music theory as a scholarly
discipline did not establish itself in the United States until much
later. Early twentieth-century college music majors studied "har-

mony" and "keyboard harmony" rather than theory; and sight-singing was taught as a separate course called "solfeggio." The systematic teaching of musical analysis was also very rare, even though the books of Donald Francis Tovey were becoming known and respected in the United States. The typical college-level course that pretended to address musical analysis was concerned primarily with preexisting "forms" of music, rather than true analysis—hence the typical course title "Form and Analysis." Unfortunately, at the turn of the millennium, this situation is only slightly improved.

Amazingly, Alfred Mann's translation of the *Gradus ad Parnassum* of Fux (Norton, 1943) was the very first English translation of this treatise of 1725, the out-of-print English version of 1886 having been no more than a paraphrase. That a musicologist rather than a theorist was the translator of this major theoretical work was a symptom of the time; for as recently as the mid-twentieth century, music theory was still a branch of musicology. It was not until the late fifties that music theory began to emerge as a scholarly discipline of its own and this was manifest two decades later by the founding of the Society for Music Theory (SMT) in 1978. A year later *Music Theory Spectrum* was established as the official organ of the SMT, a journal religiously devoted to research in the scholarly areas of music theory. Of course, the *Journal of Music Theory* had been going since the fifties as a publication of Yale University, but its primary focus was and still is the history of music theory—concentrating on discussions and translations of theoretical treatises and other aspects of music theory bordering upon musicology. Even more exclusively devoted to the history of music theory is the journal *Theoria* founded during the eighties at North Texas State University. Today these are the major American journals for publication of research in the field of music theory. There are, of course, several other good theoretical journals published elsewhere, especially in the United Kingdom.

The establishment of SMT, however, was a major step toward the recognition of music theory as a separate discipline of scholarly study and research rather than just a portmanteau for the teaching of musicianship skills. Its founders were so conscious of this that pedagogy of music theory began to take a back seat to rigorous theoretical study. SMT conferences generally included a session on music theory pedagogy—until very recently just a gesture, however, for it was clear that the organization's primary subjects for inquiry were the history of theory and music analysis. The predictable backlash resulted in the *Journal of Music Theory Pedagogy* founded in 1987 at the University of Oklahoma. I served on the editorial board of this journal for a number of years.

But getting back to Goetschius, he wrote more than a dozen textbooks and numerous articles on various aspects of music theory and composition, based for the most part upon precepts derived from the works of the classical and romantic symphonists, and he is remembered by a full-column entry in the 1958 edition of *Baker's Biographical Dictionary of Musicians*. The most nearly "modern" composers whom he considered were Ernest Chausson (1855–1899) and Vincent d'Indy (1851–1931). Thus, it was clear that the works of Stravinsky, Bartók, *Les Six*, and the Second Viennese School—all contemporaries of his, whose music he could not have avoided hearing—had made no impression whatsoever upon the theoretical perspective reflected in his writings.

Goetschius strove to circumscribe and classify musical phenomena, perhaps a necessary activity for a theorist; but when too strictly applied, it is an attribute that can lead to canonic narrowness and pointless constraint. He was not above describing "the correct way" to use a particular harmony, and it was he who gave us "the three forms of the rondo," so understandably confusing to young musicians who often see that some wonderful rondos will not fall unequivocally into one or another category. He considered the full diminished seventh to be "the most wonderful chord in music" and viewed it as "the incomplete form of the dominant-ninth."

The latter idea was developed by Walter Piston (1894–1976) in his *Harmony* (Norton, 1941), an undergraduate theory textbook widely used in subsequent editions as recent as the last two decades of the previous century. Indeed, the Piston book was our theory text of choice at the University of Michigan in Ann Arbor when I taught there in the sixties. At that time my colleagues in the theory department included Wallace Berry and Paul Cooper, both of whom made significant later contributions to the literature of music theory. There was controversy over the Piston *Harmony*, engendered perhaps by the fact that the chairman of the Theory Department at that time was John Lowell, an Eastman-trained theorist who championed the theory textbooks of Allen Irvine McHose, particularly *The Contrapuntal-Harmonic Technique of the Eighteenth Century* (Appleton-Century-Crofts, 1947). (The long title was often abbreviated as *C.H.T.*)

The chief difference between the two books is the terminology for certain dominant-quality altered chords. Piston had coined the terms "secondary dominant" and "secondary dominant seventh" to describe chords such as a V^7 of V (or V^7/V), while McHose would have described the same sonority as a $II^7\sharp4$, seemingly, but not actually, ignoring the temporary tonicization of the fifth scale degree. The $\sharp4$ referred to the raised fourth scale degree such as F-sharp in the key of C major. Both methods sought to explain foreign tones in nonmodulatory passages, but Piston's secondary dominant concept seemed also to point out the phenomenon of temporary tonicization without modulation. This terminology was extended to include secondary VIIs or VII^7s, which also temporarily tonicized a scale degree other than the tonic.

The whole concept can be carried too far. To use structuralist terminology, the *transformation* of the dominant-tonic relationship (or the VII-tonic concept) to another scale degree works fine, but then to use that newly tonicized scale degree as a second point of departure for another transformation—that borders on the absurd. At that point, one should probably recognize a modulation; for descriptions such as V of IV of VI almost always lack validity. The chances are that if the passage began in C major, a brief or transitory modulation to A minor or D minor has taken place and should be recognized by the analyst.

I was thoroughly familiar with McHose's approach because it was my theory textbook when I was an undergraduate at the University of Minnesota where we called it "The Green Bible." My theory teachers there had been Earl George and Paul Fetler, but later I studied with McHose at Eastman, and he had been on the dissertation committee for my Ph.D., which I completed at the University of Rochester in 1960. I had also used the *C.H.T.* in my first college job at Kent State University in the fifties. Nevertheless, I found it easy to transfer my allegiance to Piston, partly because at that time I was a lowly assistant professor at Ann Arbor, but also because I was easily persuaded that the secondary dominant concept was preferable. By the decade of the seventies Piston's *Harmony* had almost universally superseded McHose's *C.H.T.*

Another reason why the Piston *Harmony* gradually eclipsed McHose's *C.H.T.* was that Piston drew on literature of all periods and all styles, while McHose's approach to part-writing was to use the Bach chorales as models. It is not true, however, that McHose presented no music other than the Bach chorales in his *C.H.T,* for he included many Renaissance and seventeenth-century examples to show the evolution of part-writing up to the time of Bach, and there are also examples from composers such as Mozart and Haydn. In this sense he was a kind of theoretical historian. There was also the ugly rumor that McHose used a statistical approach such as saying that the VII triad was in first inversion 98 percent of the time and that its third was doubled in 95 percent of its usages in the Bach chorales. Not so—he might argue that such a usage was "usual" or another was "frequent" or "rare;" and he would point out that "the majority of neighboring tones in combination with passing tones originate in the tonic harmony" or that "on the whole, the rare altered non-harmonic tones are found as chromatic passing tones." While he did begin adult life as a scientist—his early preparation was for a career as a chemist—his approach to music theory was intensely musical.[1]

Notwithstanding this controversy, it is interesting to note that the actual student part-writing exercises were pretty much the same regardless of which textbook was being used. They still are, for in spite of all the noise about transcending the canon and reaching beyond the so-called common practice period, four-part writing in eighteenth-century style persists as the sine qua non of part-writing in present-day freshman and sophomore theory courses. Of course, progressive theory teachers now introduce much more contemporary music and music of other cultures than in the past; and new technologies have changed the outward appearance of the theory classroom. Yet the primary objectives of skills in sight-singing, part-writing, analysis, and keyboard remain substantially unchanged. Indeed, upon examining a more recent textbook entitled *Harmony in Tonal Music* by Joel Lester (Knopf, 1982), I find virtually nothing of musical essence that is new, although the teaching approach is well organized and logical. I'm sure the author would agree, for what could be new in a book with such a title, since tonal harmony remains unchanged?

Lester uses Schenkerian graphs to explain harmonic background, and that is not a bad idea, although many theory teachers have found other paths to the same objective. He also presents many musical examples, all from the canon of Western music literature and all from the eighteenth and nineteenth centuries. Thus, since the literature of Western music remains the primary basis for the study of music theory, the tonal prototype of the freshman and sophomore theory courses endures as well.

Some late twentieth-century theory teachers strove to reach beyond the canon of Western tonal music—especially to transcend the so-called common practice period. Songs of Billy Joel, the Beatles, Simon and Garfunkel, The Carpenters, and so forth, along with occasional examples of extracultural musics began to creep into theory classrooms and even into textbooks, but only as gravy. That is, Palestrina, DiLasso, Bach, Mozart, Beethoven, Berlioz, Debussy, Ravel, Stravinsky, and others continued to be the meat and potatoes. My main reservation about bringing rock, pop, and world musics into the theory classroom is not one of quality; although I must say that I generally agree with the late Barney Childs who was "dismayed by . . . the flatulent tedium of rock music."[2] We all listen to some of this music, and pollution is not the main problem. Rather, I feel that it tends to dilute or water down the course content, so that there is not as much time and space left for the real core of Western music literature. Because we live in the Western world, its cultural heritage should be the first and foremost basis for our higher learning.

Many fine performers of the past century did not formally study harmony and solfeggio but acquired the necessary musical perceptions and skills through their musical experiences or perhaps in part from their performance teachers. The young performers of that day may have been none the worse for having acquired their musicianship skills through a kind of osmotic process, but surely many could have learned in a more effective manner. Today our schools of music advocate a more organized approach to musicianship learning manifesting the belief that theory or musicianship can be taught in such a way as to relate its course content to performance and to integrate it with the materials of music literature and history.

THE CURRICULUM

Ideally the lower-division (freshman and sophomore) theory courses should provide students with (1) the basic analytical and conceptual understanding required for future musical studies in music history, musical analysis, music education, or performance; (2) the sight-reading and aural skills necessary to conducting, teaching, performance, and composition (above all the ability to approach intelligently an unfamiliar score and to derive mentally a reasonably accurate idea of its contents); (3) the basic harmonic improvisational skills for development in such areas as jazz performance, continuo realization, music education, or theory teaching; and (4) the requisite compositional and calligraphic skills for the study of arranging, orchestration, and composition.

From the practical standpoint these four areas of musicianship learning can be reduced to

- musical concepts and analysis
- sight-singing and ear-training
- keyboard
- writing skills (part-writing, counterpoint, or elementary composition).

Curricular plans vary as to the degree of integration among these. The first and fourth areas are often linked because it is most appropriate to teach writing skills from the precepts found in actual musical examples. Keyboard is often taught separately, sometimes by a member of the piano faculty rather than a theorist; and sight-singing and ear-training may also be isolated. Regardless of the curricular plan it is generally agreed that the ideal is to achieve a high degree of integration among all four areas in order that they may be as mutually supportive as possible. For this reason, a popular curricular plan is to have them all taught in a single class by one instructor. In this way the students' theoretical understanding of a musical example from the literature may parallel their ability to (1) take it (or similar passages) down in harmonic or melodic dictation, (2) write similar passages of their own creation, and (3) perform keyboard improvisations of passages similar to those used in the example. To a limited degree it is sometimes even possible to practice sight-singing from a musical example under discussion, although the systematic practice of sight-singing requires a collection of appropriately selected materials. There are, in any case, other ways to integrate sight-singing with the conceptual aspects of analysis and writing. These are discussed later.

The student who can improvise and compose a harmonic phrase using a secondary VII^7 or an augmented sixth chord is better equipped to handle those sonorities in ear-training than the student who cannot do so. Similarly, the ability to write them, sing them, identify them by ear, or improvise them enhances a student's ability to discover them and to perceive their meaning when they are encountered in examples from the literature. The relevance of this approach to actual performance is readily apparent; and it would seem that it is best realized in an integrated one-class/one-teacher situation.

A potential drawback to the integration of musical skills by a single instructor is that faculty will inevitably vary in their perceptions, emphases, musicianship skills, and ability to integrate and communicate. In itself, this is good; for students will profit from exposure to a diversity of approaches. Yet even though emphases will vary, it is important that all areas be covered adequately and appropriately. For example, in studying the *Third Brandenburg Concerto* one instructor may be preoccupied with its motivic structure; another may be most interested in its harmonic rhythm and other features perceived through a Schenkerian approach; while a third may emphasize both the motivic and harmonic structures but be incapable of relating them to musical meaning, the performer's task, or the history of music.

From the perspective of basic skills, the instructor who is uncomfortable singing may de-emphasize sight-singing; and the orchestral player with minimally adequate piano ability may neglect keyboard skills. The ideal theory teacher, then, at least for the integrated approach, is a kind of Renaissance person with a balanced perspective—an accomplished and experienced performer who, in addition to being a skillful composer, is comfortable singing and at the keyboard; has a good knowledge of music literature and history; and possesses the communicative skills, perceptivity, and other attributes of a fine teacher.

In the world of music this kind of balanced versatility is not as rare as one might think, but it is nevertheless understandable that some schools of music choose to separate the areas of keyboard, sight-singing, and ear-training from the analytical and written components of lower-division theory in order to staff the various areas with teachers possessing the most appropriate specialized skills. Yet in such a fragmented curriculum there is the danger that there will be little or no coordination, that the instructional areas will go their own ways without adequate communication among the faculty to ensure mutual support. If this pitfall is avoided and integration is achieved, it can be very successful; but this is possible only through close faculty and administrative cooperation.

The theory teacher, whether working in the fragmented curriculum or in the integrated single-class situation, must be fully and constantly aware of the integrative potential of the four areas. Each area is discussed separately in the course of this book, but it will be apparent that one of the chief objectives of the lower-division theory course is to capitalize upon the mutually supportive qualities of aural, keyboard, analytical, and writing skills in order to relate all of them to that which we call musicianship.

THE LEARNING PROCESS

The late Swiss psychologist Jean Piaget (1896–1980), though not an educator in the American sense, wrote much that is applicable to the teaching of music theory.[3] According to Piaget's conception of the learning process, learning in the *strict* sense is defined as modifications of behavior and thought resulting from experience; learning in the *broad* sense is defined as modifications in behavior and thought resulting from experience and a complex process of maturation. Learning in the strict sense is the kind of learning experienced in the theory class, and Piaget divides this kind of learning into two different modes of experience. One is the physical experience (P) and the other is the logico-mathematical experience (LM). Physical learning, or "P learning," constitutes the discovery of the properties and qualities of things.[4] Basic sensual experiences, such as discoveries of taste and color, fall into this category. A musical example of P learning might be the discovery that an oboe has a particular tone quality that is distinguishable from all other instruments. At this level of learning there is no logical reason for the oboe to sound as it does. A reason is irrelevant. It simply is that way, possessing from a philosophical perspective the essence of "oboeness." Children as well as adults are constantly experiencing this kind of learning. The sound of a harmonic interval, such as the major third, is first discovered through P learning. A child learns to identify it simply as a particular kind of physical experience. Because it is a unique experience it can be distinguished from other similar experiences.

On the other hand, the logico-mathematical (LM) experience is the result of the subject's own physical or mental action upon things. It is not passive like P learning. It is the experience of discovering something through motor manipulation, perceptual exploration, or both. David Elkind, interpreting Piaget, says, "It is the abstraction from motor and perceptual actions that is the basis of LM learning."[5] P learning, on the other hand, is an associative process; and the individual will learn through association more and more bits of information. These include the sources of smells, tastes, sounds, and visual images, as well as information that borders on conceptual knowledge.

A young child of one or two, for example, learns her age through P learning. She doesn't really know what it means to be two years old, but she has learned to put up two fingers when asked how old she is. P learning is also utilized when she is taught her date of birth. This means nothing to her as logico-mathematical information—it is purely associative. But it is when she initiates the action of putting these two bits of P information together to discover that she is officially one year older each time she has a birthday that she has experienced LM learning. She has taken perceptual action upon some bits of information and come up with a concept. Inherent in LM learning is the potential for maturation. The nature or process of one's P learning, however, remains essentially unchanged throughout one's life, whereas the inductive and deductive processes of LM learning are constantly expanding. The individual "learns to learn" through the LM experience. To learn to teach oneself is of inestimable value to a musical performer or composer. It is the rapidity, quality, and limitations of the expansion of LM learning that mark an individual's talent or intelligence.

The developmental or maturational qualities of LM learning are manifest primarily in the number of variables an individual can successfully handle. Elkind cites the example of the child who has learned through the LM experience the concepts of "left" and "right." He has a sense of direction in terms of his own body, can correctly point to the left or right upon request and can identify his own right and left hands. However, when an adult stands facing him, he says that the adult's "right" hand is opposite his "right" hand, and the adult's "left" hand is opposite his "left" hand. He has not yet discovered the invertability variable of this concept.[6] From Piaget's approach one can project the notion that invertability becomes a part of the left-right concept only when the child initiates the action to discover it—perhaps by the inductive process of placing himself in the adult's position.[7] It follows that the Piagetian will value the child's left-right concept even before the child understands its invertability.

The Gestalt psychologist, on the other hand, would say that the concept of invertability is inherent in the left-right concept and might judge the child to be wrong in identifying the adult's hands as he did. The Gestalt approach implies an *evaluation*, as opposed to the Piagetian *valuation*. The concept of valuation is discussed later as an important step in the process of teaching music theory.

If in a rudimentary ear-training session the theory teacher presents the aural concept of the major triad simply by playing one in root position, the students are discovering its unique sound through the P experience. Musicians learn a great deal by this method. Indeed, those with the best ears can learn to identify harmonic intervals, chord qualities, and timbres almost entirely by this physical associative process. For others LM learning enters at an early stage to reinforce the learning process with quantitative assessments. Virtually all good student musicians can readily distinguish major and minor triads in much the same way that they would identify apples and oranges—passively, through the physical effect upon their senses. The major triad sounds like a major triad just as the apple looks, tastes, and smells like an apple. Inversions and harmonic intervals can also be identified by the P experience.

Some students, however, when called upon to identify the first inversion of a major triad, will supplement the P experience by taking action upon the triad. One may mentally sing the bass tone and then sing upward, matching the tones that are present to find a minor third above the bass and a perfect fourth above the upper tone of the minor third, thus projecting a preconceived intervallic structure of the first-inversion major triad against the actual tones that are present. Another may imagine the sound to be a V^6 and may mentally resolve the bass tone up a half-step to an imaginary tonic—invoking the diatonic tonal structure. In both cases the student is checking to see if the tones present correspond to a preconceived idea of what a first-inversion major triad is. These inductive processes constitute action taken upon the triad—the LM experience.

Successful theory teachers learn to guide their students toward the appropriate inductive processes. With or without Piaget's theories of learning or Gestalt psychology, teachers develop insights into the learning processes of their students. A major part of the teachers' tasks are to follow the thought processes of their students and to value their levels of conceptual thinking. The term *value* as used here is not intended to convey the idea of softhearted, dewy-eyed sympathy for student shortcomings. While it is a humane process, there is nothing maudlin about it. It is an essential step in the teaching task. Just as the adult when confronting the child with the incipient left-right concept must understand and value that concept in order to find ways to expand it, so the theory teacher, in all aspects of musicianship learning, must understand and value the various conceptual levels of the student in order to expand those concepts. One obvious example of this is the student who can aurally distinguish perfect intervals from imperfect ones, but in ear-training sessions often identifies a perfect fourth as a perfect fifth and vice versa. He has an aural conception of perfect intervals (as an interval class), and the skillful teacher will value this concept, using it as a point of departure for the finer discrimination between perfect fourths and perfect fifths.

In another ear-training situation a student may correctly identify the cadence types in a sonata exposition as authentic, half, or deceptive cadences, but she may miss the fact that they are not all in the same key. The teacher's task is to perceive and value the student's conception of harmonic motion and find ways, perhaps through a Schenkerian approach, for her to hear the underlying harmonic framework with its modulations and to relate it to a central tonality. Similar opportunities for valuation can occur in part-writing and analysis. A student may understand secondary function well enough to be able to identify secondary dominants (V of Vs, etc.) in analysis and be able to part-write them. Valuation of this conceptual level is the first step toward imparting such related concepts as secondary VII⁷s.

A beneficial side effect of the valuation approach is that it tends to preclude the discouraging experience of belittlement. Yet because it is a logical product of the LM learning process it does so without false sympathy and artificial encouragement, which can be equally demeaning. Understanding and encouragement are natural built-in factors of the valuation process, and that is why valuation is an essential component of good theory teaching.

In dealing with the theoretical concepts observed on the pages of musical scores, another facet of Piaget's theories is most useful. This is the concept of structuralism. Applicable to any field of thoughtful endeavor, it is based upon the notion stated by Piaget that any structure must manifest the properties of wholeness, transformation, and self-regulation.[8] A *structure* is all of the things that are interrelated by virtue of their belonging to a single system. This constitutes its wholeness. For the Blake scholar with a structuralist approach, all of the poetry of William Blake may constitute a structure; or, if warranted by the relationships between individual poems, all of Blake's "Songs of Innocence" might be a structure.

For the theorist, a structure might be all of the Bach chorales, or only those based upon the "Passion" melody. Or a structure might be a single scale, such as the diatonic or pentatonic. The closure, or limits, of a structure refers to its self-regulatory quality, which permits no transformations (such as transpositions or inversions) of things within the structure (substructures) that could produce anything alien to the whole. Indeed, if it is a true structure, no transformation is capable of producing anything alien to the whole.

It is not necessarily advisable for the teacher to stress structuralism per se in the theory class. However, once made aware of it no teacher is likely to question its applicability, not only to theoretical research but also to many (if not all) aspects of the teaching task. By way of example, the diatonic scale has been approached from the structuralist point of view in an article by Ramon Fuller in which, with little reference to musical practice, the scale is shown to possess the properties of wholeness, transformation, and self-regulation and the potential for encompassing the modal and tonal practices of Western music.[9]

The perceptive teacher, after becoming aware of the applicability of the structuralist approach, may realize that he or she has been instinctively utilizing structures without knowing it. The conscious awareness of the relationships of musical concepts to the structures of which they are a part may well improve one's teaching even without demonstrating structuralism, as such, to students.

One manifestation of structuralism may be seen in an approach to sight-singing. It is important at the outset for students to develop an awareness of the unique character or quality of each tone of the diatonic scale, to apprehend the "feel" or "personality" of each of the seven tones. With certain kinds of drilling this skill can become almost instinctive, so that the student can quickly sing or identify any diatonic tone. This can later be extended to the "deep scale" substructures to include all of the chromatic tones, though still related to the diatonic scale with its tonal center. Initially the teacher might center upon two or three of the strongest of the so-called tendency tones—the seventh scale degree, with its urgency to move up by half-step to the eighth; the fourth scale degree, with its need to move down by half-step to the third; and the feeling of completeness or finality of the first scale degree. Substructures can enter whenever appropriate (i.e., the strong tendencies of the seventh and fourth scale degrees within the V⁷). Next would come the complementary qualities of the first, third, and fifth scale degrees in forming the tonic triad; then the tendency of the second scale degree to move down to the first; and finally the quality of the sixth scale degree, with its somewhat ambivalent orientation toward either the fifth or the eighth scale degrees.

While this can be readily understood at a gut level by musical individuals, the more quantitatively oriented students will go beyond the visceral approach and begin to perceive the structure. When this happens (and I believe that with outstanding theory students it almost always happens), the transformability and self-regulatory qualities of the structure come into view and are manifest with such perceptions as the fact that the relationship of the raised-fourth scale degree to the fifth is a transformation of the relationship of the seventh and eighth scale degrees. This in turn may open up the concepts of secondary dominants and chromatic harmony; and a chain reaction begins. Once this structure begins to reveal itself, the potential, if not the actuality, for the understanding of all of tonal harmony is present.

This is why one may occasionally find a rare student for whom nothing in diatonic harmony seems to be really new. That student has fully grasped the structure with its wholeness, its potential for transformation, and its limitations. Of course such a student will have been or will have to be exposed to traditional explanations of altered chords, modulations, and so on; but the concepts fall into place with a readiness and receptivity that suggests that the conceptual structure was already there. This bears out the idea of intelligence being the ability to manipulate a variety of complex variables.

Such a student will be both a joy and a problem. And herein lies the raison d'être of a flexible curriculum; for that student should have opportunities unrestricted by the curricular plan of the theory class. However it is accomplished, through honors sections or individual study, fulfillment of individual potential is a major objective.

The application of structuralism to theory teaching, whether overt or implicit, is certainly not limited to the diatonic tonal system. It is readily applicable to twelve-tone music, to other twentieth-century styles, or to any body of music forming a cohesive entity. It may yield new insights into Schenkerian analysis as well as set-theoretic and information-theoretic approaches in a variety of musical styles in both tonal and nontonal idioms. It has been described as a new metatheory—a "theory of theories" by which the general principles of structuralism may apply to any theoretical problem.[10] In relation to the creative process one may raise questions about its application before the fact to the development of new compositional techniques. Art still generally precedes theory. But there is no question of its after-the-fact relevance to the comprehension of virtually any musical score, whatever the style.

Other aspects of the learning process are discussed as they apply during the course of this book, especially applications of Piaget's physical and logico-mathematical learning. Regardless of which component of the theory program is under discussion, my greatest concern is the relationship of teaching to learning. Students are constantly learning in the classroom, but they are not always learning what the teacher has intended, nor are they necessarily learning as a result of the teacher's efforts. The popular charismatic teacher may be teaching less than the solemn disciplinarian—or vice versa. Students learn from each other, from themselves, from the teacher's attitudes, from the unique directions of their own actions, and in many other ways. Many of these may be unrelated to the teacher's actions.

The question of *how* students learn is interlocked with the question of *what* students learn; and a fine teacher is more than just a catalyst in the learning process. The teacher of real excellence is also one who has given much thought to the formulation of objectives—to the question of what theoretical concepts, skills, and values are most important to a musician's future artistic endeavor.

OBJECTIVES AND COURSE DESIGN

The purpose of this section is not to list definitively the ingredients of an ideal theory course but to provide guidelines for the formulation of these components. Determining course objectives requires a good deal of self-interrogation and intradepartmental communication. The following outline suggests many of the things to be considered in this process.

Outline for Determining Theory Course Objectives

I. Theoretical and musical skills to be dealt with
    A. Level of expertise to be acquired
    B. Theoretical concepts to be learned
    C. Relationship of skills and concepts to theory curriculum
    D. Music literature to be studied
II. Relationship of course to the total school or departmental curriculum
    A. Complementing or meeting prerequisites for other courses
    B. Expectations of faculty in other areas
    C. Avoidance of *needless* duplication or encroachment upon other courses (Some duplication is inevitable and even desirable.)
III. Values
    A. Fostering independence of thought
    B. Musical values
    C. Encouraging and rewarding creativity
    D. Imparting respect for scholarship
    E. Humanistic or humane values

The decisions made in regard to the questions raised in the preceding outline vary according to the nature of the students, instructor, curriculum, department, and institution. Even if one is not able to solve all of the problems presented in this process, the self-questioning and departmental and institutional communication do much to clarify the instructor's conception of the course and its place in the total curriculum.

First to be considered is basic content. The teacher attempts to determine not only the ultimate levels of aural, keyboard, analytical, and writing skills to be achieved in the course but (in a partial and nonspecific way) the intermediate levels at various points throughout the course. Good teachers often find that they have not arrived at the point where they thought they would at the end of a given class because of the appropriate and necessary digressions in the teaching process. Thus, the intermediate levels may be viewed as guidelines rather than firm goals. Nevertheless, the overall objectives of the course remain valid.

In setting these levels one must necessarily deal with the question of what music should be heard and studied; for the ideal approach is to study theoretical concepts and hone musical skills through actual examples in music literature. Score anthologies are economical, compact, and timesaving; but since a single collection may not adequately cover the desired literature, it may also be necessary to use separate scores.

Questions to be considered in the selection of scores are the following:

- Do they contain examples of the appropriate theoretical concepts?
- Do they represent both normative and unique practices?
- Do they afford opportunities for the practice of aural skills at the appropriate levels?
- Can they be played in class (live or on recordings)?
- Do they adequately represent the desired literature?
- Are they of optimum musical quality?

It is especially true in the integrated single-class situation that the music to be studied is critical to the success of the course; but the selection of scores is also of concern to the music school or department as a whole.

Part II of the outline deals with the relationship of the course objectives to the rest of the curriculum. Obviously, most of the musicianship skills, theoretical concepts, and literature studied are of at least general concern to the other areas. Music-education faculty often have great concern for the keyboard, sight-singing, and improvisational skills of their students. The faculties of music history and literature want their students to have a thorough grounding in harmonic common practice as well as some understanding of other musical styles. Conducting and composition instructors are concerned with students' aural skills, score-reading capabilities, and knowledge of musical media such as choral voices, orchestral instruments, and electronic media. And performance teachers (in applied music as well as ensembles) expect their students to develop analytical skills and to enhance their understanding of phrasing and musical shape. Exchange of ideas within the department or school can lead not only to a closer and more purposeful musical rapport among the various musical disciplines, it can also forestall needless duplication or encroachment upon other courses. Again let it be added that some duplication and so-called encroachment can be very beneficial to students because they furnish reinforcement as well as new perspectives.

Values (part III) are imparted by the choice of materials for the course, by the teacher's apparent attitudes toward musical and humanistic phenomena, by what the school or department seems to consider important, and in many other ways—even including non-verbal communication. A music school or department has its own unique personality based upon its strengths and weaknesses and upon what it emphasizes and what it neglects. To varying degrees, the faculty members partake of the values manifest in the overall configuration and objectives of the department, for the faculty were presumably selected because of their suitability for that department. Yet each faculty member also has a set of values that is distinct from the departmental profile. Often this set of individual values, since it is unique, is of a higher order than that of the department as a whole, even though individuals may in part subscribe to the collective value system.

It is this higher order of values that one hopes to find in the teachers of freshman and sophomore theory courses, for here young musicians formulate the precepts of independent thought and creativity and the musical and humane values that will guide them for many years. The freshman or sophomore music major probably sees the theory teacher more than any other instructor in the program. Thus, it is of major importance that the entire faculty of a department or school of music be concerned with the values, concepts, and musical skills that are being imparted in the theory courses.

Most faculty would like to see the content of the theory courses support the objectives of their studios and classrooms, but they do not want to see theory take over the curriculum. Many performance teachers in this new millennium were, and probably still are, concerned about the real value of courses in theory and analysis of music. The theory teacher, then, should find ways to convince both students and faculty colleagues of the value of theory courses and of musical analysis in particular. I address this at greater length in chapter 6.

One of the most important values to be imparted in the theory class is a deep respect for excellence in music making of any kind. Creative originality should also be given its due; and this is sometimes difficult in a course in which restrictive precepts are being imparted in such areas as part-writing, counterpoint, and the study of normative musical forms. Respect for musical scholarship and independence of thought can be encouraged in student approaches to the analytical process, provided that the teacher maintains an open attitude—even to the point of allowing students to head off in directions that may prove fruitless in order for them to explore for themselves. Artistic and humane values of a more general nature may be discovered by relating particular pieces of music to literature and the other arts or to the times in which they were created. Humanistic values may also be found in the poetic or philosophical meaning of the text of a vocal work or circumstances surrounding a composer's life. Some significant overlapping with the domains of music literature and history is inevitable.

It must be remembered that values are often imparted tacitly or implicitly so that class time needed for other things need not be wasted. Finally, the teacher who has an abiding consciousness of making music—whether at the keyboard, the blackboard, or singing an interval—conveys an important musical value.

THE TEACHING TASK

Teaching music theory is an art, and, as in any art, talent is an important ingredient of success. But there are many aspects of its practice that can be learned, and even for the born teacher there is ample room for the honing of skills. There is an essential craftsmanship in every art—that which is the proper domain of the artisan. And the beginning teacher, even if not heavily endowed with innate teaching ability, can put his or her skills to the best use through the development of sheer craft. To turn it around, even the born teacher cannot succeed without some attention to the methodology of teaching.

Thorough knowledge of content is the first and foremost ingredient of the teaching task, and this is why most successful teachers seem to possess a highly organized knowledge of their subject matter. Often this appears to take the form of a structuralist approach to the discipline, whether consciously or instinctively applied. The teacher who can envision the totality or "wholeness" of the material to be covered in a given course, and the potential of that material for transformation and self-regulation, should be capable of approaching it from many of its innumerable facets. The teacher who can then, through communication, perceive each student's unique manipulation of a concept being studied should be able to intervene in the learning process by offering good advice on the appropriate inductive processes for expansion of the student's conception. In the preceding sentence the expression *manipulation of a concept* evokes the Piagetian idea of LM learning—that the logico-mathematical experience is the result of the subject's own physical or mental action upon things. The teacher's intervention proceeds from the valuation—perceiving the student's conceptual level in order either to reinforce the student's actions (if the student is on the right track) or to offer alternatives. The complex area of teaching style enters into all aspects of this configuration; but if one views the teaching task as a series of three processes—communication, valuation, and intervention (I call this the CVI process)—the following outline emerges.

Outline of the Teaching Task

I.   Communication
    A.   Content
        1. Teacher's preknowledge
        2. Organization (structure)
    B.   Discussion and practice of concept or skill
        1. Teacher to student
            a. Reveal concept or skill
                (i) Socratic questioning
                (ii) Lecture-demonstration
            b. Show dedication and enthusiasm
        2. Reading of score or text by student
        3. Exchange between student and teacher
            a. Encourage open discussion
            b. Guide through Socratic questioning
II. Valuation
    A.   Perceive student's mode of action or conceptual level
        1. Action on a musical skill
        2. Perceptual manipulation of a concept
    B.   Student–teacher dialogue
        1. Communicate understanding and valuation of student's skill or conceptual level
        2. Encourage and value student response

III. Intervention
    A. Reinforce and supplement skills and inductive processes of student who is on right track
        1. Praise
        2. Offer suggestions for expansion of concept or skill
    B. Guide student with incomplete concept or skill (the CVI process begins again)
        1. Encourage
            a. Value valid aspects of student's conception
            b. Stimulate student to find own new approaches
        2. Suggest alternative inductive processes

Although this outline is dedicated in large part to LM learning, P learning is also of importance in the theory class. Since P learning is experienced largely through associative memory, it relies mostly upon repetitive reinforcement rather than upon the CVI process. Ear-training drills for the recognition of intervals or chord qualities are cases in point. These and other aspects of teaching and learning are discussed later in specific application to the several areas of the theory course.

Teaching style, a highly individual matter, varies according to the approach that each teacher finds to be most natural and effective. And it is a constantly evolving phenomenon. One's personality has a great bearing on style, but it does not necessarily follow that students of the popular charismatic teacher learn more than other students. It is important to achieve rapport with students on both collective and individual bases and to maintain a sense of responsibility to the discipline and to the students. If one can do this with a sense of humor, dedication, and contagious enthusiasm for music making, teaching style takes care of itself.

TEACHER TRAINING, THAT IS, TRADITIONAL MUSIC EDUCATION

Since this book is about teaching, I think it is appropriate to comment on its relationship to the academic field known as professional music education. When the first edition of this book came out twenty years ago, I somewhat hesitantly showed the little volume to a friend and colleague in the field of music education. After a cursory examination, he said, "This is not music education," and I then showed it to another colleague in the music education area, who said the same thing. It appears, then, that my approach to the teaching of music theory is in some way at odds with prevailing philosophies of music education. This may not be a bad thing, and it may also be a manifestation of the ongoing conflict that has existed for more than fifty years between music education and the other academic areas of musical learning in colleges and universities.

The fundamental disagreement is about the place of course content (musical knowledge and skill) in relation to teaching skills (educational philosophy and methodology, i.e., "foundations of education"). Most musical academics appear to operate under the assumption that if teachers thoroughly know their substantive areas of musical scholarship and research or creative activity—whether it be performance, musicology, music history, theory, or composition—that they can usually learn to be good teachers of that subject. The substantive knowledge comes first and is all-important. The teacher-training establishment (i.e., music education) appears to hold the view that methodology and educational philosophy come first; and that is why musical standards are reputed to be lower in the field of music education than in the other areas.

As a beginning university theory teacher in the mid-1950s, I was surprised at the great disparity of preparation among the diverse population of my freshman theory classes. A few had obviously had private preparation in sight-singing, ear-training, keyboard, and even musical analysis; but most of them had not. I began to have the awful suspicion that public school music teachers had not been doing their job. Some of the most obvious learning experiences for students headed for careers in music were unavailable in the public schools, and I believe that the discipline of music education has not improved much over the past half century. Many basic musicianship skills are more easily learned by elementary schoolchildren than by the young adults who knock on the doors of our undergraduate music departments—I know this from my own experience as a child as well as from my own elementary school teaching experiences. The fault lies in the training of public school music teachers.

To remedy this, a few institutions of higher learning are now beginning to identify potential public school music teachers only at the graduate level so that the undergraduate curriculum is just as rigorous for them as it is for those in the substantive areas of musical study. I particularly recall the public controversy at SUNY Buffalo in 1997 when the administration abolished the undergraduate program in music education. It had been the last department on campus to follow the trend of eliminating undergraduate teacher-training programs. The vote within the department had been 15 in favor of abolishing music education, 2 against, and 3 abstentions. Two members of the departmental faculty of 22 were not present. There had been a heated editorial debate in the *Buffalo News* between a musicologist arguing in favor of the change and a professor of music education deploring it. The chairman of the department[11] had been quoted in the campus newspaper, the *Reporter*, on October 9, 1997, as follows: "Students who want to teach music will be in an excellent position to graduate from UB as music educators with strong performance backgrounds. . . . They can receive a bachelor of music degree in performance or a bachelor of arts degree with a music major." He had added that New York Teacher Certification could then be achieved after the students had acquired the B.M. or B.A. for then they would be thoroughly grounded in the liberal arts with real depth in their major field and breadth in the other arts, humanities, and sciences. He tactfully recommended other schools that still offered music teacher training at the undergraduate level, but this, I think, was just a gesture; for other schools are following this model, not only in music but in other disciplines as well.

It is my hope that by the end of the first decade of the twenty-first century, music education on the model of old-fashioned undergraduate teacher training will be offered only in the most backward of institutions. When this happens, the music teachers we send into the public schools will be highly qualified performers, music historians, theorists, or composers—capable of teaching sight-singing and other basic musicianship skills to the children who are ready to learn. College teachers of freshman and sophomore theory, then, will be able to teach the skills of music analysis, part-writing, keyboard harmony, and even counterpoint at the appropriate levels. Along with higher admission standards, remedial theory courses will become a thing of the past. Music theory will then realize its potential as an area of scholarly study in the deepest and most beautiful sense.

NOTES

1. McHose had been a pianist for silent movies in the twenties, and his keyboard improvisational skills were legendary. In his graduate course in

"Styles," he often improvised in the styles of various composers such as Sibelius, Debussy, or Hindemith.

2. Barney Childs, quoted in a eulogy for the late Barney Childs, *Newsletter of the Society of Composers* (winter 2000).

3. Jean Piaget, *Apprentisage et connaisance (premiére et seconde parties)* (Paris: Presses Universitaires de France, 1959), 21–67.

4. David Elkind, *Children and Adolescents: Interpretive Essays on Jean Piaget* (New York: Oxford University Press, 1970).

5. Elkind, *Children and Adolescents.*

6. Elkind, *Children and Adolescents.*

7. Jean Piaget, "Development and Learning," in *Piaget Rediscovered,* ed. R. E. Ripple and V. N. Rockcastle (Ithaca, N.Y.: School of Education, Cornell University, 1964).

8. Jean Piaget, *Structualism,* trans. Chanina Maschler (New York: Harper Torchbooks, 1971).

9. Ramon Fuller, "A Structuralist Approach to the Diatonic Scale," *Journal of Music Theory* 19, no. 2 (fall 1975), 182–210.

10. Fuller, "A Structuralist Approach."

11. David Felder, a composer who had replaced the former chairman, a professor of music education, in 1996.

Two

Aural Skills: Melodic and Rhythmic

In the broadest sense ear-training can be viewed as the doorway to every aspect of the study of music theory. To be thoroughly mastered, every musical and theoretical concept must be comprehended from the perspective of sound itself. A teacher can diagram voice-leading on the blackboard, can issue foolproof principles of part-writing, can show in the score of *Dichterliebe* how and why the tonic triad is absent from the opening song, and can point out that the final movement of Bartok's Sixth String Quartet is a synopsis of the earlier movements. But true understanding of these phenomena finally comes about only through the actual sound of the music. Indeed it is possible to utilize a great deal of theory-class time without reading or writing a note of music. There is no particular reason why one should have to look at the score of *Symphony of Psalms* to derive an understanding of its basic structure. If the sound of the music did not communicate that structure, it would be lacking in lucidity (and "lucidity" is a quality that Stravinsky greatly valued).

It is most enlightening and musically valid to examine its sound first—to hear the double fugue in the second movement, to hear the tonal centers of its entrances—to experience its beautiful symmetry in the way that Stravinsky intended. The practice of music analysis can be carried on very effectively without examining the score of a work until after it has been thoroughly studied by ear.

Ear-training, then, should be more than developing the ability to identify intervals, chord qualities, or rhythmic patterns or learning the skills of harmonic and melodic dictation. It is the development of the ear for the study of music, for the performance of music, for the creation of music, and for enhancing the pleasure of simply listening to music. There is no doubt that when students learn to hear and to part-write a 4-3 suspension that their level of musical consciousness is raised. Of course those students may have been exposed to hundreds of 4-3 suspensions in their experience. But when they hear them in a Baroque sonata and actually know what they are hearing—that is when they begin to share the deeply pleasurable understanding of eighteenth-century dissonance.

Not all students are immediately aware of the relevance of aural skills, and it helps to discuss it with them. One can point out some of the obvious things—the need for a conductor to be able to derive the nature of a score simply by examining it, that musicians should be able to sight-sing, and that the ability to hear and locate out-of-tune notes is very useful in rehearsals. But there are hundreds of more subtle uses of aural skills, many of which can be effectively brought out in open discussion—the need for the jazz musician (or any musician) to be sensitive to harmonic changes and to thematic development within the ensemble, how the ear can gauge the appropriate degree of crescendo from the preparation note to the suspension note in an Elizabethan madrigal, the dynamic balance of an individual instrument in relation to its role in an ensemble, the ability to listen to the other parts in contemporary choral works in order to find one's own pitches, and the intelligent planning of the extent of a *ritard* in terms of what has gone before and what is yet to come. Members of the class will have their own ideas to offer along the same lines.

Melodic dictation is the reverse corollary of sight-singing. If one can write a melody down correctly from dictation, one should also (assuming minimal vocal skill) be able to sing that melody from the printed page. Because of the close relationship of these two skills, the teacher should often coordinate the presentation of ear-training materials with sight-singing materials. The intervals that are being identified in ear-training drills should be reinforced in sight-singing practice. Indeed singing can be an integral part of ear-training drills, as is clarified later. Since many of the methods and drills for ear-training are equally applicable to sight-singing, and because instructors are often teaching ear-training and sight-singing almost simultaneously, the two are frequently linked in the ensuing discussion. However, it is important first of all to understand the role of the voice in the study and practice of aural skills.

THE SINGING VOICE

That vocal sound was probably the earliest form of music is axiomatic. One can imagine a primitive man or woman, perhaps before the full development of speech, expressing emotions or states of mind or being with nonverbal sound—possibly the slow sliding descent of a minor third with a closed mouth to express weariness, an ooh or aah melodically arched to express wonder, some other unique vocal inflection to express affection for another. As these sounds became stylized among a given group of primitives, they may have gradually evolved with increasing complexity toward a kind of music. There is no reason to think that it did not happen in this way. The present-day sounds of whales "singing" may be just that kind of individual expression of states of being—a kind of musical language for those marvelous creatures. That our music probably evolved from vocal sounds could account for the fact that the singing voice remains the most moving of all of our modes of musical expression. It hearkens back to those preverbal times when vocal sounds may have been the sole means of communicating emotions and states of being. Some anthropologists believe that language evolved from quasi-musical vocal sounds of this sort.

Thus, singing is basic to all music. Cellists, pianists, trombonists, bassoonists, and timpanists—all of them are (or should be) inwardly singing when they perform. It is for this reason that singing is so important in the development of basic musicianship skills. Not all musicians, of course, are endowed with fine singing voices. Yet all should be able to sing; and the lack of a fine voice should not prevent a student musician from gaining the musical benefits and achieving the skills of singing in the theory classroom.

The idea must be conveyed that the theory classroom is a place where everybody sings, regardless of how unwieldy or untrained some of the voices may be. The instructor need not have a well-polished voice (in fact this can intimidate) but should be relaxed and uninhibited about singing; and he or she should communicate this feeling to the class. An open attitude and a disregard for innate voice qualities can do much to encourage erstwhile nonsinging students to overcome their reluctance to allow their singing voices to be heard by their colleagues. Let them sing more or less as they will—with falsettos or any other means of negotiating difficult passages. Yet it should also be clear that good musical phrasing can be achieved with the most ordinary vocal equipment.

Toward this end some discussion of vocal technique may be fruitful. Vocal production is not an objective of the theory class, but attention to certain obvious things, such as breathing and posture, improves the musical results. A few nonsingers may actually do such things as breathe between each note or sit in absurd postures unless they are led to do otherwise. Among non–voice majors, wind players need the least attention, for the techniques of breathing with the phrase and proper support are already a part of their preparation; but some string players, keyboard performers, and percussionists may need guidance. Such students should learn that breathing with the phrase is a very natural and musical thing to do, even for instrumentalists whose breath does not control the sound. As a cellist, I can attest to the fact that many string players do breathe with the phrase, and some string teachers advocate a relationship between the bow stroke and the breath.

In the theory class the primary use of the singing voice is for sight-singing, but the teacher's singing can and should be used as a frequent alternative to the piano in many aspects of ear-training. Classroom singing and identification of melodic intervals are only two of many fruitful uses of the voice in the development of aural skills. An additional benefit of singing is that it requires attention to intonation, an aspect of ear-training that can be overlooked when using the piano exclusively. Further, since the piano's intonation is that of tempered tuning, it is possible for the voice to sing in better tuning (according to just intonation) than can be achieved at the piano.[1]

TEACHING STRATEGIES

A wide and frequently varied range of activities is important in the teaching and learning of aural skills. Nothing can be more deadly and ultimately pointless than to spend a full class period doing nothing but playing intervals at the piano for the class to identify. If the students do not begin to nod off, it is likely that the instructor will. Any single activity of this sort should be interrupted after a relatively short time with a fresh approach to the problem or with a change of topic. Learning intervals is a physical associative process. It consists of passive repetition with no real effort expended by the subject. Like some other aspects of ear-training, it is a form of Piaget's P learning; and unadulterated P learning cannot often support a long attention span because it usually isn't very interesting.

LM learning, on the other hand, because it is self-rewarding and self-generating, can support an almost limitless attention span. Inherent in the LM experience is the feeling of discovery through one's own efforts—the "eureka!" or "aha!" experience. One can easily spend a class period or longer analyzing a one-page art song or piano piece because each discovery is a unique experience that rewards the learner's efforts and provides an incentive to make further related discoveries, because of the relationship of each subsequent discovery to the total structure. It is the same thing that keeps the crossword enthusiast going until the puzzle has been completed or the mathematician fully absorbed until the structure of an equation is realized. Our minds are such that even when a topic is not of great interest to us, a glimpse of its structure can activate the LM learning process, and time seems to stop until we have completed the experience. This is why interruptions are intolerable when we are absorbed by a problem; and it is why individuals who have made great discoveries have often done so by dint of seemingly monumental perseverance.

Although some aural skills fall partly into the category of LM learning (i.e., aural perception in relation to a harmonic system), many beginning ear-training drills utilize the physical associative experience of P learning. It behooves the teacher to find ways to make P learning more interesting. One way is to vary the activities. The teacher perceives the point at which the attention span for a single activity has been exhausted and makes a change. Simply switching from playing intervals at the piano to singing them can prolong the attention span; or having individuals sing specified intervals rather than identify them can give renewed life to interval drill. The teacher can do much with these and other alternative approaches. But in a sense this is not really making P learning more interesting; it is simply leaving each activity just before it becomes unbearable, replacing it with another related activity, leaving that one in the nick of time, and so on.

It is probably not possible to avoid some use of these varied drill approaches. And in any case musicians who have for years been inured to the rigors of long hours of instrumental practice should not only be able to tolerate classroom drills but should have the maturity to envision long-term rewards for their efforts. There are other ways to make ear-training drills more interesting, and one of these is the use of games. There has been a good deal of speculation and experimentation by game-theory psychologists on just why games create incentives for things that taken in themselves may be really quite dull and uninteresting. Are obsessive gamblers motivated only by the hope of profit? In itself the throwing of dice is not the most exciting activity in the world; yet there is something mesmerizing in the game, to the point that the players are totally preoccupied.

The use of games is successful in ear-training, I think, because the students when playing a game with, say, chord-quality perception, are concerned not with chord qualities but with the game itself. The logico-mathematical aspects of this other structure—the game— take precedence over the chord qualities (which in any case had become uninteresting because of too much repetitive drill), so that they learn chord qualities incidentally to the game. But they do learn them, and usually with more relish than when confronting them in chord-quality drills.

With some ingenuity the teacher can find ways to introduce games into the teaching of most of the musicianship skills. In ear-training drill with seventh chords, for example, one way is simply to keep score of right or wrong answers (out of perhaps ten examples) with the winner taking the place of the teacher in the next game. This places the winner in a position where he or she will be practicing another skill (that of playing seventh chords in various inversions at the keyboard) while the other students continue to practice the perception of seventh chords, with another winner taking over at the piano at the end of that round.

Various interval games can be devised, one of which is to go around the class having each student in turn sing an interval to his or her right-hand neighbor. If able to identify it correctly (according to the singer of the interval), the neighbor sings one to his or her neighbor, and so on. If the neighbor fails to identify it, the singer offers another interval until the neighbor gets it, and then the game proceeds. Like many of these games, this one has the added benefit of getting at intervals from the standpoint of singing as well as hearing.

If an electronic-keyboard room is available (with a headset for each keyboard), games with harmonic dictation can be integrated with keyboard skills, such as having a student play a brief harmonic passage and having another student attempt to play it back. If the room is equipped for pairs to communicate on headsets, the entire class can pair off and play this game simultaneously, with the instructor simply monitoring from time to time. Perhaps games will not fit every teacher's personal style, but each according to his or her own approach should explore ways to use appropriately the factors of incentive and competition. Classrooms equipped with a computer at each workplace offer even more opportunities for interesting drills and games, especially if music software and Musical Instrument Digital Interface (MIDI) capabilities are present. This is discussed in detail in chapter 9.

The electronic-keyboard example manifests another approach to ameliorating the dullness of repetitive aural drills—the integration of ear-training with other areas of theoretical study. Mutually supportive approaches can readily be found for ear-training, keyboard, and analysis. Any keyboard exercise has ear-training potential, and any analytical exercise can begin with aural perception of the work being studied. These approaches can be refined and focused so that scores for a given unit are selected on the basis of their potential for correlation among several theoretical skills.

Although testing and evaluation is discussed in detail in chapter 8, it is important to mention that a test can be an effective mode of learning as well as an instrument of evaluation. It is in fact quite possible to construct ear-training tests in such a way as to furnish opportunities for students to improve their aural comprehension substantially. For one thing, the concentration and organization of ear-training materials is greater in a test than in any other classroom situation. Also, the student incentive is much higher. Because of this, some theory teachers give very frequent ear-training quizzes, sometimes without counting them toward the final grade. Others give "pretests," which are similar to the "real" tests given a few days later; the idea being that the student, having been oriented to the mode of testing and having practiced on the pretest, then performs better on the real test. Because frequent changes of approach are essential in ear-training, teachers must have a large repertoire of varied strategies. Beginning teachers, perhaps more than those with experience, must be constantly trying new tactics in order to sort out the best approaches for their overall approach through resourcefulness, imagination, and the willingness to explore.

THE DIATONIC SCALE

One of the traditional ways to teach the aural comprehension of the
diatonic scale is to assign the numbers one through eight to the
tones of the scale (from tonic to tonic in the major scale) and to sing
these numbers in repetitive exercises designed for this purpose. This
is a variation of the movable Do system, with numbers being substituted for the solfeggio syllables.

The fixed Do system has worked very well in France (and other
Romance-language countries) because the solfeggio syllables are
themselves the actual names of the concert pitches of the tones in
those languages, rather than representing scale degrees within a
tonal framework. That is, in the fixed Do system, Do means the pitch
C, Re means D, Mi means E, and so on. The system suits the Paris
Conservatory, where the students are speaking their native language—La is the French word for the pitch-class A, Sol means G,
and so forth. The same is true in other Romance-language countries.
While there has been resistance to the fixed Do system in the United
States, the last quarter of the twentieth century has seen it being
adopted by many college schools of music. Its opponents would say
that to ask Americans to use this system would be asking us to use
a foreign language when we already have a perfectly good set of
symbols for pitches. That is, there would be no more point to that
than to ask the French to refer to the pitch of 440 cycles per second
(cps) as A rather than La. The movable Do system, although it has
been used successfully in this country, also has its drawbacks, since
it is a descendant of the fixed Do system and a throwback to the
hexachord system of Guido d'Arezzo (fl. eleventh century).

Nevertheless, in our global village, fixed Do sight-singing seems
to have become an international phenomenon, so today I believe that
it should be used in our music theory classes. Thus, the chromatic
scale in just intonation with the solfeggio syllables is shown in figure 2.1.

do di re ri mi fa fi sol si la li ti do ti   te la le sol se fa mi   me re ra do

Figure 2.1

Guido devised a hexachord system of six-note scales that was widely used well into the Renaissance and is the forerunner of the modern solfeggio system. The syllables *ut, re, mi, fa, sol, la* represent the pitches of his six-note scales. These syllables were derived from the hymn *Ut Queant Laxis* (the Hymn to St. John the Baptist) by extracting the first syllable of each of its first six phrases, which happen to be arranged in regular stepwise-ascending order. The hymn is shown in figure 2.2.

Ut que-ant la - xis Re-so-nar-e fi-bris Mi- - - - ra ge-stor - um Fa-mu-li tu-o - rum,

Sol - - -ve   pol-lu-ti La-bi-i   re - a-tum, Sanct-te Jo-ann-es.

Figure 2.2

He undoubtedly devised the system to help his singers in the reading of music. One can picture him teaching his choirboys the names of the syllables as they sing the Hymn to St. John the Baptist. It follows that this must have been a widely known hymn for it to have had the strong associations of syllables with pitches. The syllables represent pitches arranged in an intervallic pattern identical to the first six tones of the diatonic scale and were used not only for convenient sight-singing of chant, but also as an aid to reading other modal music, including polyphony. The syllable *ut* was changed to *do* in the modern solfeggio system for vocal reasons—all of the other syllables begin with a consonant, which aids the voice in attacking a tone. *Ti* was added later after the evolution of the seven-tone diatonic scale, as were also the syllables for the chromatic tones.

The advantages of using the fixed Do solfeggio syllables for the practice of sight-singing are manifold. For one thing, the practice of using different syllables for two enharmonically related pitches creates an aural as well as a visual distinction—that is, a B-flat in most contexts actually is slightly lower than an A-sharp—and this leads to greater consciousness of fine intonation. String players are particularly conscious of this, but it is beneficial to all musicians to consciously realize that the pitches of the piano are in tempered tuning. Also, if the system is learned during childhood, it is conducive to perfect pitch in musical individuals. It is unfortunate that modern American music education seems to have preferred the movable Do system, for there is minimal positive reinforcement in moving from a movable Do system to fixed Do. The student has to "unlearn" movable Do before moving ahead with true solfeggio.

The scale degree number system has also come into quite common use. One way to use it that has proven successful is to invent many number patterns of three to eight figures representing diatonic pitch patterns. These can be invented in class by the instructor, but the following list shows samples of the type of patterns that can be used to help students develop aural comprehension of the diatonic scale degrees:

    1-2-1   1-2-3-1   1-2-3-4-3-2-1   1-2-3-4-5-3-1   1-2-3-1-5
    1-3-5-3-1   1-4-3-1-5   1-2-4-3-5   5-6-5-7-8   8-6-4-2-3-1

These (and many others like them) can be used in any key within a convenient singing range (the key should be varied from day to day) according to a four-step sequence of exercises as follows: (1) Teacher sings number patterns, which are repeated by the class in chorus. (2) Teacher speaks number patterns, which are then sung by the students in chorus. (3) Teacher speaks number patterns for individuals to sing back on the proper pitches. (4) Teacher dictates patterns (with piano, or voice on "la," but without numbers) for the students to identify by scale degree numbers. An interesting variation on the third step is for each student to *speak* (rather than sing) an invented number pattern to his or her neighbor. The neighbor sings it back and then invents a new number pattern for the next person to sing, and so it goes around the class until everyone has invented and sung a number pattern.

In the early stages it helps to do some number patterns every day until the students begin to develop very strong associations of the numbers with the scale degrees. At this point, after establishing a key, the teacher can play single tones within the key in any register of the piano and ask the students to identify them by letter name. This begins the process of association of scale degrees with pitch-class letter names.

As discussed earlier, the unique personality of each scale degree should be emphasized; and at first the tendency tones should be allowed to follow their natural inclinations—leading tone moving up to tonic, fourth degree moving down to third, and so on. At later stages, as the teacher gradually increases the number of tones and the complexity of the patterns, tones should occasionally be made to move against their natural tendencies, and larger intervals should be emphasized.

At an intermediate stage it is also interesting to cast the patterns (as used in step 1) in various rhythms—sometimes in regular meters, sometimes not. This utilizes the students' rhythmic memories as well as pitch-series memories and thus aids the transfer of learning to the skills of sight-singing and melodic dictation. If step 4 is done in this way, the class has in fact progressed to the skill of melodic dictation. Asking students to invent their own melodic patterns (pitch and rhythm) for classroom use (on paper or improvised) challenges their creativity and leads toward melodic composition.

The use of diatonic patterns in the major mode can be supplemented with similar patterns in the minor mode, including raised or lowered sixth and seventh scale degrees. Since it introduces a new substructure of tendency tones, this step should be taken only after the major-mode patterns have yielded very positive results observable in melodic dictation and sight-singing.

INTERVALS

Interspersed among these number pattern activities the teacher should begin various kinds of drill for the singing and identification of intervals. Intervals are of course present in the number patterns and may begin to be learned in that context. But the objective there is to learn to hear and to sing with scale-degree feeling—to move from E up to A within the key of C, not by thinking perfect fourth but through the structure of the diatonic scale and the personalities of the third and sixth scale degrees within that structure. This is key feeling, but the skills of sight-singing and melodic dictation are also aided by interval perception—the ability to sing, spell, and identify intervals, as well as to handle them in notation.

The concept of interval class should be taught at an early stage— the idea that a major seventh, a minor second, and a minor ninth belong to the same interval class (Class I) and that all intervals of a given interval class possess a certain similarity to each other. Some caveats are in order regarding the application of this concept, however. The interval-class concept can be very misleading in harmonic analysis, where the distinction between a minor second and a minor ninth may be a significant textural factor, drastically affecting the evocative qualities of the harmony as well as timbre and dynamics. In melodic analysis, reduction by interval class can thoroughly abort the profile (and hence the musical meaning) of virtually any melody. Its use in set-theoretical and Schenkerian analysis constitutes one of the major pitfalls of these analytical approaches.

Thus, when learning the concept of interval class, students should also be led to understand the special qualities of a twelfth as distinct from a fifth, a major second as distinct from a minor seventh, and so on, regardless of the fact that in each of these pairs the two members belong to the same interval class. As discussed in chapter 1, some students quickly develop the ability to distinguish among the six interval classes; and this is most helpful later on in harmonic dictation. But some may not always be able to distinguish intervals within a single interval class, like the student who confuses perfect fourths and perfect fifths. This may be most common when the two tones of an interval are played simultaneously. The students' awareness of invertability, octave displacement, and interval class helps them to overcome this confusion; for they know in advance that they are likely to confuse perfect fourths with perfect fifths, or even minor seconds with minor ninths, and thus are prepared to listen more keenly when these possibilities are in the offing. The teacher can reinforce this awareness during interval drill.

It is important that the ability to spell intervals accurately keeps pace with the ability to hear them. The teacher who forgets this may discover one day that, although the entire class can aurally identify intervals, there are some for whom this skill is useless since they cannot spell them accurately. The teacher can present certain mnemonics for spelling intervals (i.e., in all perfect fourths and fifths the two tones have the same accidentals except when the interval consists of a form of B and F), but the students should also sing intervals with letter names. That is, the teacher plays a C-flat and says to the student, "This is a C-flat. Sing an ascending major third with the correct letter names." The student then sings "C-flat, E-flat" on the correct pitches. The teacher can go around the class asking each student to do this perhaps twice a week during the interval-learning period. And this should be reinforced with written work or tests in which the students are asked to identify intervals by writing them on the staff as well as by name (as M2, m6, etc).

At the outset a good way to build the proper associations of interval sounds is to suggest well-known tunes that begin with one or another of the intervals. Since there is a whole folklore of such "crutch tunes," the students will have their own pet tunes in some cases, but some of the more common ones are given in the following list.

m3   "Greensleeves"
M3   "Old Black Joe"
P4   "Taps" or "Wedding March" from Lohengrin
A4   "Maria" from *West Side Story*
P5   "Twinkle, Twinkle Little Star"
m6   "Go Down Moses" or "Theme from Love Story"
M6   "My Bonny"
m7   "There's a Place for Us" from *West Side Story*

As soon as interval perception reaches a respectable level, students should abandon these crutch tunes and hear intervals simply as intervals.

Some suggestions for interval drill were given earlier, but another important guideline is that intervals should be played in a variety of ways in order to strengthen the students' abilities to handle them in various musical contexts. They should be played and sung as melodic intervals (two separate tones) as well as harmonically (two simultaneous tones). Melodic intervals should be played in both ascending and descending form. Intervals should be played in various registers of the piano, and students should frequently sing melodic intervals with letter names to develop interval spelling.

One of the marks of an experienced theory teacher is the ability to perceive why a student has incorrectly identified an interval. It is a skill that teachers learn gradually through experience with many students over a long period of time. Certain problems recur often enough to suggest patterns, such as the confusion of intervals within the same interval class, which was discussed earlier. Another example is seen in the case of the student who confuses tritones with major sevenths. When the teacher sees this happening frequently with a student, it can be attributed to some sort of commonality between the two intervals—in this case the fact that both the tritone and the major seventh are a half-step away from perfect intervals. The tendency of the upper tone of both intervals is to move upward by half-step (like a leading tone) to create a perfect interval (fifth or

octave). Probably this is what is causing the confusion, and awareness of this can help the student to correct the problem.

The perceptive teacher will find other examples of commonalities
among intervals as he or she begins to see the error patterns of certain individuals. Some of these apparent commonalities may be
highly speculative, but experimentation with them is still worthwhile. By exploring interval-perception problems with their teacher,
students may themselves arrive at a solution and thus achieve
greater understanding of their hearing abilities.

RHYTHM AND CONDUCTING

A number of rhythmic activities should be carried on concurrently
with the learning of intervals and the development of aural comprehension of the diatonic scale. It is these three areas together—
intervals, diatonic feeling, and rhythm—that prepare the student for
the practice of melodic dictation and sight-singing. Some general
discussion of rhythm should occur at a very early stage. This should
include consideration of rhythm as a broad shaping force, macro-
rhythm seen in long phrases and large structures, simple and compound meters, asymmetrical meters, unmetered rhythm, and so
forth. Then the class should undertake to conduct compound and
simple meters. As in the introduction of singing, it is wise at this
point to present some of the fundamentals. First among these is the
concept of the beat as a live thing that is generated by a rhythmic
pulse from within the conductor.

This concept, if thoroughly instilled, helps the students to communicate rhythm rather than to simply beat in dull lifeless patterns.
The beat patterns should be learned, of course; but the background
pulse of smaller impulses should be ever present, though invisible.
And it should be made clear that there is a threshold of the beat, a
point where the downward motion ceases in order to define pre-
cisely the inception of a rhythmic impulse. This threshold—the bottom of the beat—can be treated in a number of ways. A workable
metaphoric approach is to describe it as a trampoline upon which
the hand bounces at the precise inception of the beat. The bounce
concept may help to loosen up the student with too rigid an
approach or add precision to one whose beat is too flaccid.

When the beat patterns have been thoroughly learned in classroom practice, the students should begin to vocalize (on "ta" or some such syllable, but without definite pitch) rhythms in all compound and simple meters. Notation can be introduced at this point, reading from scores or perhaps reading the rhythms (without pitches) from sight-singing books. The teacher can explore a variety of ways to carry on conducting activities on both individual and group bases. These possibilities include having individuals conduct the class in sight-singing sessions, having the entire class conduct the teacher, and having individuals (or the class) sing while conducting.

As rhythmic skills and conducting develop, the class can begin to explore the concept of the phrase and larger substructures as rhythmic entities. Learning how to conduct the beginning of an opening phrase—how to "start" an ensemble—also conveys an understanding of the rhythmic structure over which the phrase is conceived. The concept of the antecedent and consequent phrase can lead to discussion of periods, double periods, binary forms, and the like. Gradually the class will link the study of rhythm to musical structure, music analysis, and the writing skills of music.

Repetitive practice helps in the reading of rhythms, and one approach is to use the idea of rhythmic cells. In this context the cell is viewed as a single beat within a given meter. All of the usual cell forms for that meter are placed on the blackboard and the class drills by singing (on "ta") the cells as the instructor points to them, moving from one to another in random order. At first the teacher can allow an empty beat to intervene between the recitation of each cell, but when the class grows more skillful they can be vocalized in quick succession without the empty beat. The conventional cell forms for simple meters with a quarter-note beat (2/4, 3/4, 4/4) are shown in figure 2.3.

Next are the typical cell forms for compound meters with a dotted quarter-note beat (6/8, 9/8, 12/8), as shown in figure 2.4.

After the class has developed some skill in these cell forms, the instructor can proceed in the same way, using cell forms for beats equaling the eighth-note and half-note (simple meters), and the dotted eighth and dotted half-notes (compound meters). Students may also practice these exercises on their own.

In conventional rhythmic notation, mastery of the cell forms enables the students to develop rapidly their rhythmic reading skills. The ability to identify the cells quickly aids in the reading of

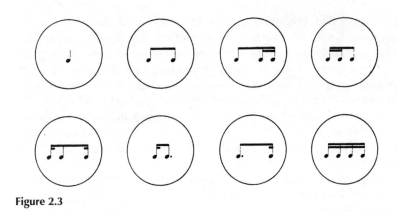

Figure 2.3

Figure 2.4

syncopations and cross-rhythms as well as simpler rhythms. As the class begins to explore asymmetrical meters, such as 5/4 and 7/8, the cells will be equally useful. At this point the principles of conducting asymmetrical beat patterns should also be presented. Other approaches to rhythm are mentioned later under the headings of "Melodic Dictation" and "Sight-Singing."

MELODIC DICTATION

Unlike sight-reading, melodic dictation is not a skill that musicians are frequently called upon to use, per se, in the practice of their art. There may be occasions when musicians hear a melody that they later jot down, but for the most part melodic dictation is practiced for what it contributes to the other skills—the ability to identify incorrectly performed notes in rehearsal, the ability to hear a passage inwardly in order to read it in rehearsal or performance, sensitivity to other parts in ensemble, and so on. In these and other ways skill in melodic dictation is manifest in other aspects of musical craft. Its importance as a basic musicianship tool cannot be overstated, and some classroom discussion may help to clarify its relevance.

Although melodic dictation relies upon all of the skills discussed so far in this chapter, its practice should not be delayed. Some melodic-dictation activities should be undertaken at early stages, even before intervals and diatonic scale feeling are fully mastered. And sight-singing should also be carried on concurrently with these other skills, using material that is comparable in difficulty with that used for melodic dictation. It is important, however, that melodies for dictation not be limited to those that are singable, for that establishes unnecessary limitations of range and idiomatic style. Although much song literature can be used, melodies spanning wide ranges from the instrumental literature should also be introduced.

The teacher should find a way to observe the students as they take down melodic dictation in order to follow their progress and to note ways in which they can improve their performance. One way to do this is to have as many students as possible work at the blackboard. In a class of fourteen or fifteen it is usually possible to have half working at the board and the other half at their seats. In playing melodic dictation at the piano the teacher should allow ample time between playings for the students to think through the melody and to write. The teacher can use the time between playings to observe progress and offer suggestions. For variety, some students can be asked to bring their instruments for melodic dictation, and the voice can be used as another alternative to the piano. Indeed, it is wise for the teacher to use his or her voice or an instrument as much as possible for melodic dictation. Using the piano or other keyboard instrument all the time tends to inculcate equal-tempered intonation, which is often at odds with the kind of intonation practiced by accomplished singers and instrumental performers.

It is important to remember that just intonation is practiced not only in string quartets and vocal ensembles, but also by wind players. Except for keyboard players, all performers utilize some form of just intonation except in instances when they are playing in unison with a keyboard instrument tuned in equal temperament. As every wind player knows, there are ways to minutely adjust the embouchure to make subtle alterations in the pitch, and singers and string players are also capable of infinitely small adjustments. Good performers make these subtle justifications almost unconsciously, so that most musicians are not even aware of the type of intonation they are practicing. At some point in the first semester of freshman theory, the teacher should find the means to demonstrate these subtleties of playing in tune. While the history of tuning systems is beyond the scope of freshman and sophomore theory courses, the students should be made aware of the fact that, even today, equal temperament is only a starting point for all musicians except keyboard players. Intonation is a part of musical craft too often neglected in beginning theory courses.[2]

In the elementary stages of melodic dictation, melodies of double period length are excellent beginning material. A melody should be played once in its entirety and then broken down phrase by phrase. An early objective in melodic dictation is to get the students to hear at least a single four-bar phrase as an entity. To test and to practice this skill the teacher can ask the class or individuals to sing back a four-bar phrase immediately after it has been played at the piano. If the students can demonstrate their musical grasp of the phrase by singing it back correctly, it remains only for them to implement the appropriate notational symbols and to write it down.

There are, of course, very talented musicians who may have difficulty with the notational component of melodic dictation and may not be able to write down the phrase even though they have demonstrated their musical grasp of it by singing it back correctly. This is where the teacher's perceptivity and skill in offering appropriate suggestions come into play. A first step is to be sure that such a student has written down all the basic preliminary things—the clef, the key signature, the meter signature—and has the correct starting note (whether or not it was given) beginning on the right beat. If these things are in order and the student seems to be organized, the teacher should now explore some of the countless ways in which musicians relate notational symbols to musical tones. The approaches to use in different situations are ultimately learned only by experience, but here are a few of the common methods that might be explored.

See if the student can identify the pitches. It would seem that if he could have done this he would have written it down, but this is not always true. The student who cannot visualize the notes in relation to the meter may be reluctant to write anything down even if he knows some of the pitch names. Perhaps such a student can begin by putting dots on the proper lines or spaces even though he cannot yet symbolize their rhythmic character. On the other hand, if he does not know the pitches, various approaches should be tried, such as relating the tones (which he can sing) to diatonic number patterns. Can he find a triad outline, or a subsidiary tonal center, such as the dominant, or can he identify all of the tonic tones in the melody? If there is a tone early in the phrase that he can identify, can he be led to spot the same pitch when it occurs later? If the student can identify certain pitches essential to the shape of the phrase, can he relate the unknown pitches to the known? Is there a melodic sequence to be perceived that gives organization and reveals the pitches of the entire passage?

Another student may have roughly sketched down all of the pitches of the phrase on the first playing, but she seems unable to symbolize their rhythmic shape. Such a student may simply require better mental organization. See if she can verbally count the beat of the phrase while it is being played. If she can do this, perhaps she can be led to put the bar lines in the proper places, to relate rhythmic cells to the beats, and finally to notate all of the rhythms. Sometimes one may encounter a student whose real problem is nothing more than poor calligraphy coupled with a general lack of organization.

Also, some students make the mistake of working in pen rather than pencil, which can only augment the messiness when corrections are made. Although notation and calligraphy are discussed in the chapter on writing skills, students should begin to learn the principles of good notation at the very beginning of their theoretical studies.

Another alternative approach is occasionally to use the "wrong note" technique. In this exercise the students look at the score of the melody being played (sight-singing books work well for this) while the instructor plays the melody with a few incorrect pitches or rhythms. The students circle the notes that were played incorrectly and tell the instructor how to correct them. The teacher can invent gamelike variants of this exercise. It teaches pitch and rhythm perception in a way that is particularly germane to rehearsal technique.

One of the basic requirements for melodic dictation is the ability to apprehend melodies in large time spans rather than a few notes at a time. This also relates to basic performance skill, for students who can span phrases and periods in their musical comprehension will be able in performance to shape phrases, periods, and larger structures more intelligently than those who think only in small groups of tones. This is why students in melodic dictation should be asked to develop their melodic memories by singing back not only phrases but periods and even longer spans of melody as their capabilities increase.

In hearing a complete double period or larger structure students should be asked to identify the cadence types at the ends of each of the phrases, even if they are only implied. If they can do this, they will begin to perceive the overall structure, will see which phrases are similar or identical to earlier phrases, and will begin to identify modulations if they occur. In short, they will be practicing the skill of aural analysis, which is discussed in a later chapter. As the melodic-dictation materials begin to imply more complex harmonies including modulations, students should be asked at various points in a dictation to sing the tonal center and to relate that tonal center to the tonal center of the opening phrase.

As soon as the class has progressed to a respectable skill level in melodic dictation of diatonic melodies in treble, bass, alto, and tenor clefs, new scales and harmonic systems should be presented. At this point relevant new concepts should also be introduced in the analytical and compositional components of the theory course; this should be paralleled by new material in sight-singing and harmonic dictation. Dictation of Gregorian chants and chants of Semitic cultures introduces the church modes and other scales, and nondiatonic folk songs of various cultures can also be presented. Most students will have quite enough to do, however, simply making satisfactory progress in melodies of the common practice tradition, so that the introduction of these diverse materials often can occur only in the final term of the second-year theory course. Special efforts should be made, though, to ensure that the two-year theory sequence is not based exclusively upon music of the common practice period.

A variety of media and historical periods should be represented, for a broad perspective on music literature and history prepares the students for in-depth study in these areas. The opening solo violin line of the Berg Violin Concerto, for example, can be a challenge in melodic dictation that can lead to significant discussion of twentieth-century styles. Melodies from the Brahms chamber works, Schumann songs, and Mozart operas, along with examples from the symphonic literature, can introduce the concepts of various styles.

SIGHT-SINGING

The materials used for sight-singing should parallel those of melodic dictation. There is in fact a strong learning transfer between the two skills, and the class that spends a great deal of time with melodic dictation certainly observes accelerated progress in sight-singing. However, although the two have much in common, sight-singing is a separate skill with its own teaching and learning problems.

At the outset it must be decided what syllables shall be sung. In working with song literature the ideal is to use the words of the song, preferably in the original language. Obviously, the sounds of the words as well as the poetic imagery are a part of the overall artistic effect. Although this is certainly the best approach to song literature, it may not always be feasible in the theory class. Most students can read English well enough to learn to read pitches and rhythms with the words, but some are hindered by trying to deal with foreign languages in sight-singing. Voice majors may wish to sing in the original language, but English translations are certainly a workable compromise for the others.

Unfortunately, most sight-singing collections, while they may admirably represent vocal and instrumental literature, and may be carefully graded as to difficulty, do not include words for most vocal examples. Thus, a syllable, such as "la," may have to be used not only for instrumental examples but for song literature as well. The syllable "la" is suitable because the L sound is a good consonant with which to initiate a tone and because the open "ah" sound is a good vowel to sing in all registers. However, if the sight-singing collection does not contain at least a few examples of vocal literature with the words, the teacher should supplement the collection with separate scores in order that the class might have some experience in singing text. For variety, the use of Elizabethan part books (or modern-score editions) creates an interesting diversion while introducing some marvelous music. As in melodic dictation, the examples should be analyzed prior to attempting to sing them. Examination of cadence types, phrase structure, form, and general style helps the students to sing more accurately as well as to perform more musically.

Group singing at the beginning of a sight-singing session is useful for warming up the voices, but the basic practice of sight-singing consists of individual performance, for in group singing an individual can rely on stronger voices around him and may not actually be sight-singing at all. Above all, it is important that the teacher, by precept and example, encourage the students to make music whenever they sing. It is not being overly idealistic to expect genuine music making in the sight-singing process. In fact it is very practical. Some students become so preoccupied with the precision of rhythm and pitch as seen in individual notes that they fail to grasp the musical qualities of a melody. The teacher should convey the idea that it is a greater musical achievement to sing a musical example with a sense of phrasing, contour, dynamics, and overall shape, even with a few wrong notes, than painfully but accurately to reproduce each pitch and rhythm without an overall feeling of having made music.

Toward this end the teacher should only rarely correct a student in the midst of singing a melody, and then only when the student will profit by an immediate correction or is hopelessly off pitch. Recognition should be given to a musical performance, even if it contains a wrong note or two. The notes should be corrected, but the musicality should be valued.

The subject of musicality in sight-singing relates to the question of choice of materials to sing. It seems to me that there is considerable assurance of musical quality if one chooses a wide variety of instrumental and vocal music from the repertoire. Music composed specifically for sight-singing, though well graded and organized, misses the mark because it seems always to be lacking the humane spontaneity of music composed as music. Thus, though it may develop technique, it does little to enhance musical values. Music qua music, on the other hand, though it too develops technique, also encourages the student to view sight-singing as a part of the real world of music and to embrace it as a part of our musical heritage.

Teachers develop individual styles and methods for sight-singing, but there are a few guidelines that are generally helpful. In singing diatonic melodies students should be led to use both interval-reading and diatonic feeling to locate pitches. Pure diatonic feeling probably produces the more musical result, since this way pitches are grasped in the structure of the harmonic system; but there are times when interval-reading is a surer means of finding a pitch. To illustrate this distinction, one can imagine leaping from the fourth scale degree down to the seventh. To me it is more musical to negotiate this leap in terms of scale degrees rather than consciously to think diminished fifth. On the other hand, the leap from the fifth scale degree up to the fourth may best be negotiated by invoking the interval of the minor seventh rather than by means of scale degrees. Individuals may vary in their choices of approaches, and often one approach may support the other; but the teacher should be ready to perceive when the alternative approach might be preferable.

Some students who have difficulty finding pitches seem to have poor pitch memories. They may sing a pitch at the beginning of a measure but be unable to recall it when it appears two or three notes later. Others, when the going gets tough, seem to lose track of the tonal center. In both cases simply explaining the situation in a careful but practical way may help.

For students who habitually fail to observe obvious cues, such as triadic outlines, melodic centering around a focal pitch, or clear sequence patterns, some extra analysis before singing may help. They can be asked to identify as many such cues as they can before beginning to sing. It is also useful at the very earliest stages of sight-singing to ask these students to state the clef, key, meter, scale degree of beginning note, beat that the first note is on, and (given the tonic note) to sing the first note of the melody, all before undertaking to perform the example. This helps to overcome the tendency to rush in without observing the most obvious preconditions.

In examples containing modulations the students should learn to establish firmly the new key in the area of the modulation. The chromatic tones by which the modulation is confirmed should be approached and left through intervallic hearing, since the old diatonic tonal center has at this point begun to disappear. One exercise to develop this skill is for the teacher to sing the example just into the modulation and then have the class (or individuals) sing 1-3-5-3-1, thus outlining the tonic in the new key.

Sight-singing should be carried on in at least the four clefs that are in common use today (treble, bass, alto, and tenor). Some teachers advocate the use of the other clefs as aids to transposition and for future research. However, time constraints in a two-year theory sequence may preclude this. In any case the four commonly used clefs are all that most musicians will be called upon to use whether going into the world of professional performance, research, or teaching. Students who show promise in the areas of composition and theory, however, should be privately encouraged to read in seven clefs.[3]

In reading rhythms, the cells discussed earlier are useful; and the class should drill on the appropriate cell patterns at the beginning of a section that presents new rhythmic problems. If, when confronted with syncopations or cross-rhythms notated with ties across bar lines or from one beat to another, the student can visualize the cell patterns that are tied together, he or she should be able to perform the passage correctly. Conducting while singing also helps, as does the practice of having one group tap the background of the beat while the others sing the rhythm.

Another exercise for both pitch and rhythm is the practice of "tacet singing." In this approach the class agrees to sing a melody together up to a given point. From that point they continue mentally singing, but without sound, up to another specified point where they resume singing aloud. If everyone resumes singing on the same pitch at the same time, it can be assumed that they all successfully negotiated the "tacet" section. The exercise has some potential for developing skills and some diagnostic function. It is most useful, however, simply as an interesting change of activity.

The "wrong note" technique discussed earlier under the heading of "Melodic Dictation" can also be used as an alternative approach in sight-singing. When a student has performed a sight-singing example creditably, but with one or two wrong pitches or rhythms, the teacher can sing it back with the same small errors the student made. If able to locate those errors after hearing the teacher sing it, the student will probably correct them in a second attempt at performing the example. This is particularly useful when the errors were the result of careless reading rather than inaccurate interval association.

As in melodic dictation, the class should begin to explore other scale systems as soon as a respectable level of diatonic sight-singing capability is achieved. In addition, score-reading activities can be undertaken—for example, part-singing of choral works or sight-singing from instrumental scores including the use of transposition. Of all the melodic aural skills, sight-singing is the most musically rewarding because it truly is a music-making activity. If approached in this sense, it can be most beneficial to the learning of musician-ship skills.

NOTES

1. See my recent book *Theories of Musical Texture in Western History* (New York: Garland, 1995), pages 3–12, for a detailed discussion of the phenomenon of just intonation.

2. For a summary of the history of tuning systems in Western history, see pages 3–112 of *Theories of Musical Texture in Western History* by John D. White (New York: Garland, 1995).

3. The legendary composition teacher Nadia Boulanger insisted that all of her students learn to sight-read in seven clefs, and there is no question that she was one of the greatest theory teachers of the twentieth century.

THREE

Aural Skills: Polyphonic and Harmonic

POLYPHONY AND ESTHETICS

As we in the twenty-first century survey the various musics of the world, we begin to realize that the polyphony of Western culture is truly unique. There are the ragas of India; the monody of Native American music; gamelans, the unique rhythms of traditional African music; oriental styles and forms, and many other kinds of musical artistry among the many cultures of the world. Yet there is nothing on earth comparable to the contrapuntal or polyphonic concepts of music in Western culture over the past millennium. The polyphonic textures of composers such as Machaut, Dunstable, di Lasso, Palestrina, Monteverdi, Biber, Bach, Mozart, Brahms, Mahler, Bartók, Stravinsky, Penderecki, and Ligeti stand as monuments of our musical culture. While it is important to learn something of the music of other cultures in our global village, the primary theme in the study of our music theory must be the music of Western history—and most of it is polyphonic.

Polyphony or *counterpoint* is music in which two or more melodies combine to form a texture that is more complex than a single line. Ideally, the various melodies in the texture are beautiful in themselves but have the additional attribute of forming harmonies together. When the rhythms of the various melodies create a feeling of independence from each other this adds musical interest, and when they also possess a variety of timbral traits, the result can be interesting and complex music. No valid study of musical esthetics

53

can avoid the subject of polyphony, and no discussion of esthetic philosophy is credible without it.

A logical sequence in the study of music theory is to begin with rhythm and melody as we did in the previous chapter, and then put these two elements together in a texture of more than one voice line or stratum to form polyphonic or contrapuntal textures.[1] Most of the music of our culture is essentially harmonic in nature. By this I mean that the affective or emotional qualities of our music are created in large part through the composite effect of two or more melodic lines played simultaneously. This is not to downplay the esthetic importance of the single line—of melody—for in any contrapuntal-harmonic texture much of the musical interest is derived from the juxtaposition of pitch, contour, and rhythm among the various melodic lines. Indeed, the writing of counterpoint is the writing of melodies. These melodies may (and should) be beautiful in themselves, but when they are heard together in the contrapuntal texture for which they were designed, the overall effect is much greater than the sum of the parts.

This being true, one can conclude that elements other than melody have contributed significantly to the beauty of a contrapuntal-harmonic texture. Among these are the composite elements of sound and rhythm, but it is the element of harmony in its vertical perspective that traditionally has been of great concern to the theory teacher. Yet the theory teacher's concern with harmony viewed vertically can lead to a common misconception in the teaching of harmonic aural skills.

This is the wrong-headed notion of harmony as a series of vertical chords marching through a phrase to arrive at a cadence point. No music, not even the simplest hymn tune, derives its essential musicality exclusively from this phenomenon. The polar counterpoint of bass and soprano, the quality of the cadence in relation to the inception of the phrase, the timbres and poetic imagery of the words, the quality of dissonance, the textural spacing of the parts—all of these contribute significantly to the overall effect of even the most homophonic music. And to reduce music as beautifully complex as, say, a Bach harmonization of the *Passion Chorale* to a series of vertical chords interrupted from time to time by cadence points—that is to miss the point altogether.

This is not to say that a reductive process cannot be very useful in ear-training. Many theory teachers have successfully practiced a kind of Schenkerian reduction (whether or not by that name) in harmonic dictation for decades. Its use requires no textbook explication, but, since it is perhaps the most common method of harmonic dictation, it is discussed in some detail later.

A responsible theory teacher with a good background in the history of music theory finds ways to introduce the high points in the continuum of polyphonic practice over the past millennium—without, of course, turning the classroom into a graduate seminar. I do not recommend a structured presentation comparable to that of a course in the history of music theory. It can be done with near-casual commentary during harmonic dictation drill or when introducing contrapuntal concepts, ideally in both situations. What follows is a brief discussion of the history of polyphony to help the beginning theory teacher organize this information.

COUNTERPOINT IN HISTORY

If we can imagine ourselves as parishioners in a medieval cathedral, twelfth- and thirteenth-century counterpoint can be as fascinating and emotionally moving as that of Palestrina, Bach, or Penderecki. The phrase structure and cadence points are engrossing to theorists, and one of the ways of tracing the history of polyphony is to examine the cadences of contrapuntal works from various periods beginning even as early as Guido's *Micrologus*. Even a student in freshman theory can understand ninth-century cadences in terms of the cadence points he or she is hearing in harmonic dictation of music in eighteenth-century style, or even in the part-writing exercises the student is creating.

"Perfection" was desired at the endings of medieval phrases, so the cadences of the ninth century concluded on a perfect interval, very often an octave or unison. If an octave or unison is approached by step in two voices moving in contrary motion, we have the beginning of the *clausula vera* (true closing) in which a third contracts to a unison or a sixth expands to an octave as in figure 3.1. The music theory student can clearly see this in the outer voices of the eighteenth-century progression of vii^6–I, and the principle of contrary motion is clearly demonstrated, as shown in figure 3.1.

Of course a unison or octave could also be approached by oblique motion where one voice remains on the same note and the other

Figure 3.1

approaches the octave or unison by step, yet the *clausula vera* with
its contrary motion became a favorite, for it persisted in various
forms for a thousand years—it is still with us today. The "Landini
cadence" of the fourteenth century was a variation on the seventh
expanding to the octave. The ascending voice (the upper voice in
two-part counterpoint) descended by step before it leaped up a third
to the final, forming first a seventh and then a sixth above the penul-
timate tone in the lower voice. Named after the famous fourteenth-
century Florentine organist, the Landini cadence began to disappear
in the pre-Renaissance, but in its place appeared a *clausula vera* with
a 7-6 or 2-3 suspension before the final. In tonal counterpoint of the
common practice period (1650–1900), the *clausula vera* became a part
of the authentic cadence (V–I) with the leading tone moving up to
the tonic and the second scale degree moving down to the tonic—
still a seventh expanding to an octave or a third contracting to a unison. (See figure 3.2.)

Another way of considering the history of polyphony is to examine the concepts of consonance and dissonance in the various periods of music history. Theorists have noticed that from the ninth
century to the present the musical concept of consonance seems to
have gradually moved from the lowest partials of the overtone series

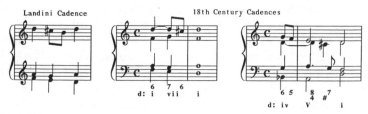

Figure 3.2

upward. That is, the earliest organum found the 8ve, P5, and P4 to be the "perfect" consonances, with all other intervals viewed as dissonances.

While there are a few problems with the theory that the overtone series presents a synoptic view of the history of consonance and dissonance, it holds up as we proceed to the pre-Renaissance period when thirds and sixths began to be viewed as consonances (though "imperfect" consonances). When sevenths became part of the tertial structure in common practice harmony, this added seconds and sevenths to the list of consonances, and by the twentieth century our ears were beginning to accept almost any combination of tones as consonant depending on the context. One of the questions that had to be asked, and Oliver Messiaen asked it—"If everything is consonant, where is the dissonance?" The two great "contraries" of harmony are the contrast of consonance and dissonance, and it is this element of polyphony that has historically been one of its greatest beauties. Thus, consonance–dissonance is the yin–yang of music. Indeed, William Blake's "Doctrine of Contraries" can be applied to harmony in Western music as well as to life:

> Without contraries is no progression
> Attraction and Repulsion, Reason and Energy, Love and Hate
> Are necessary to Human existence.
> (William Blake, "Marriage of Heaven and Hell")

There is yet another way to view the history of polyphony, and that is from the perspective of texture. In medieval counterpoint the voices crossed above and below each other quite freely. This was still happening in the Renaissance, but there began to be a tendency to keep the various voices within their own individual strata. The four-part chorales of the Baroque adhered quite strictly to the no-crossing principle.[2] Also, the voices, except for the bass, remained within an octave of adjacent voices. In some ways this vertical compartmentalization is a limitation of common practice music.

Also the number of voices in a polyphonic texture was becoming an increasingly significant factor. In the earliest organum there were only two voices, but this could be expanded into four by doubling each voice at the octave. Theorists have called this "composite organum." Throughout the ensuing millennium there was a fluctuation in the number of voices, with four being the norm in the common practice period. There are, however, many works before, after, and during the common practice period that have textures of many more voices; and the spacing of the voices is highly varied as well. At the upper end of the spectrum we have the polychoral textures of the early seventeenth century which might have as many as twenty separate vocal and instrumental parts, but this is surpassed in the late twentieth century by electronic works in which the integrity of voices may be lost entirely to be replaced by a kind of pointillism in granular textures which have been called "clouds."

Texture is also affected by the melodic style where, among other factors, we have the question of steps versus leaps. Most of the early counterpoint treatises advocated predominantly stepwise motion. Moderation in the use of leaps was the rule of thumb, but gradually Western ears began to crave more excitement in the character of melodies. By the time we get to the twentieth century we find Messiaen advocating the use of the tritone at melodic cadences—the *Diabolus in Musica* of earlier periods. There is no "evolution" here in the Darwinian sense, for each polyphonic texture in our history reflects its own Zeitgeist. The *Agnus Dei* of Machaut's Notre Dame Mass is as beautiful and moving as comparable sections of Bach's Masses, or Mozart's or Fauré's, Stravinsky's, or those of Penderecki.[3]

TWO-PART DICTATION

In order to effect a smooth transition from beginning melodic dictation, and to emphasize the linear-horizontal aspect of counterpoint, the harmonic element of aural skills may be introduced by means of simple two-part dictation. This first exposure to harmonic dictation should take place as soon as the class begins to manifest some mastery of simple melodic dictation. Thus, the introduction of two melodies heard simultaneously becomes an extension of melodic dictation and serves to emphasize the horizontal aspect of harmony over the vertical. Of course harmony and counterpoint of virtually all periods are usually conceived (composed) in terms of vertical relationships among the voices (recent research suggests that this is true even in the medieval motet). But this should not prevent the student from perceiving the end result as a musical texture of two or more horizontal lines (melodies) that, taken together, form a composite texture of harmonic beauty—a linear design, if you will.

Students are immersed early in the study of figured bass, part-writing, and perhaps species counterpoint, all of which are based in large part upon a vertical conception of harmony. Yet for the performer and the composer the best understanding of musical form—the phraseology and shape of music—is achieved by means of the horizontal dimension of music. The syntactical structure of a Mozart piano sonata is heard in terms of the relationships of interrelated events (antecedent and consequent phrases, high and low melodic points, and so on) all in a horizontal (linear) time continuum.

This is a very practical and relevant kind of understanding for musicians to achieve; and this is why, given an essentially vertical conception of contrapuntal-harmonic technique, it is vitally important to preserve the spirit of music as an essentially melodic (i.e., linear-horizontal) art. Theory teachers who come to grips with this paradox find themselves teaching musicianship in a much truer and more practical sense than those who cling unremittingly to a vertical contrapuntal-harmonic technique, which, though demonstrable as a compositional technique, tends to obscure the reality of the musical experience.

It may seem occasionally in this chapter that I have ignored my own precepts; for some of my teaching of aural harmonic skills is based upon a vertical conception of harmony. Yet its purpose is to lead toward a true understanding of music. It is a technique that can lead to artistic achievements or to mere facility, but it is an essential part of a musician's training. The extent to which the technique can be infused with art is a measure of the success of the teacher and the musical talent of the student.

The first two-part dictations may be very simple diatonic note-against-note exercises played at the piano. At first they should be within human voice ranges, such as a soprano and bass line. The bass and soprano lines of Bach chorales (omitting the inner voices) work very well and lead conveniently to four-part harmonic dictation later.

Again, as in melodic dictation, the teacher should find a way to observe the students at the blackboard or at their seats during the dictation process. If the example is several phrases long, the teacher should play it once in its entirety and then begin to break it down phrase by phrase. The students should be checked to see that they have set down all of the known preconditions correctly—the key and meter signatures, the beginning notes, and so on.

When students are observed to be on the wrong track, the teacher should use a Socratic questioning process to set them straight rather than simply telling them what's wrong. For example, if students have written incorrect notes at the cadence, one can ask them what the cadence type is. If they identify it correctly, then the teacher can pursue the questioning to determine whether they can make their written notes coincide with the cadence. If they then correctly change the notes at the cadence, one should point out that the obvious questions they have finally answered were questions that they might just as well have asked themselves. In subsequent sessions the students' progress can be observed and additional questioning used as needed.

This follow-up process is an essential part of successful ear-training. Teachers should take pains to remember the individual progress and problems of each student. In this way they can have a kind of mental communication with the students, anticipating problems and steering them toward the appropriate inductive processes. This of course is one of the shortcomings of taped dictations for use outside of class. Students may use a library of taped dictations of graduated difficulty, and for some of them it will increase their progress; but there is still no substitute for the guidance of a perceptive teacher.

In two-part dictation most students immediately transcribe the top line at about the same level of proficiency that they have demonstrated in melodic dictation. It is the bottom line that is the challenge, though some are able to hear it as a separate entity quite readily. Those who are having difficulty should be asked to sing along with the lower line (within their natural voice range, of course). Most students gradually improve as they use the sing-along technique, but they should be urged to convert this to silent singing as soon as possible.

Since the early exercises are similar to first-species counterpoint, some teachers have experimented with the teaching of beginning counterpoint as an integrated activity with two-part dictation. This, of course, means that the students will be concerned with the vertical intervallic relationships of the two voices in note-against-note counterpoint. Some students may have greater success in dictation when viewing the two voices from this harmonic perspective—as a series of vertical juxtapositions. It is important, though, to preserve the concept of two horizontal melodic lines.

Carrying the integration of counterpoint and harmonic dictation even further, one might possibly construct an entire beginning theory course around the integration of musicianship skills with the teaching of species counterpoint. In addition to harmonic (i.e., contrapuntal) dictation, sight-singing and analysis can readily be practiced upon the various species of counterpoint. It tends, however, toward a somewhat narrow approach to theory, though it might well be the best way to teach aspiring composers. In any case all students should have some exposure to Fux's *Gradus ad Parnassum*, at least to Part I, which deals with two-part counterpoint. This is discussed further in chapter 5.

As the class develops greater skill in two-part dictation, a few passing tones should be added. Then, at the teacher's discretion, the rhythms in both voices slowly should become increasingly complex and independent, and canons should be used. Exercises of this sort can be continued throughout the first year; but at a fairly early stage they should be supplemented by harmonic activities that lead directly into the course of music history from the eighteenth century to the present.

CHORD QUALITY

The discrimination of chord qualities is an extension of the hearing of intervals. Most students develop proficiency in the hearing of harmonic intervals (the two tones of the interval played simultaneously) quite early in the first-year theory course. It is at this point that the discrimination of chord qualities should begin. Major and minor triads are already among the aural skills of most students. They distinguish them on a purely physical basis—like differentiating between apples and oranges—without using a logico-mathematical process. The concept of the intervallic structure of tertial sonorities and their terminology should be introduced at the same time that the students undertake the discrimination of chord qualities—that is, the terminology and structure of the four traditional types of triads and the five types of seventh chords normally used in diatonic harmony.

As a general rule, the part-writing activities of the first-year theory course should parallel the ear-training activities; so that early in the first semester, when chord-quality discrimination is introduced, the students are dealing with pure triads in part-writing, not with

seventh chords. Seventh chords should be introduced simultaneously in both ear-training and part-writing at some point about half
way through the first year, but their terminology can be presented
at the very beginning of chord-quality discrimination.

Another activity that integrates concepts and aural activities is the
presentation of the overtone series, which correlates well with intervals as well as the concept of tertial sonorities. If it was not presented
along with the introduction of intervals, it can be presented concurrently with the concept of triads. It is an opportunity to bring in the
subject of Pythagoras, the concept of the interval as the ratio
between the frequencies of two tones, and the diatonic implications
of the overtone series. The mutually supportive integration of all
activities of the theory course is the subject of chapter 7, but discussion of various aspects of it is touched upon throughout the book.

Assuming that the class is doing well in the discrimination of
major and minor triads in root position (but with varying registers,
soprano positions, number of voices, and textures), the augmented
and diminished triads can be introduced. If the class is really solid
on major and minor triads at this point, throwing just one diminished or augmented triad into a drill made up of major and minor
triads makes it stand out like a sore thumb. The interval classifica-
tion system (see chapter 2), which would have been introduced with
the study of intervals, is useful at this point to explain exactly why
the augmented triad sounds as it does (because it is made up
entirely of fourth-classification intervals—M3 and m6). The "rootlessness" of the augmented triad should also be mentioned—
leading into a discussion of the whole-tone scale and the peculiar
affective or emotional qualities of scales or sonorities that sound the
same regardless of which tone is on the bottom. That inverting them
does not change their sound is an important fact relating to their
place in music history and is a good point for classroom discussion.

I have a preference for putting the diminished triad in first inversion when it is first presented, since that is the way it is usually
found during the common practice period. Since it necessitates the
presentation of the theory of inversion somewhat prematurely,
some theory teachers may prefer not to do this. It does correlate well
with the teaching of part-writing, however; and if this practice is
adopted, it works well to introduce the progression I– vii⁶–I⁶ along
with it. Since the most common uses of the diminished triad are as
vii⁶ in the major and minor modes and as ii⁶ in the minor mode, its

usual doubling in four-part harmony (doubling of the third, that is, the bass note, in its usual inversion) should also be introduced at this point.

Even if the teacher chooses not to introduce the diminished triad in first inversion, it is important to point out that the diminished triad as a vii triad (with the raised-seventh scale degree when in the minor mode) invariably functions as a substitute for V (or V⁷) with its strongest of all tendencies to move to the tonic. All of this touches on the integration of aural skills with part-writing and the practice of structuralism in ear-training—of which more later.

Among the teaching strategies for aural discrimination of triad qualities is the analysis of intervallic structure. The vertical deployment of major and minor thirds among the four types of triads should be thoroughly learned along with assiduous drilling on triad spelling. As in the study of intervals, teachers who are the least bit casual about triad spelling discover too late that although their students can aurally discriminate chord qualities, this skill is useless because they cannot spell them. The singing of arpeggiated triads up from a given root with letter names should be practiced frequently in the early stages, and students should be urged to do this outside of class as well. Games similar to those discussed in the previous chapter under "Teaching Strategies" can be devised to maintain classroom interest, and triad spelling quizzes should be given occasionally.

Discrimination among the five common types of seventh chords depends upon a thorough aural and conceptual knowledge of triads. Seventh chords, after all, are simply a further extension of the tertial progression; and once triads and intervals are thoroughly learned, the step from triads to seventh chords is a small one.

Structural hearing must enter into the aural discrimination of seventh-chord qualities. As in triad qualities, the students should sing arpeggiated seventh chords (with letter names) up from given roots, but they should also be aware of their potential function in the diatonic structure, particularly of the major-minor seventh chord. One enjoyable classroom exercise to develop this is to play a Mm⁷ in an SATB texture (four-part chorus) and have the members of the class sing the four parts and resolve them to a tonic according to established part-writing principles. For variety, those taking the seventh of the chord can resolve it to the third of a major or a minor tonic triad as the teacher instructs. For further classroom interest they can later learn choral resolutions to deceptive cadences in both the major and the minor modes. The process here is to write the progression in four parts on the blackboard. Transpositions can then be effected vocally, and minor changes can also be introduced.

These exercises are particularly useful for the Mm⁷ because of its strong diatonic function in its role as the dominant seventh. But structural hearing can also be used with the other seventh chords, although other teaching strategies may prove more fruitful. Since the class is now dealing with sonorities of four tones and is already familiar with mod-12 through the interval-classification table, this is an appropriate place to introduce the concepts of sets and interval vectors by which the intervallic content of seventh chords (and other more complex sonorities) is more fully revealed. Since even today it is not universally taught in our college and university music departments, I shall present it briefly here.

SETS AND INTERVAL VECTORS

A *set* is a group of tones sounded together (a chord) or several separate tones in close proximity heard as a group (almost like a chord). The *interval vector* tells how many intervals of each of the six classifications are found in the set. It is a simple method of determining harmonic quality on the basis of intervallic content. One starts with a chord or several tones that are grouped together in the context of the music, such as the one shown in figure 3.3.

This group of tones is then converted to what is called "normal order" by rearranging them in ascending order within the smallest possible intervallic span, as in figure 3.4.

Obviously this requires octave displacement to reduce all pitches to within an octave. Pitch class, then, rather than actual pitch, is characteristic of the system, just as in Schenkerian analysis. Next, the lowest pitch in the normal order is represented by zero while

Figure 3.3

Normal Order:

Figure 3.4

the other pitches are assigned numbers representing the number of half-steps by which each of them is separated from the lowest pitch, as in figure 3.5.

The resulting row of numbers (0, 1, 5, 6, 7) is called the *pitch-set* and is traditionally enclosed in parentheses. The mod-12 system discussed in the preceding chapter has been used to arrive at (0, 1, 5, 6, 7). This pitch-set can be thought of as a kind of tag or label for that group of pitches.

To find the quantity of each kind of interval (that is, the interval class) in the set, we construct an interval vector. An *interval vector* is a six-digit code, each digit from I through VI representing the six interval classes, respectively. The actual number that appears in each of the six places indicates the number of intervals of that interval class to be found in the set. The first step in building the vector is to construct a "subtraction triangle." The set we arrived at previously is placed across the top as follows:

$$0 \ 1 \ 5 \ 6 \ 7$$
$$4 \ 5 \ 6$$
$$1 \ 2$$
$$1$$

To get the second row of numbers we take the first number (other than 0) and subtract it from each of the other numbers in the set: 1 from 5, 1 from 6, and 1 from 7, thus arriving at 4-5-6 in the second row. The same is done for each subsequent row, working downward to one digit. Then using the interval-class table (the mod-12 column shown in table 3.1), we count the number of digits representing each interval class and place those totals in the six places of the interval vector.

Pitch Set:

0 1 5 6 7

Figure 3.5

Table 3.1   Interval Class Table

Interval Class	Intervals	Mod-12
I	m2–M7	1–11
II	M2–m7	2–10
III	m3–M6	3–9
IV	M3–m6	4–8
V	P4–P5	5–7
VI	Tritone	6

Of 1s and 11s in the subtraction triangle there are three; so we put the number 3 in the first place of the interval vector. Of 2s and 10s there is only one; so 1 goes in the second place. There are no 3s or 9s; one 4 (no 8s); of 5s and 7s there are three; and there are two 6s. This produces the following interval vector which is traditionally underlined: 3 1 0 1 3 2. With a little experience one learns quickly to "read" the interval vector to observe that, while there are no third-class intervals (m3–M6), there are three each of first and fifth class, meaning that the predominant intervals in the pitch-set are perfect intervals (P4–P5) and the highly dissonant half-steps (or major sevenths). That there are two tritones adds to the dissonance, and the remaining intervals are one whole step and one major third.

The previous calculations can be checked by means of the following formula, with n being the number of tones in the original pitch-set.

$$\frac{n^2 - n}{2} = \text{(total of the numbers in the vector)}$$

$$\frac{25 - 5}{2} = 10$$

$$10 = 10$$

The formula simply determines the total number of possible intervals in the set, which should equal the number of intervals represented in the vector, in this case $10 = 10$.

The system was first set forth by Howard Hanson (1896–1981) in *The Harmonic Materials of Modern Music* (Appleton-Century-Crofts, 1960) as a method by which composers could more fully comprehend the harmonic properties of twentieth-century music. His system used letters to represent the six interval classes, but a few years later Allen Forte presented a numerical version of the system in an article entitled "A Theory of Set-Complexes for Music."[4] Then in *The Structure of Atonal Music* (Yale University Press, 1973), Forte carried the system further, including the idea of interval vectors and other concepts presented here. The letters of Hanson's system are just as easy to manipulate as the numerals, but since the latter are in more common use today and since Forte has borrowed the terminology of professional mathematics, it is his numerical version that I have presented here.

The system is most often used as an analytical tool, and the critical step is the initial selection of the pitch-sets that are to furnish the basis for analysis. The rule of thumb is to group pitches together if, in one way or another, they are heard together as a discrete musical unit. Vertical sonorities (chords) form pitch-sets in themselves; but linear pitch groups, if heard as entities, can also form pitch-sets, as can combinations of vertical and linear pitches. Phrase and dynamic markings may delineate pitch-sets, and instrumentation may also be a factor. The mathematical study and manipulation of pitch-sets and interval vectors has become an active area of scholarship in contemporary theory. Having embarked upon sets and interval vectors as an alternative approach to the aural discrimination of complex sonorities, let us examine the interval vectors of the five conventional diatonic seventh chords.

MM^7: 1 0 1 2 2 0
mm^7: 0 1 2 1 2 0
dd^7: 0 0 4 0 0 2
dm^7: 0 1 2 1 1 1
Mm^7: 0 1 2 1 1 1

In comparing these vectors one is immediately struck by the fact that the half-diminished seventh (dm^7) and the major-minor seventh have identical interval vectors. Thus, they possess the same intervallic content. The immediate reaction of some students to this fact is that it cannot be true because they neither sound alike nor function alike. Yet it is true, and closer examination of the two sonorities reveals that a root-position major-minor seventh is an exact intervallic inversion (not to be confused with triadic inversion, where the pitch-classes remain the same) of a root-position half-diminished seventh. This is why they have the same intervallic content, for any two sonorities that are intervallic inversions (mirrors) of each other will have the same intervallic content—as in the major triad and the minor triad, both of which are represented by the interval vector 0 0 1 1 1 0. They are mirror sonorities.

This raises some question about the validity of interval vectors in regard to their function in representing the harmonic qualities of complex sonorities. No one reared on the harmony of the common practice period would insist that the major and minor triad sound alike. Indeed this is one of the easiest aural distinctions for beginning theory students to make. Nor can the exotic qualities of the half-diminished seventh (witness the "Prelude and Liebestod" of *Tristan und Isolde*) be confused with the strong functional character of the major-minor seventh, with its urgency to progress to the tonic.

Yet the system does have validity for modern harmony. One explanation of this paradox is that the ears of Western culture have become so attuned to the musical symbolism of functional harmony that we are capable of making much finer discriminations in music of the common practice period—to hear more sensitively—than we can when listening to new music that does not use tertial harmonic function. There may be some truth in this, but my experience in listening to and composing nontriadic music is that, while the affective qualities of two mirror sonorities will be similar, they are not identical. Thus, the reason that we are able to make much sharper distinctions between mirror sonorities in music of the common practice period is, I think, because of the function itself. We hear the major-minor seventh as distinct from the half-diminished seventh because we hear the former as a dominant within the diatonic structure.

From a phenomenological standpoint Hindemith's theory of root determination—by which the lower tone of the lowest perfect fifth in a complex sonority is defined as its root—may also be relevant here. Do we hear the major-minor seventh as more stable—and thus capable of functioning as a dominant—than the half-diminished seventh because its perfect fifth includes its root? And is the half-diminished seventh less stable in the functional harmonic system because its perfect fifth does not include its root?

For the other three seventh chords, however, for which the structural function is not as strong as in the dominant-tonic progression, the interval vectors can be useful in ear-training. The major seventh (MM⁷), for example, is the only one of the five that possesses a first-class interval. The biting minor second or major seventh is its most striking feature, and listening for this can help students to identify it. It also has two perfect fifths, but this is also true of the minor seventh (mm^7), so this fact is less helpful.

The most distinctive feature of the full-diminished seventh (dd^7) is the predominance of the third interval class—there are four minor thirds (or major sixths) in this sonority. This fact, plus the characteristic rootlessness of the diminished seventh, can be very helpful to the student. A detailed classroom discussion of the intervallic content of these seventh chords can do much to improve student discrimination of chord quality.

Correlating the spelling with the hearing of seventh chords can be achieved by drills similar to those used in interval and triad training. Again, singing of arpeggiations of seventh chords with letter names can be very useful. Also, letting students take turns at the piano playing seventh chords for dictation helps both their keyboard and their spelling ability. And, finally, giving chord-spelling quizzes can be as much a learning experience as it is an evaluation.

TRIADIC INVERSION

The hearing of triadic inversions should begin well before the midpoint in the first-year theory course. It is perhaps best to begin with a discussion of the Rameau *Traité d'Harmonie*, thus covering the theory of inversions and the concept of fundamental bass within a historical context. In addition the students should examine the use of inversions in music of the seventeenth and eighteenth centuries so as to see that even before Rameau's treatise in 1723 composers realized that a triad retains much of its original character and identity regardless of which of its members is in the bass.

In the discussion of learning theory in chapter 1, I pointed out that students may identify the first inversion of a major triad in several ways. One is to identify it physically (through P learning)—the students simply learn through association what a first-inversion major triad sounds like, just as they learn what an oboe sounds like or what a lemon tastes like.

Others may use the logico-mathematical (LM) process in various forms. From the standpoint of potential musical growth I believe that it is best to encourage students toward the type of LM learning that I call structural hearing.[5] This is generally true even for those students who appear to have no difficulty hearing inversions through P learning. The progression of V^6 to I is a good model for this, and its basis is to identify the first inversion in terms of its most natural function—to progress as a first-inversion dominant to the root-position tonic. (It is assumed that the students are already familiar with diatonic root movement through both part-writing and analysis.) Then, when isolated inversions are played in harmonic dictation, the students mentally resolve a first-inversion major triad as a V^6 progressing to its tonic, the tonic being conceived via the students' inductive process. Imagining an isolated inversion as being in a harmonic context and then checking to see if the actual sound fits the imaginary context is the essence of the process.

In structural hearing of second inversions (of major and minor triads) it works well to imagine the sonority as a cadential I^6_4 with its strong tendency to resolve to V. A third-inversion Mm^7 "wants" to resolve to a major triad in first inversion like a V^4_2 progressing to I^6. A first-inversion diminished triad can be conceived as a vii^6 within an imagined context of vii^6–I.

Identifying inversions of triads and seventh chords within a functional harmonic context (even though the context is imaginary) leads smoothly into the practice of harmonic dictation; and the students' vocabulary of harmonic progressions parallels their increasing abilities to hear inversions. To supplement structural hearing of inversions students should be asked to perform intervallic analyses of triadic inversions. This can be done according to the plan shown in figure 3.6.

Some students will need practice in step 2, locating the bass tones of various inversions. To practice this the teacher can play inversions at the piano and have the class or individuals sing back the bass tones. Females seem to have more difficulty with this than males, perhaps because the bass tones of inversions are usually not within the singing range of the female voice, whereas they are often within the range of the male voice. At first some students will sing back the root of the triad, regardless of whether or not it is in the bass. To identify the root is a skill to be valued; and the teacher's task is to build from this skill. One way is occasionally to arpeggiate the chord to call attention to its intervallic structure. Varying the doublings and the soprano positions also alters student perceptions of the bass tone. Repetitive experimentation with individual problems can yield results in the development of this essential musical skill.

(1) *Teacher plays inversion at piano.*

(Teacher Plays)

(2) *Student Sings Bass Tone.*

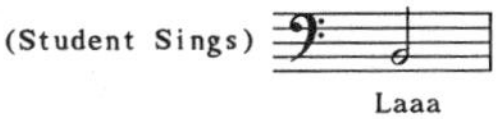

(Student Sings)

Laaa

(3) *Student sings upward from bass tone to nearest available pitch-classes found in triad.*

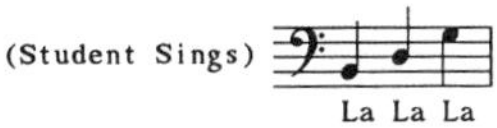

(Student Sings)

La La La

(4) *Student identifies m3 and P4 sung in Step 3.*

(5) *Student identifies first-inversion major triad.*

Figure 3.6

By and large those who have no difficulty isolating the bass tones of inversions are those who appear to have learned to hear inversions through P learning rather than LM learning. We all tend to hear vertical sonorities as single composite sounds; but it seems that some are more facile than others in making distinctions between vertical sonorities and in being able to analyze the individual tones that are present. From the standpoint of musical cognition this suggests that there are significant individual differences in the way that we hear music and, ergo, in the way that music affects us emotionally. I have found empirical evidence to support this in student responses to increasing their aural skills, some of whom have said that music became more meaningful or "affecting" after having made significant advances in their aural skill levels, particularly in harmonic dictation.

A fascinating exercise for developing aural perception of vertical sonorities is to use the voice to sing arpeggiations of major and minor triads in root position, first inversion, and second inversion. At first the teacher goes around the class singing patterns like those shown in figure 3.7 (on the syllable "la"), asking the students to identify the inversions of each group of three tones.

The students are asked to sing each one back to the teacher before

Figure 3.7

identifying it. Then, after the skill has progressed a bit, each student individually takes the place of the teacher, going around the class singing arpeggiations of the various triadic inversions. A few students will very much feel "on the spot," but the exercise stimulates interest in intervallic analysis; and after the students discover that it is harder to sing the arpeggiations than to identify them according to inversion, it becomes a kind of contest.

This, and other exercises in which the voice is used, gets at an aural skill from at least two angles; and it also correlates sight-singing with ear-training to help integrate the elements of musical craft. One must consciously know the intervallic structure of an inversion to be able to arpeggiate it vocally from scratch, interval by interval. Perhaps even more of an aid to sight-singing, it substantially increases the ability to hear and identify inversions.

Finally, as in all practice of aural skills, the element of sound must be varied to ensure that the students are capable of identifying inversions in a variety of textures, soprano positions, and timbres. At the piano, inversions should occasionally be played in more than four parts and extending beyond the range of the human voice; and all possibilities of soprano positions should be explored.

It is difficult to vary timbres in the theory classroom, but once in a while instruments should be brought to class. By this means other aspects of musical craft can be explored while studying inversions. The class can write inversions of all triads and seventh chords to be played by various groups of instruments present in the class. While the primary function of this exercise is ear-training on inversions, it also encourages students to learn instrumental transpositions and to explore the factors of timbre, texture, and dynamics through the vertical deployment of instrumental tones—another example of integrative theory teaching.

HARMONIC DICTATION

Very early in the first-year theory course, perhaps in the second week and certainly not later than the fourth, the class should begin to identify brief chordal passages played at the piano in the major mode, such as I-V-I, I-IV-I, V-I-iii-IV-V, I-vi-IV-V-I, and so on. At first they should be entirely in the major mode, all in root position, without dissonant tones, and in four-part vocal style with conventional doublings. They should be played at a normal musical pace with good rhythm so that the continuity of the phrase is readily apparent. The students will identify the chords primarily through the bass line, by means of their melodic dictation ability. That is, if they can identify the scale degree that is in the bass, they will know the Roman numeral. At this point they need not write them down. The teacher can play one for each student in turn, moving rapidly around the class. The oral responses give the teacher much more opportunity to perceive progress and problems than does written dictation.

As in other skills, Socratic questioning is the basis for most of the teaching strategies at this stage. Assuming that the students are familiar with cadence types, they should be able to identify quickly the last chord or two. If a student seems stymied, ask him what the cadence type is. If, for example, it is a deceptive cadence and he identifies it, then ask him to name the chords in a deceptive cadence. That done, he should be able to work backward from V–vi to identify the rest of the Roman numerals in the phrase. As always, the teacher should function as a catalyst to cause the student to think for him- or herself rather than to correct the student with a ready-made answer.

The students should also use chord quality to help identify the Roman numerals. Let us say that another student has identified a passage correctly except that she has identified a IV as a ii^6. Play the passage again and ask her the quality of the chord. If she correctly identifies it as a major triad, then ask her what the quality would be if it were indeed a ii chord. At this point she should perceive her error; but if not, the teacher must probe further, using other questions to advance student understanding.

When the students are skillful in hearing the short passages of three to five chords and in apprehending each passage in its entirety as a single entity—at that point the passages should be lengthened to as many as eight or nine chords. Also at this point the students should begin to write down the soprano and bass lines prior to (or concurrent with) determining the Roman numerals. For these longer passages the teacher may find it necessary to prepare the examples in advance rather than improvise them. Dictations at this point are comparable to chorale phrases of two 4/4 bars in length; and as inversions are added and dissonant tones begin to be used, they can take a form very similar to the Bach chorale style.

This is not to say that all harmonic dictation from here on should follow the chorale style. The two-part dictation discussed earlier in this chapter can lead into more complex contrapuntal-harmonic dictation in various styles; and carefully selected passages from eighteenth-century keyboard literature can be used for experience in hearing the basic harmonic motion of passages containing frequent arpeggiations. The notion of first learning to hear chordal passages devoid of any dissonance, and then gradually adding passing tones, neighboring tones, suspensions, and other types of dissonance, has been basic to college-level ear-training for at least several decades, perhaps much longer. The Bach chorales have proved to be very useful for this practice; and this has been correlated with a traditional part-writing discipline in which the procedures or rules are extrapolated (more or less statistically) from Bach's practice in the 371 chorales themselves.

This is discussed further in chapter 5, but it should be remembered that the learning of part-writing procedures should parallel the harmonic dictation activities so that students are writing the same type of passages that they are learning to hear in ear-training. The teacher should be skillful enough in keyboard improvisation to be able to begin with a two-bar phrase played without dissonant tones and then gradually to add them as needed to explain various techniques. I find it easiest simply to improvise these phrases within the style, but there is no reason why the Bach chorales themselves cannot be used, reduced to their pure triadic state, one triad per beat, and devoid of dissonance. Indeed theory teachers have used this method for many years. In a sense, it is a kind of reverse Schenkerian analysis. One begins with a reductive layer in the middle ground (the basic triads, usually one per beat, without chromatic alterations, passing tones, neighboring tones, suspensions, etc.) and then gradually as new concepts are added—simultaneously in part-writing and analysis—they are also added to these ear-training exercises. Usually passing tones are added first to the skeleton chorale, then neighboring tones, then suspensions, working toward the less common dissonances, such as the appoggiatura, escape tones, retardations, and anticipations.

This of course takes place over a period of months with many chorales. When the Bach chorales are fully fleshed out in the foreground,[6] the students will have acquired considerable sophistication
in the contrapuntal-harmonic techniques of the eighteenth century.

In addition to the study of dissonant tones[7] in this ontogenic process, chromatic tones may also begin to be added. The raised sixth
and seventh degrees in the minor mode should be added at an early
stage. Rather than explaining these as altered tones, one would
more logically think of them as being borrowed from the major
mode, thus accounting for the major dominant and subdominant
when they occur in the minor mode. Secondary dominants, secondary vii[7]s, augmented sixth chords, and the Neapolitan sixth are all
added in due course during the latter part of the first year and the
beginning of the second.

At this point it would seem logical to consider the sequence of
harmonic-dictation activities over the entire two-year theory course.
The primary harmonic-dictation activities should be correlated with
supportive aural activities (sight-singing, melodic dictation, and so
forth) and with the activities in writing skills and analysis. There are
countless ways of doing this, however, and they may vary radically
from class to class and institution to institution. It may even be
counterproductive to plan this correlation very far in advance, for
one cannot know for sure where each lesson will lead. One should
of course have long-term objectives by month, semester, and year;
but I am convinced that a teacher should not plan far ahead in terms
of lesson plans for specific days. Paul Goodman in *Growing Up
Absurd* cites the case of the young secondary school teacher who
refused to comply with the administrative directive that all teachers
should prepare ten-day lesson plans. The teacher was fired, but in
protest he brought suit against the school system, arguing that a
good teacher cannot and should not know for sure where his or her
students will end up at the end of any given class period. The dis-
missal was upheld by the court, but Goodman quite correctly
pointed out that the teacher was following a laudable teaching philosophy. From the most idealistic point of view he was in the right,
for the content of the next class does depend upon what happened
in the previous class. Goodman wrote a lengthy letter of protest to
the commissioner of education in Albany, New York, saying among
other things that "it has been my universal experience that formal
preparation of a lesson plan beyond the next hour or two is not only

unrealistic but can be positively harmful and rigidifying, for it interferes with the main thing, the contact between the teacher and his class."[8] Thus, though a lesson plan—written or not—is essential, it should be prepared for the next class only after the previous class has been completed.

It is for these reasons that I will not presume to draft a chart correlating aural activities with harmonic dictation over the two-year theory sequence. There are, however, a few guidelines that might be useful. First among these is that students should be guided to use all of the information that is available. Too often students hear and identify everything they need and yet cannot put that information together to complete a harmonic dictation.

Let us say that the dictation consists of a two-bar chorale phrase in the major mode. The student has written down the soprano and bass lines and, beginning to write down the figured bass and Roman numerals,[9] comes to a point where the fourth scale degree is in the bass and cannot seem to go on. At this point the student should be guided to consider all the possibilities and to relate them to the information already gathered.

Here is the reasoning process: With the fourth scale degree in the bass the chord could be IV or ii^6 or ii$^6_5$. How likely is it that it could be a V$^4_2$ or a vii$^6_4$, and would not the student recognize these as uniquely different from the conventional possibilities? What is the quality of the chord? Is it major, minor, or something else? And can the student hear the inversion? The student who can ask him- or herself these questions (or is guided to ask them) should be able to find enough answers to determine syllogistically what the chord is. To put it simplistically, the student who can hear that it is a minor triad and that it is in first inversion can determine that it is a ii^6.

This kind of thought process can be improved by asking the students to produce a checklist of all of the conventional possibilities when any of the seven scale degrees is in the bass. Then they can practice discriminating among these conventional possibilities. This correlates very well with keyboard practice, for they can be asked to play a short figured bass and then change certain chords without changing the bass tones. Relating this to the concept of diatonic structuralism, they will soon see that certain groups of chords, such as (IV, ii^6, and ii$^6_5$) and (V and I$^6_4$), have essentially similar functions. Schenkerian reduction can make this even clearer.

The same process can be used for identifying dissonant tones. If students hear I, vii⁶, I⁶ but also hear dissonant activity on the second chord, what are the possibilities? The most likely is vii with a 7-6 suspension. Or perhaps it is ii with a 5-6 unaccented passing tone. Again, a checklist can be made listing the various possibilities of typical dissonant activity on various sonorities. If the students really understand the possibilities for dissonance within the resolution of I$^6_4$ to V, they can with a little practice learn to aurally discriminate among the various possibilities.

Another guideline that emerges from all of this is to let aural understanding parallel conceptual understanding. The concept of secondary functions serves well to demonstrate this. Aural understanding should come first (i.e., the playing of secondary dominants and secondary vii⁷s in context) but should be reinforced immediately with a verbal articulation of the concept. By this I do not mean that the teacher should state the definition in full for the class to copy down. It works much better for the students to evolve the definition themselves in Socratic dialogue.

The students will soon learn that a good definition of a concept is rather like a mathematical formula—their opinion of grammarians is likely to rise. One of my classes arrived at the following definition of a secondary dominant: "A secondary dominant is a major triad or Mm⁷ containing a chromatic alteration; it functions momentarily as a dominant of a major or minor diatonic triad (the tonicized chord) other than I." To this they added, after further dialogue, "It is called a secondary dominant (V of something) rather than the Roman numeral of its root because it is an altered chord within a nonmodulating passage." The aspects of the definition were elicited by my questioning and through classroom dialogue. The process took more than half of a class period, whereas I could have stated the definition for them in a minute or so. But the students—all of them—were involved in the dialogue about the definition in such a way as to learn it much more thoroughly than if I had given it to them verbatim for their notes. Forming words into ideas is a *heuristic* process—one learns by doing it. And this is the essence of Piagetian LM learning—taking action upon a problem.

In the hearing of secondary dominants or secondary vii⁷s the teacher might start with the progression of ii to V and show how, by raising the bass tone of the ii⁶ a half-step by chromatic alteration, the ii⁶ becomes a V⁶ of V. From this the students will begin to understand that the chromatic alteration is often the secondary leading tone. Gradually, they will begin to listen for the linear function of the secondary leading tone—does that G-sharp go to A? Is it a V of vi? Then, when the concept of the secondary leading tone as the altered tone is ingrained, one can introduce the V⁷ of IV in the major mode in which the altered tone is the seventh of the chord rather than the third (as in V of V) or the root (as in vii of V).

The implicit guideline here is that the teacher must consider very carefully the order and sequence of the presentation of related materials. In all teaching, but particularly in ear-training, one must be sensitive, creative, and ready to change the approach at any time. When the harmonic dictation process is fully under way, the class will have become accustomed to a certain order in the dictation process. Traditionally, if one is using a chorale phrase, it goes something like this: (1) Play the phrase once at a moderate tempo in a musically expressive manner. (2) Play the phrase two or three times emphasizing the soprano line. (3) Play the phrase two or three times emphasizing the bass. (4) Play the phrase once or twice more in a musically expressive manner.

The hearing of inner voices may or may not be a problem. If the students understand their part-writing principles, there may be few choices except the correct ones. Some gifted students, however, may become aurally lazy about inner voices because they can determine them deductively rather than actually hear them. The occasional use of unusual voice-leading may help with this contingency. This is discussed further in chapter 7.

For the students, writing down the phrase consists of first writing the soprano line and then the bass line. At this point the logico-mathematical process of setting down the figured bass and inner voices varies from student to student. At one extreme are those who try to *hear every note* of the inner voices. At the other, are those who, given two notes of every sonority, can determine at least the pitch class by means of chord quality and inversion. Those who do a little of both will probably be most successful.

The teacher's task in this process is to observe the various student approaches (at the blackboard or at their seats) and to suggest new approaches to those who need it. These suggestions are, I think, best accomplished by questioning rather than declarative statements. At times, though, some respite from the Socratic approach might be in order; for any approach used to excess becomes dull and ineffectual. The bulk of this section has been devoted to more or less formal harmonic dictation. The skills acquired in harmonic dictation can transform the musician's awareness of music and are supportive of a number of other musical skills. Among these is the technique of aural analysis, which every musician, consciously or not, uses every day. It is discussed further in chapter 6, but we shall now turn our attention to the question of harmonic aural skills applied to twentieth-century styles.

MODERN HARMONY

In the section on sets and interval vectors I theorized that our Western ears are capable of making much finer distinctions in music of the common practice period than in modern music because of the phenomenon of harmonic function. Whether or not this is true, the practice of harmonic aural skills applied to contemporary styles is generally neglected in freshman and sophomore theory classes. Yet it is a skill that clearly is valued by directors of graduate programs in choral and instrumental conducting as well as in other areas. In spite of significant advances in theory teaching we still do not generally give sufficient time to aural perception of harmony of recent music.

It is a ripe area for experimentation, and many theory teachers have found interesting new approaches. One way to begin is with a discussion of styles; and this can take place by the beginning of the second semester of the first year, if not earlier. Recordings of examples of quartal harmony, twelve-tone music, clusters, triads with added tones, and so on can be played and discussed in class. Then, listening to further examples, the students can try to identify the styles by ear. This can also be correlated with modest composition projects in which some or all of the students compose brief pieces in imitation of various styles.

This broadside approach can then be followed up with more focused ear-training exercises improvised or composed by the teacher. Playing a single sonority and asking the students to attempt to identify what they are hearing in the chord can be a very useful exercise. To effect a smooth transition from triadic harmony I sometimes begin with a major seventh played in a strikingly unusual vertical deployment to exploit the factor of the textures of modern music. The student responses to the following example are quite interesting (see figure 3.8).

Several students said that they heard perfect fifths; a few said they heard one fifth played up high and another down low; while only one said that he heard two perfect fifths, one a minor sixth higher than the other. Only the last student truly identified all four tones; yet none of them perceived it as a major seventh in first inversion. It was quite surprising to them when this was pointed out; but it was an important object lesson, for it called attention to the importance of texture in modern harmony—showing that even triadic sonorities (i.e., tertial), when the tones are deployed in an unusual manner, can sound uncharacteristic of the common practice period and that the aural effect of two identical sets of pitches can be drastically affected by texture and other factors of the element of sound. It is clear that pitch class as an outcome of octave displacement is an essential feature of Schenkerian analysis and analysis with sets and interval vectors. Thus, these systems, since they ignore actual pitch in favor of pitch class, are useless in analyzing texture and other factors of musical sound. For music in which the element of sound is important to its meaning—virtually all recent music, twentieth-century music, and much of earlier music—supplementary analytical approaches must be used.

Clusters such as those shown in figure 3.9 provoke interesting student reactions when used in dictation and classroom discussion.

These three-note sonorities—"triads" in twentieth-century parlance—can be used in this form and then deployed over much wider vertical spans for further practice, as shown in figure 3.10.

Figure 3.8

Figure 3.9

Figure 3.10

My classroom discussions with sonorities like these have often centered upon intervallic content (there are several pairs of mirror sonorities here), upon how texture affects harmonic quality (sometimes more than intervallic content), affective qualities, and how one learns to identify what one hears. Sonorities with four tones and with doublings can be used in the same way. Interval vector analysis is also useful as the sonorities become more complex, though it is important to remember that texture, timbre, and dynamics can be as important harmonic factors as intervallic content—a point that can be overlooked when one uses octave displacement to find normal order.

As a supportive activity, the sight-singing of twentieth-century examples can be correlated with these harmonic activities. Twelve-tone music is particularly challenging for this, but it is best not simply to sing tone rows but to sing the music itself. Tone rows, after all, are not melodies; they are simply raw scalar materials devoid of the elements of rhythm and sound that are so important in genuine melodic material. Throughout the practice of harmonic aural skills it should be remembered that the affective qualities of our music are created in large part by the element of harmony. This is why, as students become more skillful in the discrimination of sonorities of the twentieth- and twenty-first centuries, they develop a deeper understanding and affection for modern music. Thus, the practice of harmonic aural skills upon recent music does more than expand musical craftsmanship. It also fosters a deeper and truer understanding of the music of our time.

NOTES

1. The distinction between the terms *polyphonic* and *contrapuntal* is vague at best and is virtually irrelevant, but since the former term originated with

vocal music and the latter seems to have been applied more often to instrumental textures, this may be a valid differentiation. Although the learned
authors of the many treatises on the subject over the past millennium seem
to have preferred the term *counterpoint*, for all practical purposes the two
terms are synonymous.

2. Occasionally, in a few Bach chorales, the bass appears to briefly cross
above the tenor; but in actuality, since the bass would have been doubled at
the octave below by organ or a bass instrument, this is not crossed voices.

3. For further exploration of the history of polyphony, I again refer the
reader to John D. White, *Theories of Musical Texture in Western History* (New
York: Garland, 1995), 187–400.

4. Allen Forte, "A Theory of Set-Complexes for Music," *Journal of Music
Theory* 8 (1964), 136–183.

5. The term *structural hearing* as used here is derived from Piaget's concept of structuralism, not from Felix Salzer's (Schenkerian) concept as
expressed in his book *Structural Hearing*.

6. To use Schenkerian terminology.

7. I prefer to use the term *dissonant tones* rather than *nonharmonic tones*
because the latter seems to imply that dissonance is not part of the harmony, which is clearly fallacious.

8. Paul Goodman, *Growing Up Absurd* (New York: Knopf, 1960), 245–246.

9. In analysis and harmonic dictation it seems historically accurate to
keep figured bass separate from Roman numerals. While a harmonic passage can be described in a prose paragraph as $V^6 - I - vii^6 - I^6$, in analytical
annotations, part-writing, and figured bass the passage might better be
written on two separate levels like this: $V^6 - I- vii^6 - I^6$, thus teaching the
student to view figured bass and Roman numerals as two separate and distinct concepts. This is also helpful in normal figured-bass reading, where
Roman numerals are not given.

FOUR

Keyboard Skills

Keyboard instruments have been central to music in Western culture from the early Renaissance to the present. Prior to the modern age of specialization, virtually every musician started out on a keyboard instrument—clavichord, harpsichord, organ, pianoforte, or piano, depending upon the historical period. It was a basic tool for composers, arrangers, and teachers. Many musicians learned to sight-sing as choirboys, but if music was to be a career, they also learned the keyboard.[1] Prior to the nineteenth century, kapellmeisters led their ensembles from the keyboard, and the same was true of opera directors and quite often even orchestral directors; although in the orchestra the leader might also be the principal first violinist.

It was understood that if you were a professional musician (with the exception of some singers), you were an accomplished keyboardist in addition to whatever else you did. Baroque church musicians not only had to compose and officiate at the organ or harpsichord at rehearsals and services, they also were accomplished cantorial singers, and very often played stringed and/or wind instruments as well. J. S. Bach, legendary as a keyboard improviser, was also an accomplished string player and even in his latter years continued to play a leadership role as a violinist in ensembles. Mozart, too, though famous for his piano performances, was a superb violinist and particularly enjoyed playing the viola in string quartets. Haydn and Beethoven both played the violin as well as the keyboard; and the cellist–composer Luigi Boccherini was also an accomplished pianist and guitarist. Musicians were far more versatile in those days than they are today, and this is probably symptomatic of the increased specialization in all fields of human endeavor over the past century, the same phenomenon that resulted in the disappearance of the medical general practitioner who made house calls.

Thus, professional versatility has become increasingly rare among musicians over the past two centuries, so that today it is rare for an orchestral player also to be an accomplished pianist. Even some of today's composers and conductors are not always good pianists; and among public school music teachers where keyboard skills are essential, it is deplorably rare to find even an adequate pianist. College level music schools have tried to correct this deficiency by introducing special keyboard courses into the curriculum. In addition to the keyboard component of theory courses many music departments offer separate courses designed to develop keyboard facility for nonpianists.

Such keyboard courses, sometimes called "functional-piano" or piano-class, may offer more than simply piano techniques. Supportive of the music education or music therapy curricula, they may also include such skills as piano improvisation and improvising accompaniments in various styles. Because these skills may duplicate some of the content of the keyboard component of theory classes, functional-piano classes and theory courses should be designed to complement and support each other—to avoid unnecessary encroachment and duplication. Intradepartmental dialogue and perhaps administrative help may be needed to achieve an appropriate curricular balance.

Normally, the keyboard component of the freshman and sophomore theory course includes figured-bass realization, clef reading, improvisation, and perhaps score –reading, and jazz improvisation. Of these skills, improvisation may also be an intrinsic part of the functional-piano class and may be wholly or in part relegated to that area. Piano technique itself, however, is the primary domain of the piano-class and should not be a part of the theory class. In any case it is important to remember that the emphases and perspectives of the functional-piano or piano-class teacher are quite different from those of the theory teacher, so that, for example, when improvisation is taught in both areas, the two classes can be mutually supportive and not necessarily duplicative.

THE KEYBOARD CLASSROOM

Ideally, keyboard should be taught in a situation where each person including the teacher is seated at his or her own piano or electronic keyboard. If pianos are used, the group keyboard exercises will be limited to those that can be done either individually or with all students playing the same exercise together. This is satisfactory for rote learning and for some individual coaching, but it is not the ideal way to teach keyboard skills in the theory class.

A classroom fitted with electronic keyboards offers much wider possibilities. With the use of headsets (microphone and earphones) each student can practice individually on different exercises (in the "self" or "silent" mode) without a sound being heard in the classroom itself. In addition the teacher can "tune in" on any individual or group to monitor student progress; and any two students (or larger group) can tune in on each other to work together. Also, conversations can be carried on in any of these situations.

This offers a wide range of possible teaching strategies. The only limitation is that the typical tone quality of electronic keyboards (including those that are called "electronic pianos") is sterile and unmusical, with little capability for the musical shading and nuance that is possible on the piano. As musical instruments electronic keyboards are inadequate. Regardless of this, the electronic-keyboard classroom has been of great value to the keyboard component of the theory class, though it is less than ideal for piano-class or functional piano.

A number of teaching strategies in the electronic-keyboard classroom combine ear-training with keyboard skills. Any of the harmonic-dictation exercises discussed in the previous chapter can be used as keyboard exercises. For example, with the students divided into pairs of similar abilities, one member of each pair plays a harmonic-dictation exercise and then the other member attempts to play it back. The students then exchange roles, thus developing keyboard skills as well as aural harmonic capability.

Obviously, this is possible only in an electronic-keyboard classroom in which all of the instruments (and headsets) can be paired off so that each student communicates with only one other student. Since the instrumental sound is heard only in the headsets, this allows many more students to work simultaneously than is possible in an ordinary classroom. It also produces a gamelike atmosphere in which the sense of competition stimulates the class to greater interest and to greater efforts. Also, the teacher can monitor any of the pairs of students simply by switching the controls.

A typical electronic-keyboard class might begin with the keyboards all switched to the speaker mode so that the instrumental sound is acoustically audible within the room without headsets. The teacher demonstrates the day's objectives at a keyboard and offers suggestions as to how the students can proceed. Let us say that the class is learning how to play three-, four-, and five-chord harmonic-dictation exercises in root position (four-part vocal style) of the type discussed at the beginning of the harmonic-dictation section of the previous chapter. The teacher should point out that the bass line is the critical element in these exercises and should demonstrate and have the class play several different bass lines (with the left hand) in unison. With the teacher calling out the brief chord progressions and the class playing the bass lines, the students will learn to associate the harmonic progressions (expressed in Roman numerals) with the left-hand melody of the bass line.

This should be immediately reinforced by private practice with the controls switched to the individual mode so that each student hears only him- or herself on the headset. The teacher can monitor this practice and intervene (on microphone and keyboard) whenever appropriate. After a few minutes the class can return to the classroom mode for further instructions. The next step is for the class to learn to play the three upper tones of each chord with the right hand. This is a problem only for those who have inadequate keyboard background. Right or wrong, all music departments have occasional music majors of this type—talented instrumentalists or singers who just never learned piano. They should be remedying this situation, of course, by enrolling in private piano, but in the theory class they also profit from some individual attention from the instructor. To avoid delaying class progress this should be done as much as possible outside of class.

Classroom practice playing right-hand triads in first and second inversions and root position should cover all keys and all chord qualities, but particularly all of the major and minor triads. And it should be correlated with continued drill in triad spelling. When a respectable level of classroom competence is achieved, the students should be asked to put the two hands together. Now the problem is to achieve the smoothest possible right-hand voice-leading. This correlates well with part-writing, with retention of common tones and moving the other voices to the nearest chord tones; or, as in the case of roots a second apart, moving the upper three voices contrary to the bass. There is a very strong transfer of learning between part-writing and this keyboard skill, an example of the value of integrative theory teaching.

These are a few of the methods by which an electronic-keyboard classroom can be used for teaching techniques not possible in a conventional classroom. Obviously, resourceful teachers will devise other techniques suitable for their teaching styles. Further use of the keyboard classroom is discussed in the context of keyboard skills and is detailed further from the technological viewpoint in chapter 9. It should be remembered that the keyboard classroom is an excellent place for the correlation and integration of keyboard skills with the other aspects of musical craft.

CLEF READING

The ability to sight-read in at least four clefs is indispensable for score reading and reading figured bass in early editions. As mentioned earlier, some theory teachers have advocated the use of as many as seven clefs. From a practical standpoint, however, time restrictions in a two-year theory sequence make it difficult to cover more than those clefs currently in common use—treble, bass, alto, and tenor. The soprano, mezzo, and baritone clefs can be learned later in specialized courses, such as score reading. All of the students can be presumed to have some skill in both bass and treble clefs, but there will be some instrumentalists and singers who are still in the process of developing these skills through further piano study (particularly in the freshman class). In addition, cellists, bassists, trombonists, and bassoonists will be familiar with tenor clef; and violists will be fluent in alto clef. Integration of sight-singing and keyboard can be achieved by studying the C clefs concurrently in both areas.

Surprisingly, students who already read tenor clef on their instruments may have some difficulty quickly reading the lower half of the tenor staff. This is because none of these instruments (cello, bass, bassoon, and trombone) use the tenor clef as their lowest clef, and thus the notes in an instrumental part that might be notated on the lower half of the tenor clef are usually notated in bass clef. The teacher who is aware of this will have a better understanding of these instrumentalists' clef-reading problems. To automatically assume, for example, that a good trombonist reads the lower half of the tenor clef fluently might be unfair. Most tenor-clef-reading instrumentalists are proficient in the upper half of the tenor staff and particularly the ledger lines above; but most of their instrumental passages below small A (A-220) are notated on the bass staff. (This C-clef-reading problem does not trouble violists, since the alto clef is their lowest clef.)

When introducing the C clefs in both sight-singing and keyboard, I have found it productive to ask students to try to remember the names of the top, bottom, and middle lines and to relate the other tones to them. At first, especially in sight-singing, some students try (often successfully) to read diatonic passages intervalically by ear, without really knowing the names of the letter names they are singing or playing. Since this does little to improve their clef reading, they should be asked to recite the letter names either before or during the reading process. With diligent practice they are soon reading pitches rather than diatonic intervals.

At the point when the students have begun to develop some proficiency in reading the C clefs with letter names, they should be presented with the concept of using the clefs to read (from score) parts for transposing instruments at the keyboard. For example, a page of score from Mozart's Symphony No. 40 can be projected on the screen in the classroom; and the teacher can demonstrate how the B-flat clarinet parts can be read at concert pitch by imagining them to be written in tenor clef. (Written E, top space of the treble staff, sounds concert D, and the top space of the tenor staff is D.) This also permits the early introduction of the concept of transposition, which will be new to many students.

This is a concept that can be confusing even to students who play transposing instruments, so it is wise to introduce it early and return to it frequently. Every composition teacher has had the frustrating experience of receiving a beautifully notated score from a talented student, in which some or all of the transpositions have been done in the wrong direction—even from students who play transposing instruments! A rule of thumb that seems to help is that written C in the part for a transposing instrument sounds the note of the transposition. Thus, written C on F horn will sound F, and written C on the B-flat instruments will sound B-flat. From this the students can determine the interval of transposition. It remains only for them to be sure of the appropriate octave—to remember, for example, that E-flat clarinet sounds a minor third higher than written, not a major sixth lower.

Transposition, as a part of the composer's lore, is fully absorbed only through constant use in composition and orchestration. Simply explaining the concept in class is not sufficient for the students to really learn it. It requires the logico-mathematical process of taking action upon the problem through actual use—further evidence of the validity of Piaget's theories of learning.

The real touchstone of clef reading is proficiency in switching from one to another of the four clefs. This happens frequently in actual literature but not often in exercise books designed for sight-singing and clef reading. The teacher, by selecting clef-reading examples from the advanced literature for viola and cello, can present the class with exercises that utilize all four clefs in an authentic musical context. The range of many of these examples is too wide for sight-singing; but they are admirably suited to clef-reading practice at the keyboard.

The figured basses of the seventeenth and eighteenth centuries (in early or original editions) furnishes another source, for they often switch back and forth between tenor and bass clef. This is also a good transitional exercise leading into the formal study of figured-bass realization. I have found eighteenth-century editions of Corelli's violin sonatas and trio sonatas to be particularly useful for this, but I am sure that each theory teacher will find his or her own favorite choices of music literature for this purpose.

SCORE READING

Clef reading is often neglected in theory classes, yet it is an essential ingredient of one of the most highly regarded aspects of musical craft—the art of score reading. While score reading itself may not be carried to a high level of refinement by the end of the sophomore year, it certainly is possible for most students to develop a good working knowledge of the four most commonly used clefs.

The reading of orchestral score at the keyboard is one of the most admired and most difficult aspects of musical craft. Many schools of music offer a separate course in this skill at the upper division or graduate level. Thus, the inclusion of score reading in freshman and sophomore theory courses is, in the main, preparatory in purpose and is not intended to imply an overly high expectation of undergraduate achievement in this skill. Indeed it would be worthwhile if sophomore music majors could achieve some competence merely in the reading of four-part choral score or (even better) string quartet score.

Yet some experience in orchestral score reading is important, even at the freshman level, if only to encourage students to examine scores. Keyboard majors and other students who have strong keyboard facility should begin immediately with the reading of open choral score, then string quartet score, and then should proceed into more complex instrumental and vocal scores as their progress indicates.

Perhaps the one important thing for lower-division music majors to understand about score reading is simply what it is. We have all seen or heard of certain almost unbelievable score-reading feats by great musicians of the past. Yet in many cases they were not really "reading," at least in the sense in which we usually use the word. When the great conductor George Szell (1897–1970) would astound a group of apprentice conductors by picking up an eighteenth- or nineteenth-century score and fluently playing it at the piano, he was not reading the notes as much as using them as cues—as reminders of what was already firmly established in his mind. Probably no one knew the classical orchestral repertoire better than George Szell, and if rarely he was confronted with a score he did not know from memory, he usually knew enough of it so that the notes simply triggered responses in his memory that enabled him to recreate it at the piano. Actually this is perhaps a greater achievement than truly to read an unfamiliar score note by note, for it requires an almost encyclopedic knowledge of music literature.

It must also be remembered that Szell was a consummate pianist; and it is doubtful that anyone who had acquired that level of instrumental artistry would not also have gained a knowledge of music literature vast enough to serve as a valuable crutch in score reading. In a sense then, regarding traditional repertoire, can one ever say for sure that an experienced musician is really sight-reading?

In fact reading orchestral score is almost never literal note reading. It invariably requires a mental process of rearranging in order to endow the pitches with suitable keyboard properties. Thus, it is important for the score reader to have some aural preknowledge of the work to be read. In other words, if one listens to a work enough to become almost saturated with it (as Szell was with the classical repertoire), then it becomes much easier to read at the piano. Also, if one is thoroughly acquainted with a style, like that of the classical symphony, one knows what to expect in an unfamiliar score; knows how to convert stylized accompaniment figures into keyboard figurations, where the doublings are likely to occur (in order to reduce them to single keyboard lines, if necessary); and generally knows how to convert classical orchestral textures into appropriate keyboard textures.

While few lower-division theory students can be expected to master this kind of score reading, they can develop certain skills that will prepare them for further study of score reading later on. Many of them can also learn to read at least four-part open score, such as simple choral or string quartet scores—in itself a valuable musical skill. Thus, the initial teaching of score reading in theory class can be distilled down to the following stages:

1. Aural preknowledge of a four-part choral or chamber work to be read, through individual or classroom listening. This should include discussions of style and listening to other similar works of the same period.
2. Practice in playing just the outer voices (or the two most important voices at any given point) at the keyboard, followed by discussion of the harmonies that are implied by these skeletal lines.
3. Practice in playing the implied harmonies in an unspecified texture, whether or not the actual instrumental or choral parts are realized.
4. Practice in realizing the full score at the piano.

Step 2 from the preceding list leads to another skill that is important in reading more complex scores. That is the ability to identify quickly the two or three most important parts for realization—which instruments or voices contain the essence of the harmonic or melodic motion. Then doublings and filler parts can be disregarded as the keyboard player concentrates upon those parts that are essential to a good keyboard rendition of a work scored for another medium.

Spotting the essential voice lines and eliminating the superfluous can be practiced away from the piano in classroom discussion. Indeed it is an analytical skill that is closely correlated with Schenkerian analysis; for what is Schenkerian analysis if not a reduction to skeletal lines? Thus, the practice of score reading can be readily integrated with analysis for mutual support between the two areas.

Of course excellence in score reading at the keyboard cannot be achieved without a good deal of sheer technique as a pianist. Few students other than piano majors possess this, but many instrumentalists and singers will be in the process of developing their pianistic abilities concurrently with the study of music theory. It is important that the concepts of score reading, and its relationship to the other aspects of musical craft, be imparted along with whatever performance skill each student can achieve as a score reader. Thus, each student will advance as far and as fast as possible, preparing at the same time for study in greater depth.

FIGURED-BASS REALIZATION

As stated earlier, in part-writing exercises I advocate the practice of maintaining two separate strata for figured bass and Roman numerals. That is, instead of writing I$^6_4$ below a bass note, as one would when discussing it in an expository verbal passage, the $^6_4$ should be written just below the bass note and the I should be placed directly below the $^6_4$ on a lower level reserved for Roman numerals. (See the harmonic dictation section of chapter 3, page 82.) In actual Baroque practice the figures were most often placed above the bass notes and Roman numerals were not used at all. Placing them below is for convenience in part-writing and in harmonic analysis.

This separates the harmonic analysis (Roman numerals) from the figured bass and allows the student to think of figured bass as an entity separate from the Roman numerals. This approach is also consistent with history, for seventeenth- and eighteenth-century composers (even for some time after the introduction of the theory of inversion) did not consistently think in terms of Roman numerals. Thus, figured-bass reading actually is the realization of a harmonic structure conceived in terms of intervals above the various tones of a bass line.

One can begin with classroom discussion of eighteenth-century scores in early or facsimile editions, if possible. The Corelli violin sonatas have worked very well for this—notated as they were originally composed, in systems of two staff lines, violin solo on top, bass line with figured bass below. A thorough discussion of the alternative symbols for figured bass prepares the students for a variety of methods for indicating alterations above a bass tone.

Since figured-bass reading should be closely correlated with both part-writing and ear-training, it can begin during the first semester of the freshman year. Figured-bass symbols are used in part-writing as soon as the students begin to use inversions—usually by the end of the first semester. Even before this, however, the class should be playing passages in root-position triads similar to the first passages used in harmonic dictation. (See chapter 3.) The outcome is thus a three-way integration of keyboard, part-writing, and ear-training.

From the start the class should understand exactly what the mental process is in the reading of figured bass. The essential skill is the ability to identify quickly which member of the triad the bass tone is—root, third, fifth, or seventh—and from this knowledge to determine the pitch-classes of all of the other chord tones. This two-step process should be practiced until it is instantaneous. Obviously, quick triad spelling is essential, just as it is in so many other aspects of musical craft. And, again, this is why integration of skills can be so readily achieved.

The teacher can explore a variety of ways to practice identifying the chords; but probably the best way is the most direct—to have the students actually play single chords in various inversions from figured-bass notes placed on the blackboard. At some point during the second semester of the first year, when symbols for all inversions have been learned, a series of single isolated bass notes with figures (like those shown in figure 4.1) can be placed on the blackboard of the theory classroom.

Figure 4.1

There should be a sufficient number of bass tones so that they will not be quickly memorized by repetition—at least twenty or twenty-five. An occasional tone in tenor clef should be given, and the key signature should change once or twice. The teacher then points to examples and goes around the class asking each student in turn to realize an example in four parts on the student's keyboard. After this has been done for a while in the classroom mode the students can switch to the silent ("self") mode and practice all of the examples on their own. For practice assignments the teacher can hand out a prepared sheet of many similar bass tones with figures for the students to practice on their own outside of class. Concurrently with this exercise, brief figured-bass passages of several chords should be practiced. These should be conventional formulae of four to seven chords, and they should be in all keys with occasional switches to tenor clef. Typical examples follow in figure 4.2:

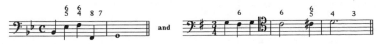

Figure 4.2

Like the previous exercises, these can be practiced in the keyboard classroom or outside of class from a handout sheet prepared by the teacher. The level and degree of difficulty should parallel the activities in part-writing and harmonic dictation. Musicality should be emphasized; and in demonstrations it is important that the teacher make a point of playing as musically as possible.

Clearly this last exercise introduces a new thought process. Whereas the isolated bass tones and figures helped the students toward instantaneous identification of the tones of a sonority regardless of which of its members is given in the bass, the practice of figured-bass formulae is a more complex and intrinsically musical process, and it introduces the concept of the musical line. The first was a purely vertical conception of harmony, while the second achieves the virtue of a horizontal-linear perspective. Yet the latter is not possible without the former.

Indeed so essential is this instantaneous keyboard response—the realization of the correct vertical sonority from a given figured-bass tone—that the student who does not achieve it (either from laziness or inadequate background and ability) will never learn to read figured bass. Once learned, however, it opens to the student a fascinating world of musical possibilities, not the least of which is the potential for authentic performance of music of the seventeenth and eighteenth centuries, not only for keyboard players but for other performers as well.

Once into the stage of figured-bass formulae, the question of line must be given deeper consideration. Undoubtedly consummate figured-bass readers such as Bach, Felix Mendelssohn, Nadia Boulanger, and Thurston Dart were capable of maintaining a consistent texture of a given number of voice lines so that suspensions and sevenths would also be properly prepared and resolved and so that improprieties of voice leading would not occur. While some musicians may be capable of doing this consistently, in the actual practice of figured-bass reading, it is often undesirable or unnecessary to do so. That is, a suspension tone should be prepared in the previous sonority and it should resolve down by step, but there are times when the preparation need not be in the same octave as the suspension dissonance itself; and there are times when the number of tones varies drastically from one chord to the next, thus implying an inconsistent texture in terms of voice lines.

Such musical liberties are taken according to the needs of specific musical situations. There are times when the sheer volume of sound of the harpsichord must be augmented in any way possible and doublings may be added almost indiscriminately. At other times it may be desirable to play detached block chords in which the voice leading seems to disappear. This aspect of the art of figured-bass realization is too vast to carry further here, though it certainly should be given some consideration in the theory class.

Yet certain aspects of texture should be considered in the teaching of figured-bass realization. The manner in which doublings control the acoustical effect of a sonority are quite important, even though they are not as clearly codified as in four-voice writing. For example, the bass tone of a V^6 can effectively be doubled at the octave in the left hand (or by means of coupling) even though it is the leading tone, but it should not appear in the right hand. And in a deceptive cadence, the third of the submediant triad should appear to be doubled (through voice leading) even though it may be tripled or quadrupled. Thus, the doubling principles and textural qualities of four-voice part-writing are operative, even though they are not followed strictly in figured-bass realization.

As soon as they have developed fluency with brief figured-bass formulae of four to seven chords, students should undertake group performances of Baroque works involving figured bass. A relatively easy trio sonata allows four members of the class to participate simultaneously, and since the instrumentation of the parts (other than the keyboard) can be varied, nearly everyone in the class can usually participate in at least one movement. That is, strings or winds can be used on the two upper parts in various combinations; and the bass line can be played by any bass instrument, such as bassoon, string bass, cello, or even tuba. Thus, the instrumentalists can change parts from movement to movement so that everyone is involved.

Of course the point of this performance activity is for every student to have a try at reading the figured-bass part. To find an appropriate work in which the figured bass is not realized (as in so many modern editions) may necessitate some research on the part of the teacher. Any good music library, however, should contain scores and parts of some trio sonatas in their original form, the score notated on systems of three staves, the two upper lines for the solo instruments and the figured bass below for the keyboard player and the instrumentalist who plays the bass line.

The philosophy behind the preparatory figured-bass formulae discussed earlier is that students will gradually learn to improvise standard Baroque harmonic patterns, so that in the context of a score they can quickly identify and play patterns with which they are already familiar. It is of course necessary to cope with the many possible variations of patterns—the dissonant possibilities in the resolution of a cadential I_4^6, for example, or the chords that may be called for as the fourth scale degree approaches the dominant tone.

If the students have gained sufficient fluency with the formulae, and if enough patterns are learned, the actual reading of figured bass is a kind of synthesis of these patterns. Figured-bass reading has been a part of the musician's craft for nearly four centuries. That most composers have not seriously composed in figured bass since the beginning of the Romantic era (Bruckner excepted) does not seem sufficient reason for us to abandon the art. There is after all a vast repertoire of fine music in which the keyboard parts were originally written by this means. Even if one does not actually utilize the skill, knowledge of figured-bass realization is a great asset in approaching many seventeenth- or eighteenth-century works, whether for performance or research.

IMPROVISATION

The experience of improvisation is essential to musical maturity. For certain kinds of musicians this is a patent fact. For others it is less obvious, but no less true. Beginning composers almost always take their first flights of musical creativity through some form of improvisation, often at the keyboard. And students of jazz will certainly have attempted improvisation, usually long before they have any training in it. Likewise, organists—recognizing that service playing requires this skill—will certainly have essayed some form of spontaneous invention at an early stage in their training.

These are obvious examples, but the experience is equally significant for singers, pianists, and other instrumentalists whose musical orientation does not immediately suggest improvisation as a requisite. Musicians who reach adulthood without having played with melodic ideas and experimented with harmonies may have stunted their musical maturity. They are the pianists whose technique is prodigious but whose note-faithful playing is sterile and dry or bombastic and unrhythmic. They are the pyrotechnical violinists who cannot play chamber music with a humane sense of music making. They are the singers who cannot learn to sing with ensemble. And they are the woodwind players whose absolute pitch cannot adjust to the intonation of an ensemble.

Psychologists tell us that children who are allowed or forced to walk too soon—before they have had the experience of creeping and crawling—are very likely to have problems later on, especially deficiency in reading.[2] This is a good corollary of what I believe happens in the development of young musicians. Without the experience of "playing" with music (of creeping and crawling, if you will), the musician may be lacking later on in important qualities of flexibility and spontaneity, which are just as important in the performance of a Beethoven sonata as they are in a jazz improvisation.

Children with access to musical instruments come quite naturally to the experience of free, spontaneous musical invention. This is the central philosophy of the Orff *Schulwerke*. It allows innate musicality to flower in quite a different manner from that of the formal music lesson. Perhaps formal training in technique and note reading should parallel such experiences; but I believe, with our current emphasis upon early formal training for young musicians, it sometimes happens that talented young musicians may be pushed so fast toward instrumental achievement that their musical personalities are not allowed to grow properly. Anyone who has heard the spontaneous "singing" of a preschool child—which often takes fascinating melodic and rhythmic turns—knows the immensity of our innate musical personalities. Is it not possible that our systematic musical training—admirable as it may be in many ways—destroys some of this talent? Are those who survive necessarily the most gifted? Do these survivors find some private way to develop their musical personalities beyond their formal training? Or are they simply the hardiest and the most determined? And, finally, can experience in improvisation at the college level be of value to music students?

The last question, at least, can be answered in the affirmative. And that is why some form of improvisation should be an integral part of the lower-division theory program. It may take a number of forms. It can grow in a traditional manner out of skills acquired in figured-bass reading. If the teacher is so oriented, it can take the form of jazz or pop improvisation, especially if the department emphasizes commercial music; or it may take the form of accompaniment improvisation, an area of particular relevance to music therapy and music education programs.

Indeed the possible forms of improvisation are virtually limitless—from the invention of jazz or pop figurations over a simple ground, as in the I-vi-IV-V vamp that is still heard from time to time in the practice rooms, to serious compositions based upon improvisation, as in Xenakis's *Strategie, Game for Two Orchestras* (1959–1962), which uses a stochastic (probabilistic) structure in which two back-to-back conductors select musical structures, or "tactics," from a complex mathematical matrix. Students should be encouraged to improvise independently (in groups or individually), but there are also forms of organized improvisation that can occasionally be used in the theory classroom. One plan, which the teacher can demonstrate, is to invent sonorities based upon a particular twentieth-century harmonic system, such as the whole-tone scale or quartal harmony. The teacher improvises two or three such sonorities at the keyboard and then asks the class to write them down from dictation, thus integrating ear-training with the activity. Then students take their turn at the keyboard (perhaps starting with those who do best in the aural identification) to try their hand at improvisation. Texture as well as pitch should be emphasized as a means to vary the sonorities. Melodies can be used also, the teacher or students inventing short melodic phrases based upon a particular scale.

Group improvisation can take many forms, limited only by the inventiveness of the musicians. One plan is to have the class clap a progressive rhythmic pattern while an individual or group improvises—either with instruments or singing—melodies that comple-ment the progressive rhythm (that is, a rhythm varied according to a plan, such as adding one impulse to each repetition of a short pat-tern, as in some kinds of African drumming).

If Orff classroom instruments are available, there are many similar approaches to improvisation that can be attempted. The students' own major instruments can also be used in various ways, such as having one student play a simple well-known melody while others improvise in keeping with a particular style or harmonic plan.

There are also ways of improvising as an outgrowth of figured-bass realization. The student who has mastered a considerable num-ber of the figured-bass formulae discussed in the previous section is ready to attempt the improvisation of small forms in eighteenth-century style. Obviously, this requires greater keyboard facility than the average; but most second-year theory students should be capa-ble of improvising an antecedent and a consequent phrase—that is, a period structure—either in simple keyboard style or in chorale style. This, too, can be integrated with ear-training. In the electronic-keyboard classroom students can work in pairs, one improvising a period structure at the keyboard and the other responding by play-ing it back after one or two hearings.

An entertaining mode of improvisation that emanates from fig-ured-bass reading is the invention of impromptu recitatives. The instructor or students select a suitable text , and each class member in turn attempts to improvise a portion of the text—singing and playing at the keyboard in eighteenth-century style. This can pro-duce considerable classroom hilarity, especially if the text is a bit anachronistic to the style. One needs only a few well-placed chords and a suitable recitation style including the appropriate clichés. This can be partially prepared ahead of time, if necessary, but some stu-dents will want to invent them on the spot. It can result in an inter-esting and amusing class session, and the recitatives produced may rival the works of P. D. Q. Bach.

If it seems appropriate to include accompaniment improvisation in the curriculum, this might be done in consultation with the areas of music education and/or music therapy. Teachers of these areas generally have their own unique applications of this skill and may be interested in receiving support from the theory faculty. Indeed their uses for music may be quite divergent from the philosophies normally found within the theory classroom. Because of this, in a large department it may be very useful for the theory faculty to confer on such questions as the following: To what extent do music education and music therapy majors receive training in accompaniment improvisation in other classes, and what is the nature of this training? Is the functional-piano class the best place for accompaniment improvisation to be taught? Are there particular needs that the theory department can fulfill in this regard? What does the theory department have in common with the other departments in their approach to accompaniment improvisation?

It may be that the other areas would prefer to teach accompaniment improvisation independently, in which case it might be omitted from the theory syllabus. However, if it seems desirable to include it, it should be integrated with some of the other components of musical craft. Knowledge of harmony is essential, as well as some sophistication in musical styles; and a certain level of piano proficiency is required. Therefore improvising accompaniments should probably be undertaken in the sophomore year.

A good way to begin is to study simple accompaniments by ear and in score to see how composers and arrangers have handled questions of style in various kinds of music, such as folk song, show tunes, and popular music. Then a few usable styles are selected for the students to practice. These could include arpeggiation of a simple harmonic passage in different styles, converting a harmonic passage to a "jump bass" accompaniment, and a texture in which a familiar melody is played in the right hand with block chords in the left. After the students have developed some facility in converting written passages to these several accompaniment textures, they should attempt to do it extemporaneously. That is, the instructor can suggest a tune that everyone knows—a folk song, national tune, hymn, or popular song—and the student attempts to improvise an accompaniment in an appropriate style. This can be done with a singer or instrumentalist on the melody; or it can be done with the improviser incorporating the melody into the texture.

An important preliminary step in this procedure deals with the aural skills necessary to accompaniment improvisation. One must know what the chords are and when they change. By the end of the first year of theory most students should have some competence in this as a byproduct of the harmonic dictation skills acquired in the freshman year. Nevertheless, some revitalization of harmonic aural skills may be in order. A useful drill that is specifically related to accompaniment improvisation is to play several tunes (melody only) that are to be used for accompaniment improvisation, asking members of the class to call out the correct Roman numerals as the melody is being played. This will develop the quick harmonic responses necessary for this skill.

One of the problems in the teaching of keyboard skills in the theory class is the question of allocation of time. It is certainly true that some theory teachers, believing in the preeminence of sight-singing, ear-training, and part-writing, would be inclined to neglect keyboard skills. In a class that meets, say, five hours a week it is understandable that one or another of the components of the theory class may be occasionally neglected. And it must be recognized that every theory teacher has particular activities that for one reason or another receive the lion's share of attention.

The integration of the components of musical craft can help to alleviate this problem. Time can be saved by teaching ear-training and keyboard at the same time through some of the methods that have been suggested in this chapter. And the areas of eighteenth-century part-writing and figured-bass realization can certainly be mutually supportive. Aside from its importance as a performance medium, the keyboard is an essential tool for composers, arrangers, teachers, conductors, music therapists—indeed for virtually every kind of musician. Thus, it is important that those keyboard skills that can be integrated within the theory program be given every opportunity to flourish.

Although some keyboard ability is a sine qua non for a career in any field of music, perhaps the greatest deficiency among nonkeyboard music majors is a lack of piano background. When a middle school student composer, instrumentalist, or singer is identified as one who may have potential for a career in music, the wise parent or public school music teacher should find some means for that student to begin the serious study of piano. Regardless of what field of music he or she ends up pursuing, keyboard background is more than an adornment or supplement to one's abilities, it is an essential skill.

NOTES

1. Haydn's early musical training was as a choirboy in St. Stephen's Cathedral in Vienna. He departed as a teenager just after he was asked to remain on as a castrato.

2. Daniel P. Hallahan, and William M. Cruikshank, *Psychoeducational Foundations of Learning Disabilities* (Englewood Cliffs, N.J.: Prentice-Hall, 1973), 91.

FIVE

Writing Skills

FREEDOM WITHIN BOUNDARIES

Throughout the history of Western music theorists and composers have written vast numbers of treatises on the writing of music—most often about how to write counterpoint. The culminating treatise of the Renaissance is *The Art of Counterpoint* by Gioseffo Zarlino (1517–1590), who drew upon his predecessors all the way back to the *Micrologus* of Guido d'Arezzo (fl. A.D.1000). The Baroque period also saw a flood of counterpoint treatises; and during this time Johann Josef Fux (1660–1741) is the most distinguished writer among these producers of contrapuntal tracts. His *Gradus ad Parnassum* elucidates species counterpoint so clearly that it has been used by composers from the time of Mozart and Haydn even to the present.

Virtually every volume among this plethora of contrapuntal treatises spoke of the "rules of counterpoint," and one can trace the development of harmony and counterpoint throughout Western history by reading these learned theses. Indeed this is perhaps the most valuable element of present-day graduate courses in the history of music theory. Yet the idea of "rules" for writing music runs counter to modern ideas of free creativity and innovation. A good composition teacher today does not want his students to be restricted by too many rules, for writing by rules produces dull, dry, and uninteresting products. Innovation is as highly valued today as in the past.

It is the balance between precepts or rules and musical creativity that the teacher of music theory must seek in the teaching of writing

skills. Such a balance was admirably achieved by Zarlino. Although
he paid verbal homage to the *auctoritas* of earlier writers, he was also
very liberal and allowed exceptions to nearly every rule he presented. In keeping with early Renaissance and medieval tradition,
Zarlino's first rule of counterpoint is that a composition must begin
with a perfect consonance, a concept that had appeared at the beginning of every counterpoint treatise since Guido. It was the most
essential bit of *auctoritas*. Yet in Zarlino's liberal view, the rule is not
inviolable; and he proceeds to justify the use of imperfect consonances at the beginning, particularly when the second voice enters
later. Of particular interest is his mention of the P4, which may not
be used by itself at the beginning but "a fourth from the beginning
of the subject to the entrance of the counterpoint," which means
entrance of a second voice (perhaps in canonic imitation) at the P4
above or below.[1]

These rules continue through chapter 39 with no notable addi-
tions to earlier treatises except that his explanations are more complete and they are bolstered with numerous musical examples with
labels such as "good progressions," "prohibited progressions,"
"tolerable progressions," and "allowed progressions." Chapter 40 is
entitled "How to Write Simple Counterpoint, Called Note-Against-
Note, for Two Voices." This chapter is particularly pertinent to the
teaching of counterpoint, for Zarlino, speaking of "general rather
than particular" contrapuntal rules, says that the composer must
use these rules by means of "his own intellect and judgment." If he
lacks these gifts, "rules and precepts will avail him little." He adds
that this is true of all learning including science, for all good teachers begin with universals regardless of the subject of study. Chapter
41 is also of interest, for its subject is the avoidance of unisons and
octaves "as much as possible." Thus, even so great an authority as
Zarlino allowed for exceptions to the rules of counterpoint, and the
modern teacher of music theory should do the same.

MATERIALS FOR PART-WRITING

Traditionally, writing skills and analytical techniques get the lion's
share of attention among the components of the lower-division theory courses. Theory teachers who are composers quite naturally
tend to emphasize writing skills, while those who are primarily the-

orists or musicologists usually have a strong professional affinity for analytical techniques. Further, analysis and writing work so well together that a very common teaching approach is to study the writing techniques of a particular historical style as an analytical exercise and then let writing assignments consist of stylistic imitations of the music being analyzed.

It was just this kind of integration that led many mid-twentieth-century theory teachers to base their lower-division courses upon the Bach chorales. Because the part-writing principles were so readily codified, because the 371 chorales were thought to furnish a kind of microcosmic view of eighteenth-century harmonic practice, and because four-part vocal style was thought to be the ideal medium with which to teach writing skills, the Bach chorales could become the basis for the entire two-year theory program. Harmonic dictation, analysis, keyboard, and part-writing were all integrated within the study of the Bach chorales. And if one could accept or overlook its stylistic limitations, it was a very effective approach. The chief textbook espousing this approach was A. I. McHose's *The Contrapuntal-Harmonic Technique of the Eighteenth Century* (Appleton-Century-Crofts, 1947).

But the reaction to this pedagogical system should have been predictable. By the 1960s many teachers had begun to recognize its illusory qualities, and soon Walter Piston's *Harmony* (Norton, 1941) began to supersede the McHose text. (See the comparative discussion of these two texts in chapter 1, pages 4–6.) While the Bach chorale approach certainly did what it set out to do—that is, to impart a synoptic understanding of eighteenth-century harmonic practice and part-writing in a style that was also usable for keyboard and ear-training—its stylistic and musical limitations were immense. First of all, it ignored vast bodies of music literature before and after the eighteenth century; second, it ignored (even within the eighteenth century) the sine qua non of all true art, stylistic individuality; third, it grossly neglected the musical elements of sound and rhythm; and, finally, its high degree of codification could perhaps inhibit the free growth of creative talent. As the reaction grew, some extremists totally abandoned the Bach chorales in favor of a free approach to music-writing skills. More temperate reactions led to supplementing the chorales with music of various historical styles and media and teaching writing skills in such a way as to utilize varied harmonic rhythms, fresh textures, and greater rhythmic variety. It began to be realized that aspiring composers need not wait until completion of their lower-division theory courses to begin to develop their musical creativity, and writing in twentieth-century styles began to be included in theory programs, particularly in the second-year classes.

The reaction against the Bach chorale approach in the decade of the sixties had a salutary effect upon theory teaching in the United States. It let in a welcome breath of fresh air and served to enlighten theory teachers regarding the rationale and purpose of our teaching. Such reactions are cyclical in nature. Today the Bach chorales are still used a great deal in lower-division theory courses; but perhaps they are being used in a more enlightened manner, and certainly they no longer form the basis for an entire two-year theory program.

Nevertheless, four-voice vocal style remains the most prevalent form of part-writing in our theory programs—clearly a vestige of the earlier Bach chorale approach. That writing skills can be taught through this approach has been proven, for there are numerous successful composers working today who were reared upon it and whose creative gifts apparently survived. While the four-part vocal style of writing remains the basis for beginning part-writing procedures, it is best supplemented with other materials calculated to furnish broader perspectives of harmonic rhythm, sound, and musical style.

NOTATION AND CALLIGRAPHY

Basic to virtually all aspects of musical craft is the understanding of musical notation. Students come to their first theory class confident in their understanding of our system of symbolizing musical sounds. After all, they have been using it for years, perhaps most of their lives. Yet it is amazing how little some of them seem to have noticed and absorbed. Can this paradox be related to the phenomenon of the fluent and avid reader of books who is nevertheless a poor speller? At any rate, a goodly number of talented musicians need much guidance in the process of setting notes down on paper.

Also, computer software for creation of musical scores has reached such a high state of development that musicians are now capable of creating beautiful engraved-quality notation on their home computers. This may be a precursor of the deterioration of the art of musical calligraphy in the twenty-first century. If so, it is comparable to the degeneration of good penmanship since the invention of the typewriter. Even so, not all theory students have access to a computer with music-writing software. Even though many students have this capability, I firmly believe that it is necessary for *all* students to learn musical calligraphy. Indeed, to be able to create good music manuscript is a prerequisite for using music software intelligently.

The practice of musical calligraphy should begin on the very first day of class, and it will of necessity be touched upon nearly every day thereafter. Since four-part writing and melodic writing may be among the initial activities, the teacher can use these as a framework for the first presentation of correct notational practice. *Everything* should be explained: how to draw clefs, bar lines, placement of sharps and flats in signatures, meter signatures, rests, stems, size of notes, indenting the first system of a piece or movement, use of space, vertical alignment, beaming, ledger lines, and so on. Among the common errors that continue to appear are meter signatures on every system, poor vertical alignment, crowding, stems in the wrong direction, whole- and half-rests on the wrong lines, and unrhythmical beaming. Some of these appear repeatedly, and it is important for the students who err most often to understand how valuable good notational habits are to a musician. Teachers should set the tone by being very careful to see that their notation is at all times exemplary. Blackboard writing should be clear, spacious, and well organized; and the notation in tests and handout materials should be carefully prepared, lest the students get the false impression that there is a certain license that applies to handwritten music—that manuscript need not be as clear and readable as printed music. If necessary, a ruler should be used in laying out notation on paper for duplication in order to be sure that irregular beams, stems, and bar lines do not detract from the appearance of the manuscript.

Soft lead pencils are probably the best writing material for students to use in the theory classroom. Pencils write smoothly and clearly and their marks are easily erased; ballpoint pens in dictation exercises are to be avoided, for they invariably lead to much crossing out, thus contributing to untidy manuscript as well as messy thinking. For special projects some students may wish to use black ink on good manuscript paper or music software such as Finale. In such cases the teacher should conduct a special session for the interested students, to begin to impart the composer's lore of inking manuscript and/or the use of music software. As stated earlier, I believe that it is best for music students to learn good calligraphy before beginning to use music software—more on this topic in chapter 9.

Inking of music manuscript is a calligraphic art that requires considerable practice, but a great deal of trouble can be saved for the student if the teacher helps at the outset with advice on materials and procedures. If composition projects are undertaken as class assignments, the teacher should spend some time on layout of the score, copying parts, and so forth. Parts copied in soft lead pencil are quite acceptable for such projects and at this stage are likely to be neater than inked parts. Whether in ink or pencil, the principles of good part copying should be followed. That is, parts should be copied on the appropriate size of manuscript paper, using every other staff line for spacious, readable manuscript; and rests for page turns should be left at the bottom of every right-hand page, even if this necessitates leaving a portion of the page blank. The importance of proofreading for accuracy should also be emphasized. Learning these principles at an early stage is of real value to budding composers and furnishes the other students with a better perspective on musical craft, as well.

Proper procedures aside, there is also the question of neatness. Neatness of manuscript contributes to lucidity of musical thought. If students can picture themselves as performers of the music they are copying, it makes them more conscious of the importance of neatness and layout—more critical of the musical quality of the music they have written. For student composers, a strong argument for neatness, accuracy, and legibility is that these are important requisites for frequent performances and publication. For the others it is an essential element of musical craft. In any case an illegible part-writing assignment stands little chance of approbation by the teacher—a point that most students will find highly persuasive.

In recent years many new notational devices have appeared, some of which are admittedly unnecessary since they duplicate usable existing symbols that are universally understood. Others, however, such as expanding or contracting beams, are useful and have established themselves in the traditions of musical notation. Students should learn these as needed. A student who has "discovered" the muted piano tone (achieved by pressing the fingers of one hand on the first inch or so of the string by the peg and then striking the key with the other hand) should not be allowed to flounder with his or her own notational invention but should be told about the generally accepted symbol for this device. For the theory teacher who is not an active composer there are several references for information on this topic.[2]

Yet notes upon paper do not music make. And this is a point that merits consideration in the theory class. Fine notation is an end in itself only for the copyist and engraver. Music is sound, and the symbols by which we communicate these sounds have little significance in themselves—only for what we can achieve with them. Also, no musical symbolism is accurate enough to produce identical results twice in a row. Some notational devices are more accurate than others, but all require interpretation, and every interpretation will be different. Some classroom discussion on the philosophy of musical notation is useful to performers, scholars, and composers alike.

PART-WRITING

It is important for the theory teacher to consider purposes and objectives when undertaking the teaching of part-writing to freshman music majors. Obviously, learning to compose in four-part homophonic vocal style is not an end in itself. What elements of musical craft are learned from part-writing? And in what ways do they apply to the art of music? First of all, there is a certain skill or flexibility in the manipulation of musical tones that can grow from any sort of compositional exercise, regardless of its mode or style. Any musician will benefit from developing this talent, but it is particularly relevant to those whose orientation is toward composition or arranging. Second, the principles of harmonic motion of the common practice period can be viewed synoptically in four-voice part-writing. That is, the fast harmonic rhythm of the chorale style is not unlike a middle-level Schenkerian reduction of a longer piece. Indeed, there have been theory textbooks written with this as the guiding principle.

Third, many basic principles of counterpoint can be imparted through the practice of voice leading; and many of these principles have both stylistic and universal (or at least very general) applications. As an example, the bass and soprano lines possess a polar relationship that is seen in a strong contrapuntal affinity for each other. That is, in good part-writing the bass and soprano, since they are the most prominent voices, should be in good two-part counterpoint quite independently of the inner voices. If this is not a universal principle applicable to virtually all musical textures in Western music (and I suspect that it is), it certainly transcends the common practice period.

Related to the contrapuntal perspective is the understanding of dissonance that one gains from four-voice part-writing. This can be as useful to performers as it is to musicologists, theorists, and composers. The performer who understands the configuration of the suspension, with its preparation, dissonance, and resolution, is in a position to interpret more intelligently the suspension figure in actual music. This is particularly applicable to choral music from the Renaissance through the nineteenth century but also applies to instrumental music of that time.

All of these musical phenomena, taken as a whole, prepare the student for one of the primary goals of the study of music theory, the practice of analyzing music. The understanding of contrapuntal-harmonic practice as seen in four-part writing furnishes the tools necessary to undertake the harmonic analysis of the music of the common practice period. Since many theory teachers believe that analysis is the primary and central activity of the theory program, this is indeed an important function of part-writing.

Part-writing should begin in the freshman theory program as soon as the students possess sufficient knowledge of notation; chord, interval, and scale spelling; and other rudiments normally viewed as prerequisites for the beginning theory course. Music departments of all sizes and types normally administer a theory placement test to all potential music majors at the beginning of the freshman year or just before. Such a test is essential, but even after this initial screening a classroom review of notation and basic rudiments is still advisable.

Starting the part-writing process can be done very well by classroom demonstration and by presentation of the beginning principles for the part-writing of two consecutive root-position triads separated by the intervals of (1) the perfect fourth or fifth, (2) the third, and (3) the second. Although there are undoubtedly several appropriate ways to state these principles, it is important that the language be consistent so that the three principles are couched in similar terms. It should also be understood that the principles apply to the three upper voices in counteraction to the bass, since the bass motion is predefined. Also, at this stage we are dealing with a texture in which the root is always doubled.

The time-honored way of stating these principles for part-writing root-position triads is as follows:

1. For roots a fourth or fifth apart, keep the common tone in the same voice and move the other two voices to the nearest chord tones.
2. For roots a third apart, keep two common tones and move the third voice stepwise and contrary to the bass.
3. For roots a second apart, move the upper three voices to the nearest chord tones contrary to the bass.

At this point the desiderata of good part-writing should also be presented. These can be related to the preceding principles, for example, by pointing out that predominantly stepwise motion and smoothness of line are achieved by moving to the nearest chord tones and that the preferred contrary motion is also a part of the preceding principles. Above all it should be made clear that the principles will later be treated flexibly, and that there will be many exceptions to them in the course of the gradual development of part-writing mastery, as there also are in the literature of music.

This mastery—that is, a comprehensive knowledge and skill of four-voice part-writing—can normally be acquired in the freshman year. To be sure, the student's eighteenth-century harmonic vocabulary may not be complete by then; but all of the basic skills necessary to carry on with additional altered chords, and so forth, should have been acquired by that time. As each new aspect of part-writing is presented, its historical and/or musical rationale should be offered to justify what might otherwise appear to be an arbitrary procedure.

For example, in the presentation of a deceptive cadence, it is important for students to understand that the reason for the doubling of the third of the submediant triad has a clear historical and musical basis—that is, the natural tendency of the leading tone is to move up to the tonic, while the natural tendency of the second scale degree is to move down to the tonic. This natural musical impulse was as true in the Renaissance *clausula vera* as it is in the eighteenth-century cadence, and in both the *clausula vera* and the deceptive cadence the tonic tone is doubled. In any case the second scale degree must move downward in the deceptive cadence to avoid parallel fifths. To move the leading tone downward against its natural tendency would be unmusical (and is highly objectionable when it occurs in the soprano) and in the minor mode would result in a melodic interval of the augmented second.

Historical rationale for this practice should be observed in actual music, where the students will soon see that such composers as Bach, Mozart, Haydn, Beethoven, and even many later composers were so strongly influenced by this convention that the third of the submediant was often doubled, not only in the deceptive cadence but also when the progression V–VI was found within the phrase.

The historical evolution of the Phrygian cadence should also be considered when it is presented as a part-writing procedure. That its name comes from the Renaissance *clausula vera* of the third church mode and that (unlike the Dorian mode) it could not be given a leading tone by means of *musica ficta* are important points to understand. The musical impulses that resulted in the historical development of the Phrygian cadence are relevant to its use in part-writing. The teacher can also prepare for the study of augmented sixth chords by pointing out that if one were to add a leading tone to the iv⁶ in the Phrygian cadence (by chromatically raising the fourth scale degree), one would be creating an Italian sixth.

Virtually all of the musical phenomena learned in four-voice part-writing can be related to examples in the history and literature of music. This is its justification in the curriculum. But how strictly should the teacher insist upon the many rules of part-writing, such as the avoidance of parallel fifths or placing the cadential I⁶₄ on the strong beat of the measure? Quite strictly, I think. But it should be understood that four-voice part-writing is not real music. It is simply an efficient device by which musical principles can be imparted to students. Students write real music in other activities within the theory program and later in composition courses; but the purpose of part-writing exercises is to impart the contrapuntal-harmonic principles of the common practice period in as musical manner as possible in order that these principles can be applied to the study and analysis of music literature.

One of the virtues of part-writing is that students also gain compositional practice in the manipulation of musical tones. But one should not overrate this virtue. For the development of genuine compositional talent, it is necessary for the student to begin to write freely in styles related to the twentieth and twenty-first centuries. To emphasize this point the teacher can occasionally modify the strictness of the discipline of part-writing by illustrating ways in which Bach, Mozart, Beethoven, or another distinguished composer departed from conventional practices. For example, in the chorale *Freuet euch, ihr Christen alle* (No. 8 of the 371 and final movement of Cantata No. 40) Bach deliberately used numerous parallel fifths, perhaps as a symbol of *unbounded* religious joy. (See figure 5.1 and in the second measure note the parallel fifths in the soprano anticipation against the 8-7 passing tone in the tenor. There are at least four instances of this within the chorale.) Debussy's famous statement that "rules are created by works of art, not for works of art" can be a guiding principle in maintaining an appropriate perspective upon the practice of four-voice part-writing.

In general, the sequence of presentation of material for four-voice part-writing follows the same ontogenic process as the harmonic dictation described in chapter 3. That is, the four-voice texture is gradually fleshed out in a kind of reverse Schenkerian process. Thus, the close integration of harmonic dictation with part-writing is a very natural outcome. One begins with unadorned root-position triads, one to a beat, and the harmonic language is then gradually expanded over a period of two or three semesters until a texture similar to that of a complex Bach chorale is achieved. The actual order of the presentation of concepts may vary from teacher to teacher, but a typical plan is first to add a few first inversions beginning with the primary triads. Guidelines for doubling are important at this stage. The cadential I$^6_4$ can be the initial second inversion to be introduced, and once this is done, discussion of dissonant (nonharmonic) tones can begin. Next would come seventh chords, fol-

Chorale *Freute Euch, Ihr Christen Alle*, First Phrase, J. S. Bach

Figure 5.1

lowed in course by passing second inversions, third inversions, and, finally, altered chords. Altered chords are a broad subject and will extend from the second semester well into the second year. It starts with secondary dominants and secondary vii⁷s and moves thence to the Neapolitan and the augmented sixth chords, and finally to those altered chords that begin to transcend the common practice period, such as augmented triads and ninth chords.

Modulation can be introduced fairly early, certainly before the introduction of secondary dominants, but must be presented in connection with musical form so that the relationship of secondary tonal areas to the home tonality can be understood in terms of the time continuum of an entire piece of music, not simply a chorale phrase. Obviously, before students can understand secondary dominants, they must understand the concept of tonality and what constitutes a modulation.

The integration of part-writing with harmonic dictation can be done very effectively through blackboard drill as well as in the testing situation. A harmonic-dictation exercise in four-part vocal style can be given with half the class at the blackboard, the others working at their seats (in a typical class of fifteen, there is usually blackboard space for about eight students). In observing the students' progress, teachers will quite often find that errors are caused not by aural but by part-writing problems. By correcting these while the students are at the blackboard teachers may be getting at the root of aural problems at the same time that they are teaching part-writing. And they are setting students on the right track with an immediacy that tends to inhibit the forming of bad habits. That is, because they are watching their work at the blackboard, they can catch errors almost as they occur and prevent the negative reinforcement that comes from repetition of errors.

Perhaps the one most important part-writing activity is the take-home assignment. This can take a variety of forms, such as the filling in of inner voices, with bass, soprano, and figures given; the written realization of a figured bass; or the harmonization of a soprano line, such as one or two phrases of a chorale melody. My preference is to require that figured bass be included, as well as a harmonic analysis (in Roman numerals) placed on a separate level below the figures. In addition many teachers ask the students to circle and label the dissonant tones. It is important that these be corrected and returned to the students as soon as possible while the assignments are still very fresh in the students' minds. The teacher's reinforcement, positive or negative, begins to lose its effectiveness in direct proportion to the length of the time lag after the assignment is turned in.

While four-voice part-writing should not be viewed as genuine musical composition, this is not to say that part-writing exercises cannot be truly musical. Within the limitations of the style, students should be urged to make them as beautiful as they can; and the best ones should be played or sung in class in as musical a reading as possible. The teacher should also give compositional advice from time to time that goes beyond the mere promulgation of part-writing principles. Beauty of individual lines, the polar counterpoint of soprano and bass, the judicious use of dissonance and chromaticism, and the harmonic rhythm—all should be given careful consideration regarding their impact upon the overall musical effect. But sometime early in the sophomore year, if not sooner, the class will profit from writing of a different sort—creative activities more directly related to twentieth- and twenty-first-century composition.

STYLISTIC COMPOSITION

The teaching of composition, as such, is not an objective of the lower-division theory courses. There are, however, several activities that fit very well into the theory program at the same time that they prepare students for the possibility of later concentrated study in composition. Chief among these is the practice of stylistic composition. Perhaps "stylistic" is a misnomer, for all composition is stylistic in that all music is somehow related to the music of the past, else there would be no commonality of musical language. Music that is totally new—if it could be written—would be unintelligible. All composers use existing music as a point of departure from which to build their own unique musical languages. Thus, composing in various styles in the theory class can help to establish a stylistic base for future composers at the same time that it teaches stylistic elements of significant historical movements in music literature.

A worthwhile exercise in stylistic composition is to ask the students to compose in a medium and texture other than that of four-voice part-writing but in the harmonic language of the common practice period with which they are already thoroughly familiar. This can be done from the latter part of the freshman year on. Its purpose is to expand the students' writing perspectives beyond the textural and stylistic limitations of four-voice part-writing. The harmonic and contrapuntal knowledge gleaned from part-writing is applied to the writing of a piano piece, accompanied song, or ensemble piece.

One student might imitate the style of *Widmung* by the Lieder composer Robert Franz, another the *Trällerliedchen* from Schumann's *Album for the Young*, a third could emulate the style of a minuet from an early Mozart string quartet, and so on. The pieces should be short and at least some of them should be performed in class. As a first exercise in stylistic composition, it is an enjoyable classroom activity. Because of time limitations such exercises cannot be assigned very often within the two-year lower-division theory sequence. They should occur, however, at least once each term, gradually working toward twenty-first-century styles. In each case the writing assignment should be linked to conceptual and analytical study of music from the period being imitated. In particular this should include Impressionistic music, thus furnishing a corridor into the twentieth century perhaps during the latter part of the sophomore year. In such an exercise students can begin to explore ninth, eleventh, and thirteenth chords; the device of planing; tritone relationships; whole-tone passages; modality; and so on. They will be examining the music of Debussy and others at the same time that they begin to imitate it.

Following that, each student might be given an assignment to compose a short piece utilizing twelve-tone technique. This, too, should be correlated with conceptual study through an analytical approach to music of the Second Viennese School. It should be understood that twelve-tone technique does not in itself mandate a style. As analytical studies reveal differences among twelve-tone composers, the teacher should value and encourage student creative efforts for their originality or for their consistency of style. Consistency of style may be important to foster at this stage; for until compositional technique reaches a higher level of development, innovation may be at the expense of other desirable qualities, such as idiomatic writing, control of texture, and instrumental balance.

Thus, while those with truly creative gifts are bound to explore interesting new possibilities, the theory class is the place where compositional skills can begin to be imparted. For example, when the class first undertakes the writing of music for small ensembles, the instrumentalists in the class can be asked to demonstrate their instruments, illustrating timbres, range, registers, and idiomatic capabilities. This, along with exposure to instrumental transposition, can begin to lay the groundwork for the concentrated study of composition and orchestration in other courses. The students learn a great deal from classroom performances of their instrumental pieces, and those who wish to experiment have the opportunity to assess the degree of success of their innovations.

Time allowing, the class should explore other twentieth-century and contemporary styles in addition to Impressionistic and serial composition. Movements from such works as the Bartók *Microcosmos* and the *Forty-four Violin Duets* or the Stravinsky *Three Pieces for String Quartet* can be used for analytical studies and then serve as models for further creative projects in stylistic composition. American composers, particularly very recent works of the twenty-first century should also be included in such activities. Those students who are interested in jazz or studio work might be encouraged to attempt a particular type of arrangement for available instruments.

Whenever possible, student creative efforts should be played in class. But, as mentioned earlier, scores and parts should be meticulously prepared. To attempt a classroom reading from poorly prepared parts is a waste of time, and the teacher should make it very clear as to what the standards are for classroom performance. This, too, begins to build a foundation of compositional discipline that is of great value in later studies.

It is important that the gifted student with genuine ambitions as a composer be given opportunities beyond those that are normally possible in the classroom situation. Such students may feel restricted by stylistic composition exercises and may manifest a desire to develop their own musical personalities. They should be guided toward the private study of composition at an early stage. Or, if this is not possible, the teacher should offer private help outside of class. For some, if not all student composers, concentrated study of composition should not wait until the junior year but should begin as soon as the interest and talent is apparent. It is clear that stylistic composition can help to build a foundation for later study, but in special cases it should be supplemented by the serious study of composition in the hope of developing a unique creative gift.

There is no greater achievement for a department of music than to foster successfully the talent of a truly gifted composer. It is a responsibility that should be met with flexibility and understanding. Some music curricula, however, do not allow for the private study of composition in the freshman year; so it has frequently happened that talented composers are left to flounder until they have completed two carefully structured years of theoretical study. This approach could have a restrictive or stunting effect upon a talented musical personality. In any case it is a waste of time, for it takes years to develop a composer; and there is no reason why concentrated study in composition cannot be undertaken concurrently with the study of freshman or sophomore theory.

While the writing activities of the theory program may not constitute the study of composition in the truest sense, they are invaluable in the building of a foundation of musical discipline for composers, performers, and scholars alike. One of the most valuable of these activities is the introduction to contrapuntal skills.

COUNTERPOINT

There remains considerable controversy as to how and when counterpoint should be taught in the undergraduate music curriculum. Many teachers in the mid-twentieth-century tradition held that the formal study of counterpoint should begin with eighteenth-century counterpoint, but only after the student has completed the two-year lower-division theory sequence. The rationale for this is that eighteenth-century counterpoint is best learned after having acquired a good knowledge of harmonic common practice. There is much to be said for this point of view, for eighteenth-century counterpoint, if written stylistically, does indeed rely upon the principles of root movement of eighteenth-century harmony. The part-writing principles imparted in the theory class can thus be an excellent point of departure from which to undertake the study of eighteenth-century counterpoint. Another point of view holds that, since students receive a large dose of eighteenth-century harmony in the two-year lower-division theory program, the study of counterpoint in the junior and senior years should therefore be based upon a different style period. This argument is used to advocate the study of sixteenth-century counterpoint; and, when the perspective on Renaissance music is broad enough, it is a worthwhile curricular approach. Fortunately, the practice of basing the sixteenth-century counterpoint class entirely upon the limited style of Palestrina seems to be disappearing, thus allowing greater contrapuntal freedom and a more authentic approach to Renaissance style.

In the latter decades of the twentieth century the practice of teaching species counterpoint in an abstract, nonstylistic manner became fashionable. This point of view came primarily from teachers saturated in Schenkerian thought and perhaps emanated most directly from the book *Counterpoint in Composition*, by Salzer and Schacter, which forcefully argued that species counterpoint is based upon the very concepts that led to Schenkerian analysis.[3] While this is a plausible point of view, it is nevertheless most difficult, if not impossible, to teach counterpoint in so abstract a manner. Whatever else it is, counterpoint is music; and no music of any period is lacking in those unique musical gestures by which we identify it as belonging to a particular style period. This is how Zarlino viewed counterpoint, and this attitude is manifest also in the *Gradus ad Parnassum* of Fux. To teach counterpoint without the element of historical and musical style is to dehumanize it and divorce it from musical reality.

But species counterpoint, when taught in a more traditional manner, can be immediately meaningful to students as well as an important link to the later concentrated study of either sixteenth- or eighteenth-century counterpoint, or, indeed, to the study of Schenkerian concepts. Two-part species counterpoint can be introduced in the second year of the lower-division theory program. Some teachers may feel that this is crowding things a bit—that with the aural, analytical, and keyboard skills that need to be acquired in the first two years, counterpoint can wait till later. Yet the *Gradus ad Parnassum* should be a part of the musical experience of every undergraduate music major; and since some students will not study counterpoint later, it should receive some attention in the lower-division theory program. After all, Bach, Mozart, Haydn, and Beethoven all attested to the usefulness of the *Gradus*, not to mention the numerous twentieth- and twenty-first-century scholars and composers who held it in high esteem.

I do not mean to suggest that the sophomore theory class should be turned over to the study of counterpoint. Yet somewhere in the second semester, time should be found for an introduction to two-part species counterpoint. It can be done without a text, though certainly the English translation of the *Gradus* should be placed on the reserve shelf of the library. Second-semester sophomores will soon see that they have already acquired the information presented in the introductory "Dialogue" (Preliminary to the First Part). The book is in three parts, each of five chapters. Only the First Part (dealing with two-voice counterpoint) can conveniently be presented in the sophomore theory class. The Second Part deals with three-voice counterpoint, and the Third Part with four-voice writing, both of which must remain for later study. The five chapters in each part deal in turn with each of the five species of counterpoint.

The method of teaching it requires no explication here. Fux has already done that very well. In conjunction with this study, however, it is useful and illuminating to examine several examples of two-part Renaissance counterpoint. Fux's contrapuntal precepts are a distillation of sixteenth-century practices, and to see these principles in operation in such works as the two-part *Canzonets* of Thomas Morley or the two-part motets of the Lassus *Magnum Opus Musicum* makes species counterpoint much more meaningful to the class.

There are also great opportunities for integration of musical craft with this contrapuntal study. The original Renaissance examples as well as the student exercises can be sung in class for sight-singing practice and can also be used for two-part dictation. Some students may wish to set actual texts, and this of course is very much in keeping with the style. If this occurs, the teacher should explain the principles of Renaissance English prosody as seen, for example, in the Morley *Canzonets*.

Traditionally, the study of counterpoint has been viewed as an upper-division activity, not to be undertaken until the student has completed the two-year lower-division theory sequence. While this is undoubtedly fitting for three- and four-voice counterpoint, the early introduction of two-part species counterpoint serves several important purposes: (1) It offers an early introduction to the craft of counterpoint that is invaluable to beginning composers. (2) It forms a basis from which to depart in later counterpoint classes. (3) It introduces students to a style and texture normally not emphasized in the lower-division theory courses that could be useful in later study. (4) It offers a fresh approach to the integration of musical craft with conceptual study.

While I have hitherto attempted to avoid mandatory statements regarding course content, I am convinced that this is an important additional component of the lower-division theory program. The traditional objections on the grounds of time constraints are discussed later under the subject of the integration of musical craft in chapter 7.

ARRANGING

For students in certain programs, orchestration and/or arranging will be studied in a concentrated manner at the upper-division or graduate levels. Although there is not time in the lower-division theory program to present a detailed explication of orchestral instruments and their capabilities, some instrumental and choral arranging could well find a place in the lower-division theory courses. If presented in the sophomore year, it need not necessitate the presentation of new harmonic concepts, and it may suggest possibilities of new career avenues for some students. Not all types of departments will find this appropriate; but it is particularly fitting for schools with programs in music business or commercial music. Arranging is also useful in the fields of music education and music therapy.

It should be approached in the simplest, most practical manner possible. One way is to divide the students into groups of three or four, each group comprising a workable combination of instruments and voices. The teacher then assigns one specific piece, such as a folk song or show tune. Each student then produces an arrangement for his or her group. In this way there are three or four arrangements for each combination of instruments and voices. When performed in class, these illustrate not only the unique product of each individual but also the things that are possible with the various instrumental and vocal combinations.

The teacher must take care to choose the combinations carefully, allowing for the presence of both harmonic and melodic instruments. Harps and guitars are very useful, but it might be refreshing to also include electric guitars or keyboards and other instruments not normally found in the conservatory environment. This might also afford the opportunity for a brief presentation of jazz chord symbols and guitar tablature—information that is not usually presented in the theory class but that is significant to a great many musicians. The relationship of these devices to Baroque and Renaissance notational symbols can also be pointed out.

In its simplest form the arrangement of a tune need be nothing more than an instrument or group of instruments playing the harmony and another instrument and/or voice on the melody. Methods of expanding from this basic format can be discussed in class in terms of each combination of instruments, prior to undertaking the writing of the arrangements. Ranges, transpositions, and idiomatic capabilities of all available instruments should be presented; and then the teacher should clearly set forth the guidelines of the assignment. At this stage limitations are important, for the students will learn more and will have a greater sense of creative achievement if their parameters are very clearly defined.

As in all writing assignments, great care should be taken with the preparation of scores and parts. Success of the classroom performances depends upon this, and no arrangement should be read unless it is clearly legible and follows appropriate notational procedures. The potential composers and arrangers in the class will profit from strict adherence to this policy. Obviously, the use of music software should be encouraged at this point, especially for student composers who will learn to extract parts from score on the computer. This is discussed further in chapter 9.

Choral arrangements present problems quite different from instrumental arrangements, and it is sometimes difficult for students to find a suitable style and texture for a choral setting of a well-known tune. One frequent pitfall is to gravitate toward a texture derived from part-writing exercises, a style that is usually inappropriate for a folk song or show tune because of the fast harmonic rhythm and other factors. One solution is to combine the voices with accompaniment instruments, but the teacher can also suggest ways in which the harmonic rhythm and texture of the choral setting can be varied to achieve the appropriate style.

Another difficulty to be overcome is the devising of appropriate figurations for the accompaniment (harmonic) instruments in either instrumental or choral arrangements. The teacher can present several typical piano figurations for classroom discussion prior to undertaking the assignment. Of particular importance is the clear implication of a bass line that is present in every good accompaniment figuration. Schenkerian analyses of accompaniment figurations reveal the contrapuntal lines that are hidden within the broken or arpeggiated chords of good piano and guitar figurations.

The teacher's choice of tunes to be arranged may be critical to the success of the assignment. The intensive classical emphasis that generally pervades the classroom of a good theory teacher can be considerably relieved during the arranging assignment by choosing tunes by such composers as Scott Joplin, Paul Simon, John Lennon, or Billy Joel. Our vast heritage of folk song is also a good source. But whatever tune is chosen, the arranger should strive to preserve the essence of the tune's original intent. To achieve this within a fresh and attractive musical setting is the objective of good arranging.

The relationship between analysis and the writing activities of the theory class has been apparent throughout this chapter. To understand the inner structure of music is essential to composition, to performance, to musical scholarship, and of course to the teaching of music. All of these depend upon analysis, and it is to this that we next turn our attention.

NOTES

1. Gioseffo Zarlino, *The Art of Counterpoint,* trans. Guy Marco and Claude Palisca (New Haven, Conn.: Yale University Press, 1968), 55.

2. In particular I recommend *New Music Vocabulary* by Howard Risatti (Urbana: University of Illinois Press, 1975). Gardner Read's *Thesaurus of Orchestral Devices* (New York: Putnam, 1953), though older, is useful for twentieth-century music in general. They may be out of print but should be available in a good music library.

3. Felix Salzer and Carl Schacter, *Counterpoint in Composition* (New York: McGraw-Hill, 1969).

Six

Analysis and Theoretical Concepts

RATIONALE

We call our discipline music theory, and this is the name of the course that is offered to our music students in the freshman and sophomore years of college. But do we really deal with theories of music? A theory is a proposition, or set of propositions, that can be tested. A theory of music, then, is a proposition, or set of propositions, about music that can be tested. Properly speaking, we deal with pure theory only in the area of musical analysis. Virtually all the rest of the lower-division theory program is musical craft of one sort or another.

This is not to say that theory does not enter into musical craft, for all of the phases of musical craft depend to a significant degree upon the discipline of analysis. Can one sight-sing successfully without perceiving phrase structure? Can one realize a figured bass without perceiving the harmonic structure? Can one take down a harmonic dictation or part-write a chorale phrase without mental processes of analysis? Can an instrumentalist sight-read a new work without exercising some sort of analytical skills? Can one perform or conduct a musical work without first having learned how it is put together?

Since the answer is no to all of these questions, this points to the fact that analysis is the central activity of the theory class. It is quite proper that this should be so, for analysis is an essential preliminary and ongoing activity in virtually all forms of music making. Consciously or not, a fine performer is constantly making sophisticated analytical judgments and evaluations in the course of rehearsing or practicing and even in the final performance.

I say "consciously or not" because the late Millard Taylor once told me, "Courses in theory and analysis of music are a complete waste of time for performers." Millard was a popular teacher of violin at the Eastman School for thirty-five years as well as an internationally known concertmaster and recitalist, so I paid attention to this comment. He was also a good friend with whom, as a cellist, I had played a number of chamber music concerts, so I knew him quite well; yet I did not for a moment believe that he was correct in his condemnation of analysis courses. Because I respected him as a teacher and performer, I devoted considerable thought to his assertion and came to the following conclusions.

There are some deeply gifted performers who possess or develop an approach to musical interpretation that, in whole or part, is an internal and perhaps subconscious process—a nondiscursive approach. They cannot talk about it and are often suspicious of those who do, yet I believe, in his own way, that Millard Taylor analyzed music all the time, not only in rehearsal but also in performance. This was not something he could talk about, much less write about, and perhaps for him theoretical courses in music analysis would not have helped; yet he knew very well how music was put together, and his interpretive decisions were based upon carefully considered analytical judgments. That his analyses were nondiscursive in nature makes them no less valid than thoughtfully argued treatises in which major musical works are dissected and synthesized.

There are other fine performers, just as deeply gifted, for whom a consciously rational and analytical approach to interpretation is the only way, and others who lie somewhere in between. We are all different and this is why every performance of any great work is and should be a new and interesting experience, even if we have heard the work a hundred times before. Courses in the analysis of music can help every musician, for the more music a composer, performer, or scholar knows, and the better he or she knows it, the more likely it is that this musician will produce something of lasting value.

Freshman and sophomore music majors are no exception to this, yet many of them find the subject of analysis onerous when confronted with it in the theory class. What then are the teaching strategies that can enhance the appeal of analysis? How can the theory teacher find a link between the fascinating analytical judgments of the performer or scholar and the seemingly tedious tasks of the theory classroom? How can students see that the formal study of analysis will not only sharpen their perceptions as scholars, composers, and teachers but will also make them better performers? As I have said before, the favorite activity of every musician is the making of music, whether creating it or recreating it; and next best is listening to music.

TEACHING STRATEGIES

Thus, a good way to start—to capture student interest—is to begin with aural analysis. The theory teacher who walks into the classroom prepared to perform or to play a recording, armed with a set of questions about what the students will hear in the music, stands a good chance of capturing and holding student attention.

The simplest procedure is simply to play a piece of music and then say, "Tell me what you have heard in this piece." The first time the teacher will probably be met by a long silence, for most students are not accustomed to being asked such open-ended questions. Teachers usually ask leading questions; and as often as not they virtually answer their own questions before the students have a chance to. This happens because teachers make the mistake of thinking that silence in the classroom is bad. The silence makes them uneasy, and they seem to forget that they have just asked a question. But answering questions requires thought; and thought takes time and is usually carried on in silence.

The teacher who continues to talk after having asked a question may very well be tacitly communicating the following message to the students: "I don't think you have an answer, and if you do it's probably not the one I'm looking for, so I'm going to give you lots of clues, even to the point of almost telling you the answer that I want."

The students' silent reaction to this might very well be, "You have contempt for our abilities, you seem insecure about your teaching, and monstrously egotistical about your own knowledge and opinions." The savvy students, who have seen teachers like this before, quickly deduce the desired answer from the teacher's chatter, raise their hands and deliver the answer, gain the teacher's approbation (such as it is), and will have learned nothing. Indeed they will have been partner with the teacher in the experience of mutual contempt. Hardly a model classroom situation.

The situation is quite different if the teacher allows the necessary time after the question and then shows respect for student responses by valuing them and responding with related questions. Let us say that the teacher has played a recording of Stravinsky's *Symphony of Psalms*. To ask what the class has heard in it is a perfectly good way to begin, but then the teacher should allow time for the students to come to grips with the sounds they have heard and to engage in worthwhile classroom discussion. Even the most obvious responses are valuable, such as, "I heard woodwinds" or "the piece has three movements." But there will also be more perceptive responses, such as, "I think the middle movement is a fugue." At this point the teacher might encourage the students to carry that perception farther by asking, "How many voices are there in the fugue?" or "What instruments first present the subject?" As facts begin to accumulate about the second movement, a second playing of just that movement would be useful.

At that point more detailed and musically perceptive responses should be forthcoming. Some students will perceive that it is a double fugue in which instruments present one subject in the opening exposition and the chorus presents another complete exposition later. The interrelationships of material from the two expositions can now become the subject for discussion, with the teacher leading when necessary—not with answers but with questions. Some students may perceive that the tonic-dominant tonal relationships characteristic of the Baroque fugal exposition are also present here—cast in a twentieth-century idiom—and some may begin to glimpse the impressive symmetry of the texture and growth process of the movement.

The object of this activity, aside from hearing and learning a major twentieth-century work, is to illustrate that those things ferreted out through detailed analyses are in fact living musical phenomena that can be heard. Time allowing, every piece of music to be analyzed should be approached in this way, for it brings the discipline of analysis down from the icy heights of abstract speculation to the rich physical realm of sound. Only after the work has been experienced should the score be opened.

Since many if not all of the students in the lower-division theory courses will later take an upper-division course in form and analysis

or analytical techniques (certainly those who intend to pursue graduate work should do so), much of the analytical work done in the
theory program tends to be preparatory in nature. The disciplines
of traditional harmonic analysis, Schenkerian analysis, and set and
interval vector analysis all fall into the general category of description. That is, having performed a rudimentary analysis by means of
one of these methods, one still must consider the elements of
rhythm, melody, and sound in much detail before undertaking the
more important step of synthesis and evaluation. By learning these
descriptive skills, the students are acquiring tools for later in-depth
study of musical analysis, but such work is itself generally preparatory in nature. The lower-division theory teacher does not normally
attempt to build a true and comprehensive analytical model.

But then, who does, or did? Certainly not Schenker or his disci-
ples, for the limitations of Schenkerian analysis were well publicized
during the late twentieth century.[1] Set and interval vector analysis
also ignores texture, timbre, dynamics, and (in the main) rhythm. It
is true that some theorists dealt separately with one or another of
the musical elements including sound, but invariably as a discrete
phenomenon—rarely in an approach that acknowledges the interdependence of the musical elements.[2]

Lower-division theory teachers, by the manner in which they
approach the subject of musical analysis, indeed by their general
musical posture, can help to alleviate this problem of excessively
categorical musical thinking. Whenever possible, the teacher should
point out the interrelationships between harmony, rhythm, melody,
and sound. For example, in dealing with part-writing principles it
is virtually impossible to ignore rhythm, for certain formulae (the
obvious example is the cadential I⁶₄) must be cast in specific rhythmic
frameworks. But the elements of sound and melody also enter into
part-writing and should be given their due. The *tessiture* of the
voices, choices of textures, and character of the lines are cases in
point. If the teacher can bring out these interrelationships in day-
to-day class work, it then becomes easier to approach the subject of
analysis with a consciousness of the interdependence of the musical
elements.[3]

The class should have been introduced to the interval-class system
and interval vectors as freshmen. As mentioned in chapter 3 (where
it is explained in some detail), this can be useful in developing harmonic aural skills as well as in analysis. In analysis, however, it is a

tool that is of particular use in dealing with modern harmony and with complex sonorities of any period.

Teachers have found a variety of solutions to the question of when and how to introduce Schenkerian analysis. Many theory teachers do not introduce it at all in the lower-division program, while avid Schenkerians of the late twentieth century were sometimes known to base the entire two-year sequence upon it. A more moderate approach is to teach the rudiments of Schenkerian notation in the sophomore year as a preparation for the later study of analysis. Whenever it is introduced, it is most important that it be placed in the proper perspective regarding its use and function. Occasionally, students have been left with the absurd notion that its purpose is reduction—that the object is to reduce a piece of music down to a few chords. Since the *process* is one of reduction—strongly emphasized in learning Schenkerian notation—it is easy for students to assume that this is also its rationale. A teaching strategy that helps to offset this misconception is to conduct a kind of classroom analysis in which the class finds the background lines of, say, the Prelude of the first Bach Cello Suite (G Major) or the first Prelude (C Major) of *The Well Tempered Clavier*, but without using a formalized Schenkerian approach. This done, the teacher can then demonstrate how the lines can be more graphically and systematically illustrated by means of Schenkerian notation. This shows the genuine purpose of Schenkerian analysis, puts rationale ahead of process, and demonstrates the real meaning of middle-ground and background lines.

The follow-up strategy, then, is to demonstrate the practical utility of understanding these lines. The most effective way is for the teacher to perform the work just analyzed, demonstrating how knowledge of the lines contributes to a more meaningful and musical performance. Or the teacher can ask a student to perform, with the class offering suggestions and comments on interpretation based upon the Schenkerian analysis.

The traditional classroom setting for the subject of musical analysis has the teacher at the piano and the students at their seats, each with a copy of the score in hand. The class is presumably prepared with pencil annotations written into the score, and the teacher is ready to play at least excerpts from the work, if not the complete piece. An obvious and very workable teaching approach is for each student to recite in turn, gradually working through the score. The dynamics of the classroom in this setting are conducive to free and open discussion. The teacher can solicit class responses to each student's recitation and can interject analytical solutions along with a good deal of Socratic questioning. At the same time, the teacher can also play each excerpt before, after, and during discussion.

The bulk of the observations made at this stage is descriptive in nature. That is, harmonic analysis or even perception of normative structures does not usually enter the domain of evaluative judgment. It is the teacher's task to carry the discussion beyond the descriptive stage at appropriate times in such a way as to lead the students to begin to see a synthesis of their observations. This is at once the most significant and the most difficult analytical stage.

Let us say, for example, that the class is examining Bartók's Sixth String Quartet, perhaps as a final analysis project in the second semester of the sophomore year. The preliminary and descriptive stages of analysis have yielded a fund of information pertaining to harmony, sound, melody, and rhythm. An overall tonal center of D has been established and explained; the recurrences of the *Mesto* theme have been discussed; the first movement is discovered to possess traits of the classical sonata form; the fourth movement is found to be a kind of synoptic view of the entire piece; Bartók's unique use of timbres and textures has been discussed; characteristic chord forms have been revealed; and other aspects of the musical elements have been brought under consideration.

It is at this point that the teacher must lead the students to see a meaningful synthesis of these musical perceptions, above all, to make significant judgments regarding style. Here are some questions that might elicit these kinds of judgments: (1) Which musical elements contribute most to the "uniqueness" of this piece of music? (2) Is the work stylistically different from other works of this composer, and if so, how? (3) Is the work unique among analogous works of its time in history, and if so, how? (4) Into which category of historical-musical tradition does this work fall? (5) Is it distinctive among the other works in this tradition, and if so, how? (6) Are the growth process and shape of this work unique among other works of this composer or among analogous works?

If the teacher can lead the class to apply these questions to Bartók's Sixth String Quartet, the class may decide that the elements of sound and rhythm are chief among the special stylistic features of the work. And this can be perceived in the use of fresh timbres, unusual string techniques, and remarkable textures, such as that in

which the cello plays in its highest register in an impassioned
melodic passage with wide quasi-glissando leaps while the violins
tremolando below against balalaika-like strumming in the viola (middle of second movement, see figure 6.1).

Figure 6.1

Discussion then might turn toward a comparison of Bartók's use
of sound with that of his contemporaries. Was he an innovator in his
use of timbres and textures? Was he a pioneer in the development
of new string techniques? What other Bartók works also reflect these
features? By dealing with questions of this sort in classroom discussion after the class has made a detailed descriptive analysis of a
work, the teacher is demonstrating a most important point—that the
object of analyzing music is not to find all of the descriptive material, such as chord forms, normative structures, harmonic analysis,
or whatever. These are simply the means to an end. The object of an
analysis is to draw important musical insights or make significant
evaluative judgments that are useful to musicians or scholars. If the
class can be left with a sense of purpose in regard to the analysis of
music, the teacher will have achieved a great deal indeed.

THE HISTORICAL-STYLISTIC APPROACH

By linking analysis to style and to history it is possible to teach
important theoretical concepts in such a way as to make those concepts more meaningful (and therefore more memorable) than if they
are taught as rather arbitrary abstractions. To cite an obvious and

extreme example, one could quite readily teach the concept of figured bass outside of any historical context by approaching it purely as a matter of musical craft—a skill to be learned. To most modern theory teachers this would be absurd, for one would inevitably wish to illustrate and examine seventeenth- and eighteenth-century usages of figured bass; and it would be only natural that this would lead to discussion of the features of Baroque music that led to the development of figured bass.

Virtually every concept discussed in the theory class can be meaningfully linked to music history and musical style. If, for example, the subject is phrase structure, the class should examine and analyze a variety of cadence types from the literature including not only the obvious examples that can serve as models for part-writing but also those that are unique and problematical. When the subject of cadences comes up in connection with phrase structure, it should be possible to trace briefly the entire history of music from the cadence points in Guido's *Micrologus* up to the twenty-first century— examining examples of all cadence types from the literature along with the practice of writing them in common practice style.

A similar thing can be done with the concept of dissonance, that is, the class "discovering" that the intervals of the fourth and fifth were considered consonant during much of the period in which organum was written; that thirds and sixths began to be viewed as consonances in the fourteenth century, leading toward the adoption of triadic contrapuntal textures in the Renaissance, wherein the intervals of the fourth, second, and seventh were the chief dissonances. This can lay the groundwork for the study of dissonant practices of the common practice period at the same time that it offers fine opportunities for the examination and analysis of distinguished works from our musical heritage.

The so-called common practice period has been mentioned frequently throughout this book. It is that period of approximately 1650 to 1850, during which musical practices of composers in Europe and England arrived at a state of development (or crystallization) that allowed for ready codification of contrapuntal-harmonic practices. It is this aspect of easy codification that results in the musical techniques of the common practice period being used for the traditional approach to the study of music theory.

There have been criticisms of this approach. It has been charged that the musical scope of the common practice period is too narrow;

that it teaches a style that, if it ever existed, is not practiced today; and that students saturated in the period of 1650–1850 are unprepared in the music of both earlier and later styles. With the recent emphasis upon "world music" and ethnomusicology, even the practice of limiting theoretical study to the music of Western culture has been attacked. It should be remembered, however, that in today's postmodern and neomodern environments there are many composers who are returning to techniques of the common practice period—diatonic textures, triads, and so forth—while trying to dress them in new clothes. Compatible with this is the movement toward writing "audience-friendly" new music, using techniques of the Classical and Romantic periods, so that the theory-teaching biases of the recent twentieth century may now be old hat.

Yet there may be a certain validity to these criticisms. It is true that some theory teachers have limited the scope of their lower-division theory courses to a historical period that is clearly too narrow. This is a pointless economy, and it is unnecessary. The attractive feature of the common practice period is that it is a culmination point in music history—a point of arrival. I used the word *crystallization* a little earlier—and around 1750 there was indeed a crystallization of harmonic practices, seen at its best in the music of J. S. Bach. Rhythm also reached a point of arrival at about the same time, with the system of meters and bar lines that had developed out of Renaissance practices exercising great control over most composers. At the same time there was a fascinating reaction to this in the music of such composers as C. P. E. Bach, Mozart, Haydn, and Beethoven and continuing in the music of nineteenth-century composers even up to the time of Schoenberg. Thus, music both before and after the common practice period is in one way or another linked to the eighteenth century. If one teaches a theory course based upon the music of the common practice period without drawing upon its links to music before 1650 and after 1850, the scope of the course will indeed be too narrow and the aforementioned criticisms would certainly be valid.

It is extremely important, then, that theory teachers have a perspective of music history that enables them to allude at any time to musical practices before and after the common practice period that are relevant to the theoretical concept under discussion. When discussing sonata form, the teacher might appropriately point out that the normative structure promulgated by both Czerny and Marx around 1840 is in a sense a fictive design statistically based (more or less) upon the sonata movements of Beethoven. Because this is no more than a kind of statistical mean, there are many sonatas of Beethoven and others that significantly depart from this normative pattern. The manner in which this normative design influenced such later composers as Brahms, Bartók, Prokofiev, and Stravinsky should be highly relevant to the study of sonata form and offers a good opportunity to broaden the scope of the theory course beyond the music of the common practice period.

The study of theoretical concepts, then, is bound up with the study of musical style, and no study of musical style can be carried on without analytical skills. As mentioned earlier, the technique of finding sets and interval vectors (see chapter 3) could well be learned early in the two-year theory sequence, and the rudiments of Schenkerian analysis can be learned during the sophomore year. The skills of traditional harmonic analysis should have been gradually acquired throughout the two-year theory sequence, and the students should also have developed skills in perceiving phenomena of musical sound and rhythm. What remains to be done is to integrate all of these skills and techniques into an analytical methodology that can cope with the integration of the musical elements of rhythm, melody, harmony, and sound.

INTEGRATIVE ANALYSIS

Theorists tend to concentrate unduly on those elements of music reliant upon pitch, particularly upon harmony. It is understandable that this would be so, for harmony has been more thoroughly systematized than any other element of Western music. In fact, harmony (along with its close relative counterpoint) is the only element of music that throughout history has consistently been the subject of theoretical study. This is not true of rhythm and sound because those musical elements do not lend themselves well to neat conceptualization and thus cannot be so readily studied. Schenkerian analysis and set theoretical analysis both emphasize pitch and/or harmony to the virtual exclusion of the other elements of music. Traditional systems of analysis have always centered upon the examination of harmony at the microanalytical level and as it relates to the overall structure.

To be sure, music in Western culture is unique among the musics

of the world in that its melodico-harmonic structure is basic. This
has been true at least since the time of Guido d'Arezzo. But this does
not mean that the element of sound, for example, is less important
than harmony as a musical element. After all, music cannot exist
without sound; and where there is sound there is also timbre, texture, and dynamics. And where there is organized sound for a
length of time substantial enough to be music, there is also rhythm.
The musical elements of rhythm, harmony, melody, and sound are
thus interdependent, and it is logical to treat them as such within
the discipline of musical analysis.

But by what teaching strategies can one do so within the theory
classroom? Most of all, I think, by using a systematic approach to
analysis. By this I am not advocating the exclusive use of any one
system, such as Schenkerian analysis or set theoretical approaches.
These may be incorporated into the teaching approach, but if so,
simply as tools at the descriptive level of analysis. The plan can con-
ceivably be designed by the teacher and may well be modified
according to the nature of the music under discussion, but it should
have some features generally applicable to nearly all kinds of music.
As mentioned earlier, one should certainly begin with aural analysis
in order to allow the class to experience the work as music and to
emphasize the relevance of analysis to the musical experience. A
checklist system works very well. Four headings can be placed on
the blackboard: (1) rhythm, (2) melody, (3) harmony, and (4) sound.
Then the students can place their observations under the appropriate headings, perhaps noting from time to time that certain observations might fall under two or more headings as a result of the
interdependence of the musical elements. By avoiding the use of the
score at this stage, the students are required to use their ears in a
manner that correlates very well with the formal practice of aural
skills.

After the lists have become quite sizable the teacher can steer the
discussion toward some integration or synthesis of the data written
on the blackboard. At this point, if not earlier, a fifth category, form
(or structure or growth process), can be introduced. This may lead
to conclusions regarding form, historical or individual style, affective or psychological observations, the nature of the performance,
and so on, the objective being to complete a kind of cursory macroanalysis before digging into the score itself.[4]

The next step is to open the score and begin the microanalytical process—the ferreting out of fine details of harmony, rhythm, melody, and sound. Here too a checklist process can be used, perhaps making separate lists of the four elements—once at a microanalytical level, again at a middle level, and finally at the macroanalytical level. Microanalysis includes observations of the smallest details of harmony, rhythm, melody, and sound. Middle-analysis deals with relationships between phrases and other medium-sized units—anything that fits neither the very small nor the very broad categories. Macroanalysis deals with events that can be viewed within the total time span of the composition—the broad perspective of the piece. A checklist of the four elements can be used at all three of these levels.

As the class begins to deal with these checklists of the four elements, their interdependence becomes apparent. It is the integration of these descriptive observations that is the essence of musical analysis. In many cases it is virtually impossible to deal solely with a single element, such as pitch. Indeed it is the overlapping of the musical elements that leads to important observations regarding, for example, the source of the emotional or affective qualities at a given point in the music. The class may observe that a certain climactic point is not so much the result of a special harmonic device as it is a rhythmic, textural, dynamic, or timbral phenomenon.

While pitch is an important element in the music of today, the other elements of music often contribute just as much to the overall effect. It is for these reasons that the theory teacher must find ways to transcend the traditional emphasis upon harmony. Harmony must still be learned, but it should be viewed in the proper perspective—as one of the four coalescent elements of music.[5]

THEORIES AND CONCEPTS

Analysis and theoretical concepts are grouped together here because of their affinity in the learning process. One certainly applies theoretical concepts to the analysis of music, but one also learns theoretical concepts through the analytical process. Musical and theoretical concepts are also learned through aural, keyboard, and writing activities. Their integration in the theory class is discussed in the next chapter. But one deals directly and often exclusively with theoretical concepts in the process of analyzing music.

The theory teacher should consider the manner in which concepts or theories of music are evolved and elucidated in classroom discussion. As an example, let us take the D-sharp minor Fugue (VIII) of Volume One of the *Well-Tempered Clavier* of J. S. Bach. We can use it to describe a fugal exposition to a sophomore theory class and to explain the concept of the tonal answer. The class has been asked to analyze the first fourteen bars outside of class in preparation for classroom discussion. Although the exposition ends in the middle of bar 10, the teacher has also asked the students to account for the entry that occurs in bar 12, since it can be viewed as a redundant fourth entry in a three-voice fugue. (It has the appropriate tonal configuration to be an answer to the third voice.) The class has previously listened to and discussed the complete Prelude and Fugue without the score.

The setting is as was described earlier—the teacher at the piano prepared to play excerpts in the course of discussion and the students at their desks with the annotated scores in hand. The teacher begins by asking, "Where does the exposition of this fugue end?"

Several students are ready with the answer, and student A responds, "At the third beat of bar 10."

TEACHER: *Why there?*

STUDENT A: Because at this point all three voices have presented the subject.

TEACHER: *How long is the subject?*

STUDENT A: Two and a half bars.

TEACHER: *Then there is a subject entry every two and a half bars?*

STUDENT A: Umm, no, the third voice doesn't come in right after the second.

TEACHER: *Why not?*

STUDENT A: I'm not sure, but I suppose Bach wanted to make the exposition longer.

STUDENT B: No, it's for a modulation.

TEACHER: *Why do you need a modulation?*

STUDENT B: To get back to the tonic for the entrance of the third voice.

STUDENT C: Yeah, the second voice modulates to A-sharp minor, so now we have to get back to the D-sharp minor tonic for the entrance of the third voice.

TEACHER: *The second voice modulates? But I thought the second voice had to answer in the key of the dominant. Shouldn't it already be in the key of A-sharp minor?*

STUDENT C: No, it actually starts in the key of the tonic and on the tonic chord itself. In fact it leaps from the fifth scale degree up to the tonic note. Then it modulates.

STUDENT A: Oh, I see, that's a clear-cut cadence at bar 6 where the second voice ends—an authentic cadence in A-sharp minor. Then the next two bars have a real purpose, don't they? They get us back to D-sharp minor for the entrance of the third voice. But why doesn't the second voice start right out in the dominant?

[No one responds and the teacher allows the class to savor the silence in the hope of an answer. Then he cautiously proceeds with more Socratic dialogue.]

TEACHER: *Well, let's look at the subject itself. It doesn't modulate, does it? It simply ends in D-sharp minor. Does that give you any ideas?*
STUDENT D: Well, I remember your telling us about several types of tonal answers. This is one of them, isn't it? The leap of tonic to dominant is answered by the leap of dominant to tonic. You said it would go to the wrong key. If we used a real answer here, the third voice would be in the key of E-sharp minor and that doesn't sound right.
STUDENT B: Well, why didn't Bach modulate back to D-sharp minor just as he did here? Then you could have a third answer and the third voice could be in D-sharp minor again. He put in the two measures anyway.
TEACHER: *Okay, I think you understand the problem, but you've got to think like eighteenth-century listeners, too. They expected the opening emphasis on the tonic and they expected to hear the key of the dominant pretty soon, too. All eighteenth-century music—just about—moves to the dominant. Eighteenth-century ears would have been very puzzled if it didn't. But listen to what happens if I put in a real answer.* [Teacher plays an altered version of the first five bars, using a real answer as in figure 6.2.]

Fugue No. VIII, W.T.C. Volume 1, J.S. Bach
(First Five Bars Altered to use a Real Answer)

Figure 6.2

STUDENT D: That doesn't sound right. It's too abrupt. Bach's way
is better.
TEACHER: *What! Better than mine?*

[Laughter]

TEACHER: *Listen to this fugal exposition.* [Teacher plays the opening
of Bach's "Little" organ Fugue in G Minor through the
entrances of the first two voices; see figure 6.3.] *Shouldn't that
fugue have a tonal answer? It begins with the leap of tonic to dominant, just like this one. But look, here's the answer and it's a real
answer.* [Silence]

Figure 6.3

STUDENT A: This one sounds right, too.
STUDENT C: I guess Baroque composers didn't always follow their
own rules.
TEACHER: *Tonal answers are a pretty long-standing practice. Even sixteenth-century composers used them in imitative choral works. Look,
here's one in a Canzonet by Thomas Morley, an Elizabethan composer.* [They examine the *Canzonet.*] *There is a reason for Bach
using a real answer here in the G Minor Fugue. Listen again.* [The
teacher plays the opening of the G Minor Fugue again.]
STUDENT C: Wait a minute. In the D-sharp Minor Fugue the subject doesn't modulate. Does this one modulate to the dominant?
STUDENT A: That's it! You got it! But it's a kind of implied modulation. You don't get any C-sharps, but the subject is so long that
Bach can get our ears to hearing D minor in time for the answer
to actually be in the key of the dominant.
STUDENT B: Yeah, that's why he could use a real answer here. The
other one still had to emphasize the tonic at the beginning of
the answer.

STUDENT D: But if the subject modulates, and the answer is real, that means that the answer will modulate, too. The third voice would end up in A minor, and that won't be right for a fugue in G minor.

STUDENT C: I'll bet there's another extra section at the end of the answer to modulate back to the tonic. What do you call those sections in a fugal exposition where there's no subject?

TEACHER: *The generally accepted term is* codetta. *Let's use that, but the important thing is to understand the function. But let's see if you're right. Let's look at that G Minor Fugue to see if there is a* codetta.

And so the class proceeds to the score of the "Little" Fugue in G Minor to track down *codettas*. Note that almost all the teacher's lines were questions and yet the concept of the *codetta* evolved. The teacher did not announce that a *codetta* was such and such and did not define tonal answer, although it had been discussed at an earlier session. The term *codetta* was introduced only when a student asked for a term by which one could refer to that particular musical phenomenon. The class understood the concept even before they had a term for it.

Note also that the teacher reached beyond eighteenth-century practice by discussing an early example of the tonal answer (Thomas Morley's *Canzonet*). The teacher might also have alluded to twentieth-century fugues (such as the first movement of the Bartók *Music for Strings, Percussion, and Celesta*) and led the discussion toward an understanding of why twentieth-century fugues are unlikely to have tonal answers, though they may have *codettas*.

The teacher should not necessarily respond to every student comment. It often happens in classroom discussion that the students themselves respond to each other, as was the case here. The teacher should intervene when the discussion goes too far afield or should insert a probing question. But for the most part it is better if the students can carry on the discussion with little teacher intervention. With some teachers the problem is that they say so much that the students do not need to grapple with the problem under discussion. The teacher is doing it for them. This gets back to Piaget's theories of learning, wherein LM (logico-mathematical) learning consists of abstracting from perceptual (or motor) action. That is, one learns by taking action upon a problem. The students in the preceding discussion learned about tonal and real answers, *codettas,* and fugal expositions through the active process of analysis. They grappled with the exposition of the fugue and emerged with a durable concept or two. It was a process of abstraction from perceptual action. If the teacher had simply presented the concepts as preestablished principles, the students would not have remembered them, if indeed they even understood them. The teacher's role is not to present concepts but to create the right environment for the students to come to grips with the problems out of which the concepts emerge.

In this case the teacher achieved this by presenting the appropriate materials as well as by asking questions. The introduction of the G Minor Fugue, which on its face did not fit the emerging concept, caused the students to struggle with the problem until they saw the differences between the two subjects, thus resulting in their learning that among eighteenth-century fugal subjects that begin with the leap of tonic to dominant, it is only those that do not modulate that require tonal answers, while those that modulate to the dominant can accommodate real answers.

Concepts pertaining to rhythm and sound can also be brought out in this sort of discussion, though often they are not so concrete and precise as those evolving from harmonic phenomena. As the preceding analysis of the Bach fugue (Fugue VIII, *WTC,* Volume 1) moves forward, however, both rhythmic and textural factors should be introduced. The dotted-rhythm mutation of the subject that occurs in the middle voice at bar 24 can be related to the comparable place at bar 48; and the textural component of invertible counterpoint can enter into the discussion. For even in keyboard works in which there is no timbral contrast, consideration should be given to other factors of sound, such as dynamics and texture.

The concept of secondary dominants causes problems for some students when it is first introduced. However, if the students can discover the phenomenon through the analytical process, perhaps even before they have a term for it, a subsequent classroom discussion of the concept is much more meaningful. That discussion can then center upon the dialectical task of formulating a definition for secondary function, after the class has already observed and grappled with the actual musical phenomenon. Virtually every theoretical concept to be learned in the lower-division theory program is best approached in this way—through observation, analysis, and evaluative discussion—but always in terms of real examples from music literature. This principle cannot be overemphasized. Theory textbooks were written in the past century in which the authors created their own artificial examples rather than drawing from the literature of Western music, and this distorts the reality of music. While a teacher with strong keyboard skills certainly should improvise examples of various harmonic phenomena and should teach students to do so, the use of examples from the literature shows that normative phenomena such as an augmented sixth resolution in which all of the voices "follow the rules" are not as prevalent in the literature as one might think.

NOTES

1. See Eugene Narmour's *Beyond Schenkerism* (Chicago: University of Chicago Press, 1977); Charles Rosen's *The Classical Style* (New York: Viking, 1971); and my brief communication, "Analysis and the Interdependence of the Musical Elements," *Journal of Music Theory* 22, no. 1 (spring 1978): 134–136.

2. Robert Cogan and Pozzi Escot's *Sonic Design* (Englewood Cliffs, N.J.: Prentice Hall, 1976) is a case in point; and Jan LaRue in *Guidelines for Style Analysis* (New York: Norton, 1970) purported to integrate the musical elements.

3. I have attempted to outline a methodology that achieves this type of musical integration in *Comprehensive Musical Analysis* (Metuchen, N.J.: Scarecrow, 1994).

4. I coined the terms *microanalysis, middle-analysis,* and *macroanalysis* in the early 1970s and they were promulgated in my book *The Analysis of Music* (Englewood Cliffs, N.J.: Prentice Hall, 1975). Regrettably, they have been misused since then, particularly the term *macroanalysis.*

5. This section on integrative analysis is drawn in large part from my book *Comprehensive Musical Analysis* (Metuchen, N.J: Scarecrow, 1994).

SEVEN

Musical and Pedagogical Integration

THE MUSICAL UNION

This is not to be confused with Local 802 of the American Federation of Musicians, but if we categorize the musical elements as (1) rhythm, (2) melody, (3) harmony, and (4) sound, it becomes immediately apparent that no single element can exist separately in a musical context. That is, even the simplest monody must have a rhythmic and melodic character and implies a harmonic context; and to be realized in actual sound it must use the timbres and dynamics of an instrument or voice. Thus, there is a union or synergy of the musical elements in all music, a fusion that cannot be ignored either in the analysis of music or in the teaching of music theory.

In the past century at least one writer on musical analysis avoided consideration of this interdependence by simplistically defining melody as "the profile formed by any collection of pitches."[1] By this definition even a serial tone-row is a melody. Obviously, no ordered set of pitches can form a melody unless the set is given a rhythmic character; and the element of sound that includes timbre and dynamics is indispensable to any melody. Nor is harmony lacking, for every melody, at least in Western culture, implies a harmonic character, even if it is not explicit. It is interesting to note that even in the period of a single generation one can perceive pronounced changes in scholarly approaches to such things as musical analysis and theory teaching. Today this synergy of the musical elements is almost universally accepted and understood.

The theory teacher who is consciously aware of this musical union encourages students by precept and example to sight-sing with musical taste, giving attention to phrasing, dynamics, and even to bringing their conceptual knowledge of cadences and harmonic implications to bear. In other words, a major objective is to sing musically. The same musicality should be found in keyboard activities; and in writing projects, the teacher should insist that the students give attention to the relationship of cadences to phrasing and to include dynamic markings.

THE TEACHING UNION

Forgive me, but this too is not to be confused with the American Federation of Teachers (AFT) or the American Association of University Professors (AAUP). At this point it becomes clear that I advocate a lower-division theory program in which musical craft and conceptual knowledge are presented in such a way as to be mutually supportive in the learning process. Having discussed most of the components of lower-division theory, I shall now consider the question of their synthesis in the theory classroom.

One of the chief objections that some theory teachers have raised in regard to the integrated teaching plan is that there is not time enough, even in a class that meets five days a week, to cover the four areas adequately. Ear-training alone, they argue, can well occupy the bulk of that time if it is done well; and the same might be said for the other areas. In response to this problem some schools have instituted computerized ear-training programs and programmed learning devices by means of which students can use nonclass time for drilling in such areas as ear-training, thus allowing more classroom time for conceptual and analytical studies and writing skills. Some of these were experimental programs in the late twentieth century, but now have proven their value. They are discussed further in chapter 9.

However, even if the students can partake of a large amount of outside drill using new electronic technologies to improve their skills, it is essential that a certain amount of time be spent in class on those aspects of the program that fall into the area of musical craft. Technology cannot replace a skillful and dedicated teacher, especially for those students who, in spite of demonstrated musical talent, have difficulty achieving adequate skill levels in such areas as ear-training and keyboard. Listening tapes and computer programs should of course be readily available for independent student use; but I have found that even when the students use them (and many seem to have tremendous inertia in this regard) they do not help as much as the tutoring of a skillful teacher. Theory teachers who are willing to give a few extra hours a week for private or small-group ear-training or keyboard sessions are much appreciated by their students and will see clear improvement in students' skill levels.

There are also timesaving devices that can be used in the class-room. And because these are of an integrative nature they serve also to support conceptual learning. Indeed, to remove ear-training and keyboard entirely from the environment in which conceptual and analytical studies are carried on would be a great mistake, for genuine understanding of musical concepts cannot be acquired without the aural and even tactile experience of actual music. To understand a piece of music the way a musician should, one needs to live with it aurally as well as to understand it conceptually.

STRUCTURAL CONCEPTS IN MUSICAL SKILLS

At a number of points in the preceding chapters references were made to analytical perceptions as a part of the process of learning musical skills—for example, analyzing a sight-singing example prior to attempting to perform it can be a great help in the actual sight-singing process. Such an analysis can be done in various ways. The class can collectively analyze an example in open discussion followed by individual sight-singing of the same example. Or, a student can analyze an example for the class prior to singing it at sight. The students should be made aware of the fact that analysis is an ongoing part of the process of sight-singing—that a good sight-singer not only glances ahead to perceive phrase structure several measures (or even phrases) ahead but is analytically gauging each interval or rhythmic configuration that he or she is about to sing. The good sight-singer prepares high points in advance, not only in terms of breath and vocal technique but in terms of musical qualities; and modulations are preobserved and prepared for accordingly.

Indeed, the ability to sight-sing (or sight-read upon instruments) in a musical manner is closely correlated with the ability to comprehend in advance the musical structure of relatively long periods of time—phrases, periods, or even lengthier units of musical structure. Thus, there is a tacit analytical process occurring during the sight-reading process. Technical skills being equal, those who are skillful in this tacit or even subconscious analysis are those who can sight-read most musically. They can shape lines in terms of perceived structure, and the tones that have just been played or sung are intelligently related to those that are yet ahead. One is not always aware of this process; and the use of the word *subconscious* a moment ago alludes to the fact that some excellent musicians do not admit to using analysis in performance. Yet they do use it, perhaps constantly.

The theory teacher, by increasing student awareness of this phenomenon and by having students consciously practice analysis in relation to sight-singing, integrates structural concepts with performance in a way that can have a beneficial effect upon the students' progress in the applied-music studio. It also correlates with the conceptual components of the theory program in a meaningfully musical way.

A related skill that should be mentioned has to do with the awareness of other voices in a musical texture. The ability to sing in ensemble is an essential skill, not only for singers but for instrumentalists as well. Intelligent sight-singing of Bach chorales in four parts or more difficult imitative textures requires analytical perceptions more sophisticated than simply finding one's own pitch from another voice. The musical execution of the dissonant tone of a suspension figure, for example, requires that the singer be aware that he or she is indeed on the suspension tone—an analytical perception—so that the voice can perhaps swell into the dissonance and diminuendo on the resolution. This is a skill that fine choral singers are well aware of, but it is equally relevant to instrumentalists. Thus, ensemble sight-singing in the theory class can build musical skills important to both vocal and instrumental chamber music.

I think that most good performers are aware that analysis is a useful tool, but many of them think that they use it only in rehearsal and practice sessions—how loudly to play this passage in relation to that one, how to bring out this high point, how best to prepare for this recapitulation, and so on. That they do use it also in actual performance is what lends an additional element of beauty and spontaneity to an outstanding performance. Perhaps most important of all, the students' awareness that they are learning skills and concepts that can be used in actual performance brings renewed relevance to the theory classroom.

Another example of skill integration, briefly mentioned in chapter 2, is the relationship between sight-singing and melodic dictation. Sight-singing, of course, is actual music making, while melodic dictation is not. Yet these two skills are very closely linked, and the teacher can capitalize upon this correlation by keeping the two skills more or less parallel in level of difficulty. Most musicians have a more natural flair for sight-singing than for melodic dictation, perhaps because the latter is not normally practiced in day-to-day musical activity, while the former is. Yet the two skills are complementary in that each is the converse of the other. That is, a student who can sight-sing a melody should, given the proper instructional environment, be able to take down from dictation another melody of equal difficulty. Conversely, the student who can take down a melody from dictation should be able to sight-sing a melody of equal difficulty.

The writing skills developed from melodic or harmonic dictation make the student more conscious of notational devices when they are encountered in sight-reading (beam groupings, ledger lines, stem direction, etc.). This increases facility in sight-singing and also supports the student's writing activities. Harmonic dictation, of course, is closely correlated with the concepts that unfold in the activity of harmonic analysis. This relationship between harmonic concepts and harmonic dictation should be one of the chief concerns of the theory teacher, for it is perhaps the strongest single correlative phenomenon to be observed in theory teaching. It is for this reason that the harmonic concepts observed in analysis, and reinforced through the study of excerpts from various periods, should simultaneously be practiced in harmonic dictation. Indeed, to fully understand harmonic devices such as the augmented sixth chords, the student should confront them in analysis, harmonic dictation, part-writing, and keyboard activities.

Since they seem to be a favorite topic for theory teachers, let us take augmented sixth chords as an example by which to demonstrate the integration of these activities. The first introduction of the concept could occur in any one of the four activities. Let us say that the class is reviewing the part-writing and history of the Phrygian cadence, using the blackboard and piano for illustration. (See figure 7.2.)

TEACHER: *You see, it's really just a specific kind of half-cadence in the minor mode. This minor IV chord in first inversion progresses to a root-position dominant; but it's the major sixth expanding to the octave that gives it the name Phrygian cadence. How do you think this happened?*

STUDENT A: It must be from the Phrygian mode, but you're not in the Phrygian mode, you're in the key of A minor.

TEACHER: *So?*

STUDENT A: So it must be a name that came down to us from older music.

TEACHER: *When in music history did composers use modes?*

STUDENT B: I think they still do, don't they? But the Renaissance period is the one they talk about in music history. They call it modal counterpoint or modal polyphony.

TEACHER: *Okay. We can't take time now to follow up on your comment about the contemporary use of modes. You're quite right, and we'll discuss that later. Actually, it's the Renaissance that I want to discuss now. What was a cadence then—I mean in its simplest form?*

STUDENT C: Oh, it's that Latin term—*clausula vera*; it means true close.

STUDENT B: A sixth expanding to an octave.

TEACHER: *Do you see anything like that here on the blackboard?*

STUDENT D: Yes, the F and the D expanding to the E octave; and that E would be the final of the Phrygian mode if we were in that mode.

TEACHER: *Good; now do you see where the term Phrygian cadence comes from?*

STUDENT A: Yes, but did they—I mean the Renaissance people— think that E sounded like the key of the piece? It sounds like the dominant to me.

TEACHER: *I think they did, but they didn't understand "key" in the way you do, even though they were evolving toward functional harmony. In some of the modes, like Dorian, they used* musica ficta *at the cadence to create a leading tone. They raised the seventh scale degree a half-step.* [Teacher plays a Dorian *clausula vera* with and without the raised seventh and writes it on the blackboard.] *What's the difference between these two?* (See figure 7.1.)

STUDENT D: The one with the raised seventh sounds more like eighteenth-century music—more tonal. The other one sounds— well, sort of ancient—archaic. I don't think it's tonal.

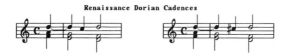

Figure 7.1

STUDENT A: That's because the raised leading tone creates a feeling of dominant. That major sixth really contains two notes of the dominant triad, E and C sharp, plus the G is the seventh of the dominant seventh. It's just that there's no root—no A.

TEACHER: *Okay. Now, will someone come to the board and change that Phrygian cadence in the same way—the minor IV chord in first inversion progressing to the V in A minor.*

STUDENT B: That's going to sound funny, but I'll do it anyway. (Refer to figure 7.2.)

[Laughter, but he goes to the board and changes the D to D-sharp, thus unknowingly creating an Italian sixth.]

TEACHER: *Fine. And will you* [indicating student A] *play it at the piano for us? Play it the old way first, and then play it the new way with the D-sharp.*

[Student A does so.]

STUDENT B: It doesn't sound as funny as I thought. I've heard that progression before.

TEACHER: *Right, and it has a name. It's called the Italian sixth, the word "sixth" referring to the interval of the augmented sixth, in this case the interval from F up to D-sharp. Actually, Renaissance composers would be very unlikely to apply* musica ficta *to the Phrygian cadence*

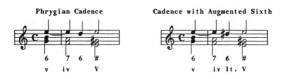

Figure 7.2

although I've seen an example or two in Gesualdo. With that D-sharp it doesn't sound much like sixteenth-century music, does it? They are used commonly in the eighteenth century, and there are a couple of other variants of augmented sixths: the German sixth [plays one at the piano in four parts in context], *which sounds very similar to the Italian sixth, but a little richer and fuller; and the French sixth* [plays a French sixth, four parts in context], *which is the most dissonant of the three and perhaps for that reason the easiest to distinguish by ear. Now, will you* [indicating student D] *go to the piano and transpose this Italian sixth progression on the blackboard to the key of C minor?*

[Student D does so, but with some difficulty.]

TEACHER: *Good; we'll be doing this in keyboard next week—with all three nationalities of augmented sixths. They're also the subject of the next chapter in your textbook, so go ahead and study that tonight. And I want you to find some examples of augmented sixth chords in the anthology. Look for them in the minor mode and with the lowered sixth scale degree in the bass. You'll find one near the beginning of the first movement of Beethoven's Fifth Symphony, in the first and second movements of the Schubert B-flat Major Piano Trio, and see if you can also find some Mozart and Schumann examples.* [Teacher sees that student C has a question and acknowledges him.]

STUDENT C: Isn't the interval of the augmented sixth the same as the minor seventh?

TEACHER: *To the ear it is. So tell me, why is it spelled as F up to D-sharp? Why an augmented sixth instead of a minor seventh? Why not E-flat?* [Waits quite a while. Finally student A, who knew the answer all along but was reluctant to appear more knowledgeable than student C, raises her hand.] *Yes?*

STUDENT A: It's because of how the lines move. The D-sharp wants to go to E—like a leading tone—and the F down to E. If you spelled it as E-flat, it wouldn't look like it wanted to go up to E. An E-flat there might want to go down to D.

STUDENT C: And they all have the interval of the augmented sixth doing just that, don't they—I mean regardless of their ethnic background? [Laughter] Do they always progress to V?

TEACHER: *That's for you to find out tonight, among other things. Read the text and then make a harmonic analysis of the examples found in*

*the anthology—just two or three chords on either side of the aug-
mented sixth chord. On Friday be prepared to write your own examples of augmented sixth chords in the context of four-part choral style,
and tomorrow we'll use them in aural skills.*

Note that throughout this discussion the teacher, while furnishing
quite a bit of information, strove to have the students answer their
own questions by means of their own concept manipulation. Whenever possible, the teacher asked questions rather than answered
them. Note also that the discussion brought in points of music history and utilized several musicianship skills, including keyboard
and aural skills. Also, it was clear that future assignments would
relate the augmented sixth chords to harmonic dictation and to part-
writing. This integration of the elements of musical craft with analysis and conceptual study creates an ideal environment for musical
learning. Understanding of augmented sixth chords is not complete
without the aural component; and, conversely, the treatment of augmented sixth chords in keyboard and harmonic dictation is inadequate when it is not accompanied by the conceptual and analytical
approach.

The teacher, of course, could have found a variety of other
approaches that might have achieved the same integration. To begin
by simply stating that the essence of the augmented sixth concept is
the expansion of that interval to the octave is a possible approach,
but it deprives the students of the learning opportunity that comes
with concept manipulation. The concept is given to them ready-
made and thus (and this is a manifestation of Piaget's theories) is
less likely to be truly understood and retained. By the approach
used in this dialogue, the students' interest was maintained because
they were involved in the development of the concept.

A strong attraction for musicians is the introduction of musical
craft, for making music is what it's all about. In later sessions keyboard skills can be brought in much more significantly. Students can
be asked to come to the piano and improvise passages containing
augmented sixth chords, while the class can be asked to take such
passages down as harmonic dictation or to identify the "national-
ity" of the augmented sixth chord that was used. Game-like competition could be added by letting the student who does best at the
harmonic dictation take over at the keyboard for the next improvisation. Thus, the two chief ingredients of this approach are (1) concept

manipulation by the students and (2) integration of conceptual learning with musical skills.

Aside from the fact that this is a very musical approach to the study of both historical and theoretical concepts, it also is efficient. It saves time and space. Rather than have separate keyboard sessions and lab sessions for aural skills on the grounds that there is not time in the regular theory class, this approach integrates keyboard and aural skills in such a way as to augment both conceptual learning and musical craft.

It sometimes happens, however, that a teacher working with this integrative approach to music theory neglects one or another of the four areas of aural skills, keyboard, part-writing, or analysis. It is only natural that teachers tend to emphasize those things in which they are most interested or most skillful, at the expense of other components of the program. One way to minimize this is to utilize scheduling in such a way as to ensure that keyboard (for example) is practiced once a week. Teachers might do this by scheduling a five-day-a-week theory class to meet on Wednesdays in the electronic-keyboard classroom.

This is not to suggest that keyboard should be taught in an isolated way without integrating it with the other components of the theory program. Integration can still take place in the electronic-keyboard classroom so that, for example, harmonic aural skills are also practiced there in association with keyboard skills. (See chapter 4.) This organizes the classroom week in such a way as to mandate that the teacher work at certain things at certain times. And by integrating concepts with skills one maintains the thread of continuity in the learning of concepts. With separate keyboard and ear-training classes it is much less likely that they will be appropriately coordinated with analytical, conceptual, and writing activities, with the result that time spent on keyboard and aural skills interrupts the learning process rather than supports it.

At the beginning of this chapter I made some feeble jokes (puns, I guess) about "the musical union" and "the teaching union." While jokes should never be explained (if they're truly funny, it's unnecessary), I would like to point out (parenthetically) that humor can play a valuable role in the class room. A *relevant* bit of humor captures interest for the topic under discussion and may be a device for retaining information in the memory. The term *mnemonic* comes to mind. Humor should be spontaneous, however, never contrived, and above all should be relevant.

At the same time, a teacher telling jokes simply for the sake of being entertaining often is playing the fool simply to curry favor with students. The popular and entertaining teacher is not necessarily the best teacher. I have known extremely serious teachers who rarely strove to be witty, in some cases because they knew such an attempt would be futile, yet who were superb teachers whose students learned more than in any class led by an "entertaining" teacher. Enthusiasm for the subject matter is very contagious.

The relatively recent phenomenon of student–teacher evaluations has too often led teachers to ingratiate themselves to their students in self-demeaning ways detrimental to real learning. The university of the twenty-first century is heir to some profound changes in the student–teacher relationship that evolved during the last quarter of the previous century. Not all of these changes were for the better, and it is to this topic that we direct our attention in the following pages.

NOTE

1. Jan Larue, *Guidelines for Style Analysis* (New York: Norton, 1970), 69.

EIGHT

Evaluation

THE EVOLVING ACADEMY

The first edition of this book was written in the latter part of the decade of the 1970s and published in 1981. At that time few could foresee that currents begun during the student protest days of the late 1960s and early 1970s would lead to profound changes in the university during the final two decades of the twentieth century. To vividly illustrate the inception of these transformations, let us go back to the year 1970 and the campus of Kent State University.

It was a surprising scene for the bucolic campus of a state university. There was a small contingent of young Ohio National Guardsmen on the right side of the field, not in tight formation and not terribly concerned about what was happening down field. There, on our left, perhaps forty yards from the guardsmen, were about thirty students chanting antiwar slogans and shouting at the soldiers. It was spring, a sunny May 4th, the first Monday in May. We were returning from lunch in the old Student Union Building—the vice president for research and myself, associate graduate dean. We had stopped at the Parade Ground to join a group of students and faculty watching these strange goings-on at a distance. The scene returns to my memory as a surrealistic tableau.

Occasionally, one or another of the guardsman would throw a tear gas canister in the general direction of the students so that there were several smoking canisters in the middle of the field, but there was no barrage of gas sufficient to discourage the students. A few daring young fellows would sometimes leave the student group to dash to the center of the field to pick up a smoking canister and hurl it back at the soldiers. But this, too, was essentially a harmless gesture, or so it seemed.

This went on for a while and we were just starting to continue on our way to our offices in the Administration Building when we heard gunfire in the woods beyond the soldiers and saw another squad of guardsmen firing rifles at an unseen target in back of the new Architecture Building across the Parade Ground. My immediate reaction was that the soldiers must be firing blanks as a crowd-control measure. I could not believe that real bullets were being fired on our campus. I have seen recent newscasts in which riot troops used rubber bullets, but in those days soldiers carried only lethal ammunition. I should have known this from my army days.

Confusion seemed to reign on the Parade Ground and the crowd of observers now broke up while we hurriedly returned in puzzled consternation to the Graduate School Office. There we found the staff crowding around portable radios listening to a variety of confused reports most of which turned out later to be false rumors: Weathermen (the militant arm of the Students for a Democratic Society, or SDS) had infiltrated the campus and were sniping from campus roofs, large numbers of students had been shot, guardsmen had been shot, FBI agents were here, more troops and tanks were being sent from Columbus. . . .

It was only later that we learned a part of the truth. Four university students had been killed, one had been permanently maimed, and several others had been wounded by the gunfire. The student victims had not been involved in the protests but were simply passing between classes. It was not long before the campus was temporarily closed and for months its future was in grave doubt. Because of courageous actions by some of the faculty and students, the university survived, but it would never again be quite the same. No American college or university would.

This historic episode in the little Ohio town of Kent was a kind of benchmark in the turbulent era of the civil rights movement, the Vietnam War, student activism, and the peace movement. It also marked the beginning of a period of profound change in higher learning. Beginning in the late sixties and early seventies, university students had been increasingly assertive about their role in the academy. I recall an anonymous treatise from that period, obviously written by a graduate student or students, entitled something like "The Graduate Student as Slave." It was circulated throughout our nation's academic community and even drew some commentary in the *Chronicle of Higher Education*.

It portrayed a typical university campus metaphorically as a Southern plantation with its patrician slave owner, managers, and slaves. The slaves were the graduate teaching assistants (TAs) who had no rights, were paid a mere pittance, and who did the bulk of the scut-work in the institution—teaching the large classes and lab sections, grading papers, and doing other menial tasks for professors. In the meantime, the faculty, the plantation gentry, lolled around drinking coffee brought to them by the TA slaves, did their research, and occasionally taught a graduate seminar.

It was a clever piece of satire. Exaggerated, of course, as good satire usually is, but nevertheless touching upon some repugnant truths about the contemporary university. In the decades that followed, unionization of graduate assistants became a reality, student governments tried to exert real power, and students at all levels became increasingly assertive. Gone were those luxurious times—if they ever really existed—the halcyon days of a faculty whose authority was unquestioned by a docile student body.

During the late sixties and the decade of the seventies, the academy began to bend over backward to be responsive to "student demands" which were often "nonnegotiable." Honors colleges were established which allowed creative students to design their own curricula, in some liberal arts institutions (mostly private) grading was abandoned, special programs such as majors in "Black Studies" or "Far Eastern Religions" were created, the term in loco parentis was bandied about pro and con, faculty became increasingly responsive to "student needs," and, almost universally, institutions began to require each faculty member to invite written evaluations from their students in each class at the end of each academic term.

Although most of these more or less new ideas possessed some intrinsic value, almost all of them went too far in the direction of liberalizing higher learning. It was to be expected that there would be a conservative reaction in the opposite direction, a backlash. This came in the late seventies and early eighties in the form of reestablishment of solid, almost classical core curricula—a prescribed body of courses that were required of all undergraduate students regardless of their majors. Most of the institutions that had deemphasized or abandoned the conventional grading system began to reverse themselves. In loco parentis ceased to be a controversial topic, and

conventional majors became preeminent once again. Yet it had been
a period of healthy reassessment and to the present day there has
been a vigorous ebb and flow of these ideas throughout the academic community.

EVALUATING FACULTY

The university was profoundly affected by these changes but one of
the vestiges of this turbulent period was the concept of student–
teacher evaluations, or STEs, a trump card which students have used
for the past quarter century. At the end of every term each student
fills out an evaluation sheet, a questionnaire, for each class taken.
These are collated and the statistics become a matter of public
record for use by administrators in evaluating the faculty. The students, then, are grading the faculty, and these grades have a positive
or negative effect upon future faculty careers.

It is well known within every college and university that these student–teacher evaluations are invalid and unreliable. They are useful
to administrators, though, for they can pay attention to them or not
as they see fit. Even students who have done well in a class are not
good judges of teaching effectiveness, but, as I show later, most of
the students who have done poorly give the professor a low evaluation. This has had a coercive effect on the faculty over recent decades
and many of them began to give higher assignment grades and final
grades than the students deserved so that they, the faculty, would
receive good STE scores. Often they made the course content easier
so that the students would appear to be doing better and thus have
a good feeling about the course. Some students who should have
failed were passed. This meant that over the years the average grade
climbed higher and higher so that by the end of the twentieth century, grade point averages (GPAs) have become relatively meaningless. Thus, among the educational innovations of the 1970s and
1980s, this one has continued with unabated energy, and it is the
chief cause of grade inflation. The idea of students evaluating faculty, perhaps a well-intentioned notion, has become institutional-
ized and overemphasized to the point that today it is a cancerous
affliction within the academy.

College and university faculties and administrators have known
for years about the many published studies that show that these

ubiquitous student–teacher evaluations are statistically invalid and unreliable. Worse still, rather than improve faculty teaching and student learning, they tend, over repeated use, to *lower* the quality of the course content and the level of the learning experience. Student–teacher evaluations have caused grade inflation, watered-down course offerings, and a state of mutual contempt between college students and their teachers. Sadly, they are also beginning to be used coercively by unscrupulous administrators to "target" dissident or outspoken faculty, a serious threat to academic freedom.

Most of the proponents of STEs are administrators and they have garnered some studies to support their position, but there is strong evidence that STEs are not only useless as instruments of evaluation, they are harmful to the learning experience. Recently, Ceci and Williams at Cornell University have found that "student ratings are far from the bias-free indicators of instructor effectiveness and quality that many have touted them to be. Students can make or break the careers of instructors on grounds unrelated to objective measures of student learning."[1] Their methodology was to have Professor Ceci teach the same course in exactly the same way with identical course content and materials for two consecutive semesters. The only variable was that the second time he changed his speaking style, "spoke more enthusiastically, varied his pitch, and used more gestures."

Student performance was about the same in both classes. That is, the tests and final grades revealed no evidence of any difference in levels of learning or teaching effectiveness between the two classes. Yet his student ratings improved dramatically the second time![2] The second group of students found that, in spite of using identical content with the same course materials and the same textbook and lectures, the course was judged to be much better in (1) instructor's level of knowledge, (2) organization, (3) fairness, and (4) quality of the textbook. I emphasize that the level of student learning was about the same in both courses. Thus, the Cornell rating instrument of 1995 is worse than useless, it is misleading and seriously flawed.

A recent study by the University of Washington's Office of Educational Assessment collected data from STEs of several hundred UW courses and found unequivocally that professors who grade higher receive better STE scores than professors who are tough graders. Anthony G. Greenwald, one of the investigators, concludes that "evaluations may encourage faculty to grade easier and make course work loads lighter."[3] This is clear evidence that STEs cause grade inflation and superficiality of course content, but it also shows that courses in our colleges and universities now manifest a kind of marketplace attitude in which professors are coerced into treating their students like customers to be satisfied.

"The student in college is being treated as a customer in a retail environment, and I have to worry about customer complaints," says an assistant professor of marketing at one of the SUNY colleges.[4] In order to get good STE ratings and thus keep his job, this faculty member admits to watering down his course content, giving easy multiple-choice tests, and currying student favor by giving extra credit for absurd reasons. Other faculty entertain students with refreshments and try to create an environment in which students raised on MTV and *Sesame Street* will feel very much at home. All this to get good ratings from the students—in order to keep their jobs, they must corrupt the academy.

Having written and spoken a great deal against the use of STEs, I have had ample opportunity to explore faculty opinion on this matter. Even faculty who invariably receive high scores on their student–teacher evaluations believe that they are meaningless or harmful. Students with whom I have spoken on this topic are equally distrustful of STEs—some, usually the better students, are downright cynical.

A respected educational research scholar has blasted the use of student ratings of professors.[5] This "well-meant practice," he wrote, "poisons faculty/student relationships, inhibits free expression, and erodes the quality of instruction." Student–teacher evaluations have caused grade inflation and watered-down course offerings—a condition in which too many faculty teach only for high ratings and most students study only for grades. Yet there still are some devoted faculty who maintain high standards and strive to share their research with their students in spite of the fact that this may lower their student ratings, and thus cause them to lose opportunities for salary increases and/or promotion and tenure.

At a large state university where I taught for many years, the STE instrument was (and I think still is) a twenty-item questionnaire using a "Likert-type" scale. That is, each item gives the student the choice of a score of 1 through 5. The lowest choice is 1, 3 is average, and 5 is the highest. The first nine items are summarized in a composite analysis as the "Instructor Evaluation" and address such questions as objectives, communication, expectations, availability and concern for students, enthusiasm, facilitation of learning, stimulation of interest, and encouragement. The other eleven items address other student perceptions of the instructor and other aspects of the course, while on the back of the rating sheet the students are invited to offer personal comments about the quality of the course and the instructor. The rating sheets themselves are anonymous and confidential and are returned to the instructor after a statistical summary sheet has been prepared for each course by the Office of Academic Affairs. This summary sheet becomes a matter of public record and is prepared and disseminated in the subsequent semester at the same time that the rating sheets are returned to the instructor.

In the fall of 1996 at that institution, I taught a class in "remedial theory," a course designed to bring new but deficient graduate music students up to speed in basic theoretical aspects of music, knowledge which should have been acquired as early as the freshman and sophomore years, if not before. This course was known fondly among some of our students as "dummy theory," and our most marginal entering graduate students were enrolled in it. On my midterm examination that semester, 40 percent of the remedial theory students received a grade of D or lower, and for a final grade, 20 percent received C or lower. (C, of course, is considered an unsatisfactory grade at the graduate level.)

It is not surprising, then, that I scored only slightly above average on my STE for that course—the composite analysis of my "instructor evaluation" was 3.23 on the Likert scale of 1 to 5. By contrast, in the previous semester I taught the graduate analytical techniques, a core course in which I had competent students, many of whom received final grades of As and Bs for the course. The composite analysis of my "instructor evaluation" for that course was 4.41, a very good score. Many faculty colleagues have described similar anecdotes and the Cornell and University of Washington studies cited earlier make similar points.

The moral here is well known to most faculty members in the world of higher learning—STE ratings do not indicate the quality of the learning experience in university classrooms. Since it seems clear that they are useless and even harmful to the academy, why do colleges and universities still use them? A faculty colleague may have hit on the reason. He wrote, "Administrators are paid . . . to keep their political bosses happy. Anything that looks like it's data-based

. . . no matter how flawed, will do. Student ratings of faculty serve that bill."[6]

While some university administrators have sought alternative ways to evaluate faculty teaching quality, the fact is that STEs furnish what some seem to consider to be the only significant measure of teaching effectiveness in spite of the fact that it has been widely known for years that they are invalid and unreliable. Peer evaluations might be useful, but they are fraught with pitfalls such as bias and ignorance of a narrow discipline. Yet even this has never been seriously or consistently explored, for in my forty-plus years of teaching in four major state universities and two private colleges, no administrator or faculty colleague has *ever* asked to visit any of my classes for the purpose of evaluating my teaching.

As one music faculty colleague used to say ironically, "If you're getting good grades (i.e., 4s and 5s) on your STEs, you're not doing your job." And, of course, some winners of annual teaching awards *are* getting 4s and 5s. In the eyes of many of the committee members who select the recipients of these awards, it is the only criterion. Because of the absurd faculty strivings for high STE scores, the average scores are extremely high, so that a teacher who eschews destructive and unethical STE score mongering often scores below average on a curve. Further, many of the administrators who decide promotion, tenure, salary raises, and other faculty perks give credence to these unreliable STE ratings in spite of the irrefutable evidence that they are damaging and worse than useless.

There are several likely victims in this process: (1) The most tragic is the fine dedicated teacher–scholar who, for some of the reasons cited previously, receives average or below average STE ratings; (2) the well-trained and gifted teacher–scholar who is seduced into becoming a kind of academic prostitute in order to get high STE ratings; (3) the sometimes-well-meaning administrators who are undermining the learning process by appearing to take STEs seriously; and (4) the students themselves who, given the chance to corrupt the system, do so, and thus are cheated out of what should be a joyous period of learning and intellectual growth.

Because STEs are still being used in the twenty-first century, the controversy continues. An article in a recent issue of the *Chronicle of Higher Education* suggests ways in which STEs can be made valid and reliable—apparently the author has no hope of seeing them abolished. Speaking of the ubiquitous STEs, the author, a professor emeritus of English at California State University, writes:

Colleges and universities now put a great deal of energy and expense into elaborate bubble sheets that serve nobody's ends well. Instead, institutions should devote their efforts to producing holistic information for administrative purposes, and detailed analysis of their own performance for the teacher's own use. If that happened we might actually see systematic improvement of college teaching—which is supposed to be the goal of the entire operation.[7]

While I have used specific universities and the discipline of music theory as examples, I am speaking in general terms about all of American higher learning. The university, our society's most valued institution, is being damaged not only by STEs but also by the movement toward treating students like customers to be pleased and catered to. Many steps could be taken to correct the situation, one of which would be to abandon the use of student–teacher evaluations. But this will not happen until the faculty (and perhaps the students as well) begins to fully realize the gravity of the situation and take a stand in favor of the academy as a place of learning.

GRADING STUDENTS

As to the grading of college and university students, it is a necessary evil, but the grade inflation that has resulted from the use of STEs has made student transcripts virtually unreliable as a measure of student achievement. No longer do grades of A or B in English courses necessarily mean that this student is a literate person who is knowledgeable of some of the great works of English literature. Indeed, the grade of B could very well mean that the student is deficient in that area, and a grade of C, which used to be the average grade, invariably means today that the student is incompetent in this area. During my undergraduate days 3.5 to 4.00 averages were earned only by a small group of elite intellectual achievers, and prospective employers and graduate schools could rely on those averages as a true indication of student quality.[8] All but a small percentage of today's college students have become grade mongers who expect to receive all As and Bs and find ways to punish professors who do not reward them in kind.

I have said earlier that letter grades are a necessary evil, but there are some institutions that are experimenting with a modification of the no-grades system of the seventies used at some private colleges. That is the practice of writing evaluative statements for each student in each class in lieu of letter grades.[9] The system is receiving mixed reviews, but some employers and graduate schools are finding it more revealing than grades and grade point averages. Yet here also there can be a kind of grade inflation as professors feel coercion to endow their students with false feelings of success. That is, it is just as easy to overstate a student's intellectual achievements in a written evaluation as it is to give him or her an undeservedly high letter grade.

Of course we want our students to feel good about themselves, but, as discussed earlier, teachers often go too far in this direction, even to the point of hiding failure. From kindergarten through high school, many teachers strive to impart false feelings of "self-esteem" to their students instead of assessing them realistically and impartially. The public schools even have invented the term "social promotion" for passing an unqualified student on to the next grade.

The results are grade inflation, low learning levels, and academic achievement that appears to be much higher than it really is. Then, when these students come to the university, they expect the same kind of treatment. For things to flow smoothly in the academy, faculty members are pressured not to rock the boat. The path of least resistance is to give higher grades. Having made these points, let us now turn our attention realistically to the problems of student evaluation—bearing in mind the strictures and injustices to which faculty may have to adjust.

THE NATURE AND PURPOSE OF EVALUATION

One of the most difficult and, at times, tormenting tasks of the teacher is to evaluate students in the form of grades for permanent records, tests, daily assignments, or classroom activities. To grade reasonably and with a proper sense of responsibility requires that the teacher decide for him- or herself what the purpose of grading is. Obviously, those grades that are recorded permanently on student transcripts have a clear-cut purpose—to let others, such as potential employers or graduate admissions committees, know the strengths and weaknesses of students. But there are other and perhaps more important purposes of evaluation, one of which is to let the students know how they are doing, what their strengths and weaknesses are, and how they can improve. Further, and this is addressed later, there is positive learning value in a well-written test.

Assurance that students are aware of their deficiencies early enough so that there is time to correct them before final grades are determined is a serious responsibility of the teacher. An effective way to do this is to give frequent tests covering all of the components of the theory program. Such tests should be difficult enough that no one in the class gets a perfect score, for the students who do so have not been tested—that is, no weaknesses have been revealed. On the other hand, the tests should also be easy enough so that even the weak students can see areas in which they have achieved something. Students who get almost everything wrong have also not been tested—that is, no strengths have been revealed.

In keeping with the integrative approach, tests can include several of the four components of lower-division theory. A format for written tests can be devised that examines students' skill in harmonic dictation, melodic dictation, part-writing, analysis, and conceptual knowledge. All teachers have their own preferences for a format, but one model frequently used at the freshman level begins with interval dictation. To distinguish between the students' abilities in hearing and spelling of intervals it is important to identify separately the skill of hearing (in which the answers consist of M3, P4, m7, and so on) and the skill of spelling intervals (in which the students are asked to write the pitches of the intervals on the staff). This can be done by asking for both kinds of answers for each interval.

The second part of the test can be a melodic dictation administered more or less as in classroom drill, testing both rhythm and pitch perception as well as the perception of phrase structure. The third part can consist of a harmonic dictation; if its texture is appropriate, it will furnish an assessment of part-writing ability as well. The final portion of the test can consist of a brief analysis with a set of questions dealing with related concepts.

In addition to covering several areas this model helps to integrate such things as part-writing with harmonic dictation, or analysis with structural concepts. Sight-singing and keyboard skills must be measured separately by means of individual private sessions. Such tests should be given frequently throughout the term for diagnostic as well as evaluative purposes. In most instances a sensitive teacher is aware of the strengths and weaknesses of most students; but there are times when a test can reveal the need for a new approach. One common example is the student who scores almost perfectly on identification of intervals by such symbols as M3, P4, but who does very poorly at writing them on the staff. Obviously, that student needs to learn to spell intervals in order to make the most of a good ear. Another student may reveal that part-writing difficulties are inhibiting progress in harmonic dictation, manifest by incorrect voice lines within the correct harmonic structure. The diagnostic procedure should occur frequently throughout the term, and it should be coordinated with individual counseling and tutoring in order for students to concentrate on those areas that need the most improvement.

Tests that concentrate on only one of the four components of the theory program are also useful. Let us say that a fugue from the Well-Tempered Clavier has been analyzed in classroom discussion in the sophomore class. The students have learned the conventions and terminology of eighteenth-century fugal writing by this process and should now be capable of using this knowledge in individual analysis. A fugue from another period (Mendelssohn, Brahms, Bartók) can be assigned for outside study. The students can analyze it, annotate their copies of the score, and bring them to class for an open-score test on the fugue. The students' incentive to do a thorough job of preparing is much greater in this instance than when they are simply preparing for classroom discussion.

Part-writing should also be tested occasionally by an instrument other than the integrative test discussed earlier, because that method, since it relies in part upon the students' ability to hear a harmonic dictation, in some cases may not be a completely valid test of part-writing ability. Such a test should include a variety of approaches to part-writing in order to pinpoint the students' problems and to test the scope of their ability. It might include a chorale-type "fill in" in which a figured bass and soprano are given; a figured bass in which the students realize soprano, alto, and tenor lines; and a soprano line to be harmonized in four parts. In all cases the class should be asked to include the harmonic analysis showing all notable harmonic phenomena, such as modulations, altered chords, and secondary dominants. Testing of such skills as sight-singing and keyboard should be done on an individual basis, with five or ten minutes scheduled for each member of the class. To simplify the logistics and to avoid a second private test, keyboard and sight-singing can be scheduled for the same session (in an adjacent room), with each individual assigned a block of perhaps fifteen minutes.

In sight-singing the students may be told that they should study a particular chapter in the sight-singing book with the understanding that one or two examples (perhaps one using alto or tenor clef) will be selected from that chapter for the test. It might be argued that this is not really testing sight-singing since they will have prepared all of the examples in the chapter. However, I believe that in preparing that many examples they will be improving their sight-singing considerably; and the incentive is very great because of the testing situation. The many patterns that they will learn, even if by rote, will broaden their pattern vocabulary, thus increasing their sight-singing ability. Another method is to have the students practice sight-singing a specific chapter and then select the test examples from another source with examples containing similar problems and level of difficulty. This will perhaps be a more valid test but may not generate as much incentive as the other method. Either way the students are learning melodic patterns, and sight-singing is in large part the recalling of patterns from visual cues.

The individual keyboard test might include a number of skills, such as realizing figured bass, playing chord patterns, or harmonizing familiar tunes. While the teacher may wish to test all of these skills at the end of the term, it may be better to test only one or two at a time earlier in the term. In testing figured-bass reading the class should be told to practice certain patterns in a variety of keys, with the understanding that the test example will be similar to those patterns but not identical to any of them. For chord patterns and harmonization the class can be given the specific test material but asked to learn it in a variety of keys—say, up to three sharps or flats. They will not know, however, what key will be requested at the test. Thus, as in the sight-singing test, they have the incentive to learn the patterns thoroughly. In keyboard and sight-singing tests the teacher should vary the material from student to student to minimize the unfair advantage that later-scheduled students might have by conferring with those who took the test earlier.

THE TEST AS A LEARNING EXPERIENCE

Implicit in the foregoing is a conviction that tests should be used for learning as well as for evaluating. Every test should be designed so that the students can come away with a sense of having accomplished something more than just having given correct answers. The adrenaline flows during a test, and student incentive is at a peak. Why not capitalize on this condition by constructing the test in such a way as to create an optimum learning situation? If, as Piaget said, learning takes place when the subject manipulates the concept, then let us design tests in which the responses are found primarily by means of concept manipulation rather than by rote learning. Tests in musical analysis can readily be designed to achieve this. Since students vary in their speed of performing preliminary descriptive tasks, such as assigning Roman numerals, finding interval vectors, drafting Schenkerian analyses, and labeling dissonant tones, it seems fair to allow them to do this in advance. For example, after having analyzed a couple of classical sonatas in class the students are told that on the following Monday they will have an "open-score" test on the "Waldstein" Sonata, first movement. They may fill their scores with as many annotations as they wish, and they may have the full weekend to analyze the movement prior to the test. Because it will be a graded test, the class has high incentive to prepare thoroughly—some will even work in groups. It will seem to many of them that advance knowledge of the test material is a great opportunity (there may even be a feeling of "beating the system"), and they will often prepare more thoroughly than for classroom discussion sessions.

The test, then, consists of questions utilizing the descriptive material already gathered but requiring concept manipulation. Here are several sample questions pertaining to the first movement of the "Waldstein" that call for manipulative efforts:

1. Locate and describe the second tonal group, relating it to the normative structure of the sonata form, and describe the ways in which it is most remarkable.
2. Describe the beginning of the development section in terms of key area, melodic material, and macrostructure.
3. Describe the secondary key centers in the development section and explain their rationale.
4. In the recapitulation the second tonal group begins at bar 196. What is *conventional* about the next sixteen bars in terms of normative practice? How does Beethoven get from A major to C major? And what is remarkable about this key relationship?

5. Relate the use of the third relation in this work to the early nineteenth century and to one or two works by Beethoven's contemporaries.

First of all, this mode of testing ensures that most students prepare in advance. And the process is such that they learn a good deal from the preparation itself. Second, the nature of the questions requires the students to draw directly upon the material they have prepared—not simply to spout back ready-made answers. They must grapple in a new way with familiar material. In question 1, for example, they may already have determined that the juxtaposition of C major and E major is unusual, but the question seeks a relationship to the overall structure, which is probed even further in questions 4 and 5. Questions 2 and 3 deal with the development section in ways that require creativity of thought and synthesis of data. Note also that question 5 reaches beyond the work in question to relate it to a composer (such as Schubert) who used the third relation in similar ways. This adds a historical context and draws the students into a broader consideration of the concepts under discussion.

Part-writing examinations can also be designed to relate practice to concepts. For example, the test can begin with the realization of a figured bass in four parts, followed with questions about the concepts utilized in the realization. Let us say that such a progression is in C minor and contains a Neapolitan Six moving to a vii^7/V followed by a I$^6_4$–V–I cadence. Appropriate conceptual questions might be (1) What is the justification and rationale for vii^7/V moving to I$^6_4$ rather than to V? (2) Without changing the bass line, what chords might be substituted for the Neapolitan? (3) Without changing the bass line, what chord might be substituted for the vii^7/V? (4) Add at least three different types of dissonant tones to this passage and describe their use below.

A thorough response to question 1 in the preceding paragraph would deal with the concept of the cadential I$^6_4$ as an embellishment of the dominant and could also bring in the rhythmic element and its relationship to the cadence. Questions 2 and 3 require brief answers but will cause students to think in terms of harmonic function in a way that is applicable to ear-training as well as to part-writing. And the description of dissonance called for in question 4 subjects the student to the heuristic process of articulating definitions—a likely route to clearer understanding.

In ear-training tests one way to capitalize upon student incentive is to give practice tests. Students will welcome them because they offer the opportunity for learning in a test situation without the hazards of grading. Students can thus receive advance orientation to a specific kind of ear-training test without the pressure of an impending grade. Undoubtedly, grades on the real test will be improved by this method. Administered a few days before the real test, a practice test identical in format to the real test (1) puts students at greater ease in the real test, (2) identifies problems that can be addressed by last-minute drills, (3) furnishes practice in all areas, and (4) increases confidence. Although grades are not recorded, some of the incentive associated with a real test is nevertheless present. Also, the students are conscious of a specific opportunity to improve their performance on the real test.

RATIONALE FOR GRADING

My frequent reference to incentive in the testing situation relates to the fact that students are intent on getting the best possible grades they can. Conscientious students are also eager to learn in order to expand their potential within the field of music. And, if this is not too optimistic, more often than not they are aware of the important contributions that the theory program can make to their overall musicianship. Thus, while grade mongering and its unpleasant side effects will always be with us, one looks hopefully for a majority of students who are interested in learning for its own sake.

Student concern about grades is perfectly understandable. Competition in outstanding graduate schools and for positions in the field of music or music education is very tight in the twenty-first century. And strife over grades is compounded by grade inflation, as discussed earlier. Professors too have gone along with this, as is demonstrated by the fact that such honors as magna cum laude are now granted only to students with GPAs of 3.7 or 3.8, whereas forty-five years ago a 3.5 GPA was sufficient for that distinction in many schools. This indicates that grading in the fifties was more stringent than today, and outstanding students are now under greater pressure to distinguish themselves.

Designing tests as instruments of learning is one way to make the best of this situation. Another is to be sure that one is testing the appropriate body of knowledge or skills. And a third is to be sure that the grades that are awarded truly represent student achievement and ability. The previous section addressed the question of how tests can be used as learning experiences. Let us now consider the problem of validity in testing and test design.

TEST DESIGN

To begin with, there is a high correlation between general ability (i.e., intelligence) and musical talent. There is evidence to suggest, however, that the categories of musical talent—rhythmic perception, pitch perception, digital agility, timbral discrimination, quantitative ability, musical memory—do not correlate uniformly with intelligence. I have no data to indicate just how this works, but every experienced music teacher has seen examples of the music student who has high abilities in several of these categories but appears to be innately deficient in others. Pioneering research in locating areas of the brain that control specific abilities and responses bears this out. It appears, for example, that the part of the brain that controls musical memory is distinct from that of verbal memory and of quantitative ability.

Thus, it is possible for a student to possess a superb rhythmic sense but an inadequate ability to discriminate pitches. Generally, however, there is both an acquired and an innate correlation among the abilities collectively called musical talent. While becoming musicians, we develop all musical skills, though to varying degrees. But this collection of abilities usually correlates positively with intelligence. Indeed, since musical talent consists of the coordination of a number of complex variables, and since intelligence has been termed the ability to manipulate and coordinate many variables, it is logical to expect that the deeply gifted musician will also be highly intelligent.

In designing theory tests the teacher must determine which musical skill is to be tested and then must find a way to isolate that skill in the testing process. Otherwise, the various abilities of a gifted music student may confound the tester. That is, correct answers may be found by means of a skill that the test was not intended to measure. The integrative theory test discussed earlier manifests some difficulties in this regard. For example, when a melodic dictation is given and a student omits a bar of the melody in transcription of it, how does the teacher know if this is caused by rhythmic problems, pitch problems, or both? It helps if the student puts the rhythms down and omits the pitches (or vice versa), but sometimes students do not do this, even if they are able to do so, unless they have apprehended both the rhythmic and the pitch elements. Thus, it may at times be necessary to test rhythmic ability separately from pitch discrimination.

Melodic dictation is the coordination of both of these factors, and it is important that this coordinative ability also be measured. But at early stages the teacher may wish to test rhythm separately by such a method as dictating rhythms on a single pitch at the piano (tapping or other purely percussive sounds should be avoided because durations are too imprecise). After the teacher is assured that the class is generally competent in purely rhythmic dictation, the rhythmic and pitch elements may be combined in melodic dictation.

The question of validity enters into harmonic dictation as well. Bright students with high quantitative abilities usually do well in part-writing because the concepts and principles are essentially quantitative. When such students are not equally gifted in pitch discrimination, they may find ways to compensate in harmonic dictation. For example, they may be able to fill in the inner voices of a harmonic dictation by means of part-writing principles without really having to call on aural skills. This should not necessarily be discouraged, for we all find ways to compensate for our shortcomings. If one can hear the soprano and bass and can identify chord quality and inversion, the inner voices can be deduced in all but those instances where exceptional part-writing practices are used. On the other hand, since such students are already demonstrating a certain quality of aural skill, they should be encouraged to extend that ability even further.

Actually, a harmonic-dictation test can be designed to measure, among other things, the ability to hear inner voices. One way to circumvent the excessive codification of part-writing procedures is to include occasionally such exceptional practices as unusual doublings or unorthodox textures. These should also be practiced in classroom drill; and as students see that the deductive process is not infallible for inner voices, they will begin to cultivate the ability to follow the alto and tenor lines inwardly rather than to extrapolate them deductively.

This makes good musical sense too, for most real music is full of exceptional practices. Parallel fifths, crossed voices, unusual textures, and remarkable doublings all occur within the 371 chorales of J. S. Bach. Too much stereotyping of the materials used for aural skills can result in dullness or prim but unmusical competence. And it can also lead to invalidity in testing.

Validity can also be a problem in conceptual tests with verbal answers. The questions on such tests should be written so that the students must manipulate the musical test materials in order to articulate an acceptable answer. In an analysis test, for example, the teacher may wish to measure the students' ability to perceive certain concepts in operation. Such questions as the following tend to achieve this:

1. Describe the methods by which the composer achieved contrast and heightened tension at bar 30.
2. Describe the relationships among the cadence points in this Bach chorale. How do these relationships help to define the form of the chorale?

Question 1 might elicit responses pertaining to any of the elements of music, but the respondents must come to grips with how those elements contribute to tension and contrast. This requires preknowledge as well as concept manipulation. The students demonstrate their knowledge as well as their ability to perceive the materials of music in operation. And because they are grappling with musical concepts, they learn from such a question.

Question 2 is a leading question. It suggests an answer, but it, too, requires concept manipulation; and in addition to "what?" the student must answer "how?" Questions like these challenge the inductive processes. They are not as easy to grade as clear-cut one-word responses, but student achievement is more fully revealed, and new learning occurs in the process.

Good test design should probably follow a process of several steps, something like the following:

1. Determine the skills or concepts that are to be tested.
2. Determine the general nature of the questions that best measure student achievement of these skills or concepts.

3. Decide how the test can be a learning experience.
4. Design the format of the test.
5. Write the specific questions.

The skills or concepts that are to be tested should be well established in the teacher's mind throughout the teaching process, for they are the same skills and concepts that are reflected in the objectives of the course itself. Testing is the process of measuring the degree to which students have achieved those objectives, and the type of questions that are used can have a profound effect upon the accuracy of that measurement. The format of the test can also have its effect. Should there be a few questions, all of the same type? Or should there be several sections to the test, each with a different approach? Finally, the specific questions, regardless of the format, should be written so that they require musical thinking and test the appropriate concept or skill.

It should be clear from the foregoing that the purpose of testing is not exclusively evaluative. Testing can contribute to the integration of musical skills as well as to the linking of conceptual knowledge to practice. And testing can be a strong stimulus to new learning. As a vital component of the theory program—and one that can be mishandled—it merits careful consideration on the part of the theory teacher.

NOTES

1. *Chronicle of Higher Education*, March 14, 1997, page A10, originally in *Change*, American Association for Higher Education.

2. Evaluations made with the Cornell student–teacher evaluation instrument of 1995.

3. Quoted in *Chronicle of Higher Education*, January 16, 1998, p. A12. The study, by Greenwood and Gilmore is in *American Psychologist*.

4. Robert S. Owen of SUNY Oswego, quoted in *Chronicle of Higher Education*, January 16, 1998, p. A12.

5. Richard R. Renner, "Comparing Professors: How Student Ratings Contribute to the Decline in Quality of Higher Education," *Phi Delta Kappan* (1981): 128–130.

6. Richard Renner, editorial, *Gainesville Sun*, April 16, 1997, p. 13A.

7. Edward M. White, "Bursting the Bubble Sheet: How to Improve Evaluations of Teaching," *Chronicle of Higher Education*, November 10, 2000, B11.

8. On a scale where A = 4, B = 3, C = 2, D = 1, and F = 0.

9. At Empire State University in New York State, where this system is being used, students have the option of requesting a letter grade in addition to the written evaluation.

NINE

Technology for Teaching and Learning

William E. Lake
(Copyright © 2001 by William E. Lake)

Does technology enhance teaching and learning? This may seem a reasonable question, since incorporating technology into instruction costs considerable amounts of time and money. What advantages does that cost purchase? There has been much gushing hyperbole portraying computer technology as a panacea for education. Perelman (1992), for one, predicts the demise of schools as we know them, with students buying their educations online from a variety of competing providers, resulting in better and less-expensive instruction. Computer technology seduces, no question about it. A slick, multimedia presentation will set teachers to dreaming, administrators to salivating, and donors to opening their purses. By the same token, an expert can do lots of neat tricks with a yo-yo, but that does not mean getting yo-yos into the classroom will improve learning. One might reasonably wish for hard evidence of the benefits, as opposed to glitzy salesmanship.

Research studies on the instructional efficacy of computer technology have yielded mixed results. Some show increased achievement, while others show no effect. In fact, no straightforward answer could possibly exist, because the above question itself is too simplistic (Cohen and McMullen 2000). Numerous problems confound research into this question (Clarke 1985). One stems from the breadth and diversity of technology itself. Different technologies should have different effects on learning. Another problem is the absence of distinctions among a technology per se, its application

179

(how it is employed), and the content being delivered. A technology may fail to yield the desired result due to ineffective application and/or content. It is important not to blame a technology for shortcomings in these other aspects. Individual differences among students pose a third problem. One should not expect a given technology to affect all students in the same way. Unless all such variables are controlled, results cannot reliably be attributed to an experiment's technological treatment.

That said, good reason exists to believe that technology is indeed a worthwhile addition to the instructional environment (Brown 2000a). Studies of educational methods per se have demonstrated that, among other things, providing students with (a) material in several different formats, (b) rapid feedback, and (c) greater interaction with their professors all increase learning. Computer technology excels at facilitating these. Thus, the answer to the question posed at the outset is a qualified "yes." If technology makes it possible to carry out existing instructional activities better or more easily, or if it permits implementation of previously unused educational strategies already known to be beneficial, then technology will most certainly enhance teaching and learning.

This answer treats technology as a tool, that is, an apparatus used in performing a task. In this light, computers are merely one part of a large array of tools available to assist teachers and students in achieving any educational objective. Tools cannot accomplish work, solve problems, or produce learning on their own. But the right tool can greatly increase both the quantity and quality of the end product. Conversely, the wrong tool can make success virtually impossible. Imagine trying to dig a hole with a rake! Thus, carefully selecting the right tool is a critical step.

Philosophy of Selection

Experts agree that considerable thought should go into planning instructional uses of technology. The educational value of a technology depends on "the way we approach [its] use and how we harness [it]. . . . Intelligent use is the key" (Webster 1993). "Critical discourse concerning the roles technology should play in music instruction" is too often lacking (McGee 1993). Sam Reese espouses the motto, "People and purposes before software and hardware," which means that teachers and students should not have to contort their present practices to fit a technology (Reese et al. 1998). The best uses of technology support and enhance the ways people customarily teach and learn.

People too often approach the selection of computer technology backward. The first question they ask is, "What kind of computers should we get?" The deciding factor here is sometimes completely divorced from potential uses, for instance, lowest cost or the preferences of tech-support personnel. The second question they ask is, "What music software runs on the machines we've decided upon?" After buying a selection of software to fit their hardware, they try to figure out ways to use it in teaching and learning. Ultimately, they end up wondering, "Why isn't all this great hardware and software getting more use?" The answer is that it was not selected to serve educational purposes. They have tried to adapt people to the technology rather than "using the technology to realize the visions of teachers" (McGee 1993).

The first step toward integration of technology into teaching should always be deciding on an instructional purpose. Begin by asking, "What do I do that technology could help me do better?" Do you and/or your students do tasks that involve (a) computation, such as synthesizing complex timbres or figuring grades; (b) repetition, such as making up or working simple exercises in music fundamentals; (c) revising one's work; (d) creating and/or searching databases; (e) sending and receiving messages and/or documents; or (f) juggling multiple media (texts, scores, audio recordings, videos, and the like)? Computers excel at supporting these tasks. But do not stop with present practices. Also ask, "What would I like to do differently that technology might facilitate?" Would you like students to actively engage the material, to work independently, to collaborate with each other, or to interact with experts in the field? Would you like to draw upon new and different learning resources, to meet individual students' special needs, or to try something really "outside the box"? Technology may support these as well. Ultimately, technology should lead to rethinking every aspect of the educational environment. Current practices are based on what could be done with old tools. Imaginative thinking may yield some hitherto unrecognized educational strategy made possible by new technology.

The second step is finding appropriate software to satisfy that instructional purpose. It is important to select the right tool for the job. The tool may be an existing software package, as is, or adapted in some manner, or a newly created application. Several sources provide good information about existing music software (see the list at the end of the chapter). As much as possible, review software personally to discover how well it actually suits your purpose. Do not overlook general applications (word processors, web browsers, etc.), which can serve many educational purposes. If nothing appropriate exists, some programming becomes necessary. Programming tools are becoming easier to learn. Alternatively, students in computer-science classes are always looking for projects. Tech-support personnel or colleagues are occasionally willing to pitch in and write a little code. Publishers of commercial software may also welcome suggestions for new applications or features.

The final step, selecting hardware, should be dictated by the preceding steps: Buy whatever is needed to run the chosen software. If sound educational reasons exist for wanting to use software that runs on a computer platform not supported by the department or college, the logic should convince them.[1] For music applications, the hardware will most likely entail a MIDI (Musical Instrument Digital Interface) keyboard with interface and headphones (or speakers) in addition to the standard workstation setup. As more and more applications become available on the World Wide Web, the platform (Macintosh, Windows/Intel, etc.) selected becomes less important. Web applications run similarly on many platforms.

Philosophy of Implementation

Technology must be employed throughout the curriculum to achieve its optimum potential. All credit-bearing study, even studio lessons and ensembles, should involve students in technology as appropriate. A freshman introductory course in technology, while an admirable start, is not sufficient. Technology skills and content need constant reinforcement for students to develop technological literacy. While theory courses cannot do it alone, they can make a significant contribution.

Furthermore, technology should be an integral part of the learning process, not simply an appendage. The mere availability of computers does not guarantee their use, educational or otherwise. Neither will haphazard, supplemental computer assignments develop technological competency. The institution must envision a complete picture of the technological skills students need and how those will be developed. Assignments, both focusing on the technology and employing it in a supporting role, need to be carefully sequenced. Once taught, technological skills need to be nurtured by regular practice opportunities.

Such lofty goals for technology may seem daunting. But keep in mind the adage "a journey of a thousand miles begins with a single step." Instructors would do well to adopt technology incrementally, starting with small steps with which they feel comfortable (Brown 2000b). This should promote better integration of technology and also should keep the work involved from become overwhelming. As long as those small steps represent progress toward an overarching vision, the effort will not be wasted.

Computer technology for music-theory instruction means much more today than it did twenty years ago. Early music-theory software merely drilled students on basic information assumed to have been presented in class. Nowadays, traditional drill-and-practice is only one of many functions, and its importance is rapidly diminishing. Computer software now has the capability to present information, coach complex skills, and stimulate creative and independent work. No longer should we view computers as merely remediation for students who do not "get it" in class. Now they are tools to help people with any activity associated with teaching and learning. Thus, this chapter does not restrict itself solely to discussing software with music-theory content. Much useful software, ranging from simple word processors to complex, multimedia authoring environments, is content free. Rather than adopt someone else's pedagogy, instructors can achieve better results by using some of the many, easy-to-use software tools available to support their own pedagogy.

TECHNOLOGY TOOLS FOR STUDENT PRODUCTIVITY, CREATIVITY, AND RESEARCH

Introduction

The National Association of Schools of Music (NASM) recommends that "through study and laboratory experience, students should be made familiar with the capabilities of technology as they relate to composition, performance, analysis, teaching, and research" (National Association of Music Schools 1999, 79). NASM's language here, "should be made familiar with," is woefully weak, seeming to advocate a kind of "technology appreciation," that is, a mere nodding acquaintance. Yet the reference to "laboratory experience" belies this, seeming to indicate some hands-on work. Thus, I interpret this NASM recommendation to mean that students not only should know the appropriate uses of different music technologies but also should actually acquire a modicum of skill with some of them. Of course, theory classes should not have to bear the brunt of this, for there should be a course or courses that all music majors must take to provide greater opportunities for the promotion of student literacy in music technology.

General-Use Applications

General-use applications that students will find useful include a word processor, a web browser, and an e-mail (electronic mail) program (although many do e-mail through their web browser). Knowledge of all three can now generally be assumed of students entering college. Sufficient incentive exists for most students to learn these on their own. Many universities run free supplementary training sessions for students who need help with these. If anticipated uses are rather specialized (e.g., creating figured-bass symbols in a word processor), teachers should provide students with the necessary training.

Composition

Software note processors and sequencers both aid composition but from different directions. The former approach is through the metaphor of a score; the latter through the metaphor of a recording studio. MIDI keyboards are the usual hardware for interfacing with these software packages. From that standpoint, students need to know MIDI-keyboard basics. But because their primary market is for performing musicians, such keyboards have many features that are not especially applicable to theory class work. Perhaps piano class would be an appropriate place to learn about MIDI keyboards in some depth.

Note processors computerize production of music notation,

which greatly improves the legibility of student work. In addition, most of them allow users to listen to what they have composed. This is a boon to theory students who lack keyboard facility. By note processing their stylistic composition projects, part-writing, and exercises of all sorts, they may hear their work in progress at any time. Such ear checks advance learning and enhance the musicality of the enterprise. Thus, good reason exists to devote the time in theory class to teach students a note-processing program and to require them to use it in preparing their assignments. However, note processing should not completely replace music calligraphy. Students will need to employ hand-written notation on in-class worksheets, tests, and the chalkboard. The basics of music handwriting should be taught in theory classes alongside computer note processing. A note processor may actually improve calligraphy by providing good examples to imitate.

Sequencing programs computerize production of multitrack recordings, simulating a recording studio. In addition, most of them create graphic representations (which may be analyzed) of such dimensions as register and dynamics, as well as corresponding music notation. Thus, they too facilitate working between sound and notation. The primary input device for a sequencing program, a MIDI controller (keyboard, wind, guitar, etc.), suits performance-oriented students particularly well and also provides an alternative for those whose grasp of notation is weak. Those with keyboard facility will be able to input music fastest with a sequencer, although most note processors have facilities for performance input also. Despite their different purposes, note processors and sequencers serve similar educational goals in theory classes. Because theory classes emphasize notation, I believe it is more important for students to learn a note processor than a sequencer, if time does not allow for both.

Teachers need to be aware of the effect these software tools may have on students' audiation skills. With a computer to render notation into sound for them, some students may not learn to imagine the sounds of notation on their own. When this occurs, the theory teacher must compensate for this shortcoming by means of the ear-training component of the theory classroom. More commonly, however, these programs will have a positive effect. In the initial stages, students merely observe the correspondences between notation and sound as the computer plays for them. Those observations provide experiences they can build upon, which begins a learning spiral between computer-assisted and self-audiation. Of course, this is no substitute for aural-skills training, but it can serve as a useful adjunct.

The choice of specific software products should be made by the entire music faculty, since students will presumably use them throughout the curriculum. One issue is whether to adopt a sophisticated, full-featured program or a rudimentary one. The latter tends to be easier to learn but has limited functionality. I think it is better to adopt a full-featured program. Most are fairly user-friendly in regard to simple tasks,[2] and students would not then have to switch to a different program when their needs become more sophisticated. As of this writing, Finale (Coda Music Technology) is the industry leader in note processing, but many professionals have complaints about it. Opinion is divided regarding the best full-featured sequencer. Digital Performer (Mark of the Unicorn) is currently quite popular, but several others have sizable loyal followings.[3]

Analysis

In contrast to composition, computer support for analysis is not standardized in any respect. Some shareware applications do exist (visit the Queensland Conservatorium Web site listed at the end of the chapter), but their scope is often limited to a narrow, computation-intensive aspect (e.g., pitch-class-set theory). More broadly applicable are programs designed to produce some sort of time line representation of a piece (Form Companion, Chart Creator), which can support the study of form. Students can create listening guides and/or bubble/bracket diagrams of form and coordinate these with CDs or even MIDI files. Doing so results in a much closer connection between student analyses and the sound of the music.

Research

Computer technology has become essential to the efficient conduct of research projects. Online resources are growing apace and provide information not readily available elsewhere. Online databases are far more convenient than print indexes. Students will need to learn what databases are available, where to find them, and how to search them efficiently. University libraries may hold training sessions for students, covering their own online catalogs and some broad-coverage databases. Music instructors may need to provide additional tips on how to find scores and recordings efficiently and how and when to use the various music databases. Many other formerly print-only resources exist online as well, including books, journals, scores, manuscript facsimiles, and sound files. The Web has its own unique resources as well, including special-topic Web sites, newsgroups, Web broadcasts, and interactive online projects. If students will need to consult these, an introduction to Web searching would be appropriate (Negrino 2000).

Another form of research is discovery learning, in which the learner actively constructs knowledge as opposed to passively receiving it. Projects and laboratory experiences have served this purpose for years. More recently, computers have been employed to provide students with media-rich environments in which to explore and learn. For example, the CD-ROMs by Robert Winter, each of which focuses on a single masterwork, provides a recorded performance, biographical information on the composer, historical background on the piece, a form chart, measure-by-measure commentary, a detailed listening guide, and often a quiz game, all hyperlinked together to facilitate easy navigation among them.[4] The presentation is enhanced by photos, artwork, animations, music notation, sound clips, and hyperlinks to a glossary. These resources entice students to follow their interests in many different directions, learning as they go. Experience suggests that students need guidance on how to take full advantage of such multimedia learning environments. They can quickly become overwhelmed by the quantity of information. Research shows that quite a few try to take a straight linear path through the software, as if they were watching a video (Fortney 1994). That is, they often do not stop to explore a phenomenon in greater depth, even when it interests them.

Students need encouragement to take advantage of the richness available to them. Instructor demonstrations, guide questions, and self-posttests all help, but, for students to take this work seriously, close links with class work and tests are essential. Multimedia discovery-learning activities seem to be most effective when placed in the middle of a term (Peterson 1993). If placed too early, students will not be prepared to get the most out of them.

Selection and Training

Relevance is the primary factor in selecting software tools. If students will use a tool a fair amount for class, then it is worth spending precious class time on it. Class use motivates learning and exercises skills. Major projects, such as stylistic compositions and analysis papers, provide an excellent opportunity to integrate several technologies into course work. Their learning value and the final result can be greatly improved through technology. Another factor to consider is what types of software students will likely use as professionals. Finally, to decide among competing products, read reviews (see sources listed at the end of the chapter), ask advice of colleagues, and test them personally.

Students will need training on how to use most software tools. This training should address both the operation of the software itself and how to use it effectively for class purposes. Training might be thought of in three categories determined by students' prior knowledge and the anticipated uses of the various tools: (1) No in-class training is necessary on tools that many students already know fairly well or if basic training in them is readily available on campus. Word processing, web browsers, and e-mail fall into this category.[5] (2) Supplemental in-class training should be offered on tools that students may know in a general way but will need to use for a specialized purpose in class. (3) Thorough in-class training should be provided on tools that many students may not already know but will use a great deal for class. Note processing is a prime example. In such cases, students should receive not only a step-by-step handout but also hands-on practice with the tasks they will be required to perform.

TECHNOLOGY TOOLS FOR FACULTY

Preparation

Many faculty who do not use a computer in their actual teaching do use one to prepare teaching aids on paper, such as lecture notes, handouts, worksheets, and tests. Word-processed files such as these can easily be loaded into a presentation program or converted to Web pages. In fact, most modern word processors will save files as

Hypertext Markup Language (HTML) pages, ready to upload to a Web site. With few exceptions, creating teaching materials from scratch is no easier with a computer than without. On the other hand, it is not a lot harder. The time devoted to learn any program is repaid with repeated use. Over time, the teacher can amass a collection of presentations, examples, assignments, and tests on computer. Compared to low-tech materials, these can be more quickly revised and collated into new presentations, assignments, and the like.

Presentation

Faculty spend a considerable portion of their in-class time on presentation (lecture or demonstration). Most use one or more mechanical aids to help get their points across. Even so, music theory is sometimes taught in a media-starved manner. Kindred (1993) has observed, "Teaching and learning are too far removed from the music, and often the student's knowledge is technically accurate but not complemented with a corresponding understanding of how the information applies to the music."[6] Because music analyses are difficult to convey in words alone, lectures benefit enormously from incorporation of multiple media, especially diagrams and audio examples. Technology may streamline this process. Four criteria may help place various presentation technologies in perspective: (a) logistics, (b) ease of use, (c) learning curve, (d) and flexibility.

Presentation technology used to mean merely a chalkboard and a piano. These grand old technologies usually are standard equipment in music classrooms and almost never break down or get stolen. Both are easy to use in that they require little or no setup (piano tuning excepted) and just a few intuitive steps to operate. However, they represent the two extremes regarding learning curves for the teacher, with the chalkboard having virtually none but the piano having a very steep one. The piano is much harder to learn than most modern computer programs. Fortunately, many music instructors have been climbing its learning curve for years and have achieved a moderate level of pianistic skill. Both tools are very flexible. The chalkboard grants unlimited and seamless freedom in kinds of graphic representation (text, music notation, diagrams, etc.), allows easy revision, and welcomes multiple simultaneous users.

A semiskilled pianist (and every theory teacher should be at least a semiskilled keyboardist) can play prepared examples, improvise exercises, and alter examples to facilitate comparisons. Live performance, either on the piano or some other medium (voice or instrument), offers an opportunity for the teacher to display his or her musicality, which would provide a valuable role model for students.

Both the piano and the chalkboard have drawbacks, which we sometimes overlook. The chalkboard has limited space, does not save work, requires presenters to turn their backs to the class, and leaves behind a dusty mess. The piano's drawbacks include limited timbre, quick decay of sounds, and its size, which may hide the instructor from view and thus interfere with nonverbal communication. (The last problem is circumvented with a small grand piano, ideal for the theory classroom.)

The first wave of electronic presentation technology might be called "AV" (audio-visual), meaning stereo systems, overhead projectors, slide projectors, videocassette players, and the like. These may or may not be permanently installed in music classrooms, which can lead to logistical problems either way. If left out of the classroom, they tend to be stolen or borrowed at inopportune times. If locked in a closet somewhere, they have to be moved to the classroom in time. If they have to be ordered from across campus, additional planning is required; and here the vagaries of the bureaucracy will often intrude—lost or botched requests, delivery snafus, and so forth. AV equipment varies in both ease of use and learning curve from slight to moderate, although an AV resource person may provide helpful advice. Also, flexibility can be fairly limited. For instance, examples dubbed onto an audiocassette cannot be altered, except by truncation. Comparisons between passages some distance apart on the tape are difficult to achieve effectively, and alterations to explore "what if" questions are impossible. This is where the ancient but flexible piano may actually be preferable.

Computers represent the second wave of electronic presentation technology. If a teaching lab big enough for an entire class exists, logistics may be no problem. Every student can sit at a computer, and teachers can project what is on their monitor onto a screen or send it to students' monitors. Similarly, a lecture hall wired to facilitate computer presentation will be easy to set up. In contrast, using a computer in an ordinary classroom incurs all the problems of AV technology (and then some) to broadcast its output throughout the room. Video options include extension monitors (TVs), an LCD (liquid crystal display) panel to set on an overhead projector, or a video-projection system. Audio requires connection to a stereo system or at least to powered speakers. Problems may also arise in connecting the computer to AV equipment. None of these obstacles are insurmountable with sufficient advance planning. Starting from scratch, computer learning curves are steeper than most AV equipment but less than the piano. However, someone already using a computer for other tasks should find that learning a new program or two does not take much more effort. Like any skill (including piano playing), the more computer skills are used, the more fluent they become.

A number of different types of software can be useful for classroom presentation. (1) Presentation programs (e.g., PowerPoint) can support lecturing. Computer-generated "slides" can be more colorful and dynamic than transparencies for the overhead and may hold an audience's attention better. The learning curve is slight, so time invested is repaid quickly. (2) Audio examples on CDs can be parsed in advance into clips. This saves class time in locating and playing examples. It also makes for easier and quicker switches among examples for comparison. Even better is recording audio examples direct to a single CD or hard disk (which requires a lot of disk space unless compression is used) or as QuickTime movies or MP3 files (both of which creates relatively compact files). Then one does not have to shuffle CDs to compare between pieces. (3) MIDI files can be created in a sequencer or note processor for playback in class. The advantage here is that examples can be altered quickly to see the effects of various changes. This approach has some of the flexibility of a piano, with a wide variety of timbres a piano cannot provide. (4) Multimedia software can synchronize music, graphics, text, and other media to an extent not possible by hand on the fly. Simultaneous presentation of information in multiple modes enhances learning, and it can connect concepts and music in a stunningly vivid manner. Multimedia programming is not a simple matter, however. Depending on the sophistication of the project, knowledge of an authoring tool, for example, Macromedia Director, may be necessary. Regardless of the software used, computer presentations can easily be archived and reused. Also, they can readily be made available online to students for review.

Students may also avail themselves of the same presentation technologies that their instructors use. Additionally, an online presentation area for student work may prove beneficial. This can be as simple as a community folder where students can read (and possibly comment upon) each other's essays; or as involved as individual Web pages devoted to students' multimedia projects. Most course-management packages incorporate a student presentation area.

Guest lectures can offer students important perspectives and spur their imaginations. Difficulties of time and distance have often limited the number of guest lecturers that could be brought in, but computer networks expand the possibilities far beyond the pioneering "distance learning" programs of the seventies. With a video camera, microphone, and videoconferencing software on both ends, distinguished scholars may lecture to and interact with the class without leaving their offices. In this case, a technological tool truly redefines the situation.

Whenever possible, the teacher should test electronic presentation technology in advance and then again right before class to make sure everything is working. Nothing is more wasteful or embarrassing than a lesson plan decimated by technical difficulties. Keep phone numbers for technical support personnel handy. Have a fallback plan for when the technology fails. (It will not very often, but it is best to be prepared for the worst.) Keep a sense of humor during technology failures.

Communication

Teacher–student interaction outside of class has always been a small but important part of the educational process. It traditionally has taken the form of handwritten notes, office hours, and telephone consultations. With the advent of e-mail technology, communication has become more convenient. Parties need not connect in real time. Messages travel instantly to a person's electronic inbox to be read and replied to at the receiver's convenience. If all parties check their e-mail fairly frequently, more interactions can occur than in traditional media. Important information does not have to wait until the next class meeting. Teachers may disseminate announcements or clarifications, and students may get answers to questions. Electronic communication typically results in more teacher–student interaction, thus helping students to succeed in class. From that standpoint, it is time well spent by the teacher.

Discussion

Another form of communication, class discussion, can also be enhanced through technology (Ottenhoff and Lawrence 1999). In-class discussion labors under four types of time constraints (Lake 1999): (a) The class period is of limited duration. (b) Everyone participating has to be there at the same time. (c) Participation must be strictly sequential—only one person can talk at a time. (d) It is locked in to a single pace. Online discussion may occur in real time (chat rooms) or asynchronously (newsgroups). The former sidesteps only the first time constraint—discussion may continue for as long as necessary. Students must log on at the same time but may do so from any networked computer anywhere. The participants' typed input appears on everyone's screen in the order submitted. Comments and replies may follow each other very quickly, but the computer keeps a record that can be reread if needed. Experience suggests that chat rooms become unmanageable with more than about seven participants. Software products dedicated to this purpose exist (AOL Instant Messenger). Alternatively, course-management software packages usually contain a chat facility. Both are very easy to set up and use.

Asynchronous discussion escapes all four constraints listed above. It is organized like a newsgroup, with posts sorted into topic threads. Students log on and off at their convenience, with the software keeping track of their places for them. They read sequentially through the discussion but do so at different times and rates. This allows them as much time as they need to evaluate arguments, to organize their thoughts, and to craft responses. The computer then accepts responses whenever they are ready, placing them with the posts to which they refer. One may set this up in stand-alone software or a course-management suite, both of which are easy to use. A list server, in which an e-mail sent to the list address is delivered to everyone on the list, could also be employed. A disadvantage is that list servers do not sort messages by topic. An advantage is that messages go to everyone's personal e-mail account. To access discussion in other software products, students must go to a separate location (e.g., a class Web page), which they probably will not do as frequently as they check their personal e-mail inboxes.

Instructors will want to plan ways to motivate students to participate in online discussion. One trick to get them online is to post information, such as announcements and helpful hints about assignments, that is not available elsewhere. Another is to hold office hours online, while yet another technique is to tie in-class and online discussion together. When an in-class discussion heats up and threatens to overflow the time allotted to it, transfer it online by posting (or assigning a student to do it) a summary of discussion soon after class. Conversely, the teacher can also bring up points from online discussion in class, so those who are not online may feel mildly left out. Intrinsic motivators work much better than grades. The best motivation comes from dealing with real issues of relevance to the students.

The greatest advantage of online discussion, its different time dynamic, is also its greatest disadvantage. Taking discussion outside the classroom creates time for the extended consideration necessary to deal with complex issues. Also, it allows everyone to participate as much and as often as they like. However, a large and active class will occasionally generate an immense number of posts, which can take a great deal of time to read.

A second big advantage is that online discussion is easier to guide than in-class discussion. This is not to say that no guidance is necessary. Students often know little about the protocols for a good discussion and will have to be coached (Knowlton, Knowlton, and Davis 2000). However, online discussion can be more freewheeling, since time is not an issue. Students may follow a topic where it leads them. If necessary, a new discussion thread or chat room can be opened, while the old one continues. Online discussion tends to be self policing. Monitoring participation is a snap, because an archive of all contributions exists on hard disk, obviating the need to take notes. This makes grading student contributions a much less daunting task, and the emphasis can be on quality rather than quantity.

A third advantage devolves from the equalizing effect of the technology. In electronic communication, appearance, voice, and social position are all moot, which puts everyone on equal footing. This increases participation, as well as distributing it more evenly. Students too reticent to speak in class become emboldened and have their say. However, participation imbalances will still exist. Happily, they are different from those in class. Experience shows that the greatest total participation results from a combination of in-class and online discussion.

Finally, online discussion is place shifting. People can participate from any networked computer anywhere. This allows (a) commuters to work at home, (b) distance learners to stay connected, and even (c) interested or invited persons from all walks of life to get involved.

Collaborative Learning

Many employment situations involve working in peer groups. Collaboration, like technology, may increase learning if properly employed. Thus, many faculty are placing some emphasis on group work in their courses. This might take the form of group presentations, group compositions, or discussion groups, among other things. Computer technology can support these efforts (see Sullivan 1994 for examples related to writing). Group communication can be furthered by e-mail, Web-based discussion areas, and/or chat rooms. Group presentations may employ the presentation technologies mentioned above or may be placed online.

Individualizing Instruction

Students come to college with different backgrounds. They learn in differing ways and at differing rates. Technology has great potential for addressing those differences. Computers might help identify student needs and then provide catch-up instruction or enrichment work as appropriate. They might offer various approaches to suit different learning styles (e.g., linear versus nonlinear) and allow students to proceed at their own pace. Unfortunately, this potential is largely untapped at present. Some drill-and-practice software does well diagnosing difficulties and prescribing remedial work within the confines of its subject matter (usually music fundamentals or ear-training). But none deal comprehensively with theory or aural skills, and none address learning styles. Nonetheless, an instructor who desires to individualize instruction will find today's D&PS useful as part of a plan to meet differing needs of students. This will be discussed further under "Supplements to Classroom Instruction."

Assignments

Homework may be submitted, marked, and returned electronically. It can be submitted as an attachment to an e-mail message or deposited in a secure drop folder. This approach saves paper. It may also save the students some time, if an electronic shell to get them started is provided. For instance, a note-processed shell for a part-writing exercise might include the first chord, the bass, and perhaps part of the soprano. Online submission works better with some types of assignment than others. Anything normally done on computer works best, since it already exists in electronic form. Of course, multimedia assignments are best presented via computer. Word-processed essays can easily be read and evaluated online. (Markup utilities exist, but it is easier to simply insert comments in a different font or style to distinguish them.) Note-processed compositions or exercises are not so easy to markup in the traditional manner, but verbal commentary can be typed separately. Some D& PS allows students to e-mail records of their work within the program to the instructor. Certain types of exercise do not translate well into an electronic format. For example, chord-analysis and figured-bass symbols are difficult to create without a special font and they are sometimes bothersome to align under chords in an electronic score. Such analysis assignments are still best submitted and marked on paper.

Testing

I must say at the outset that, because cheating is easy and rampant with online testing, many theory teachers will prefer to avoid it. Yet in-class testing can take up a lot of class time, including not only the duration of the tests themselves, but also the review to prepare the students and posttest feedback. For teachers who are willing to cope with the possibility of cheating, technology can help ease that time crunch.

Online-testing applications automate quiz creation and delivery. They usually offer several possibilities for question format, such as matching, fill in the blank, multiple choice, calculated, and essay. Randomization features normally include (a) answer order within questions, (b) question order, and (c) question selection from a designated pool. Questions may incorporate graphics (including music notation), sound, and/or short videos, although student responses may not. Tests can be timed or self paced. Automatic scoring (not applicable to essay questions) and record keeping are very convenient. Students may view their scores and any feedback the instructor builds in almost immediately. The software stores the quizzes and results for future use and study. Often, extensive statistics are available.

The greatest advantages of online testing are rapid feedback and time saved. With automatic grading and feedback, students find out what they did wrong while they still remember their erroneous thought processes and thus have a much better chance of correcting them. The instructor's time spent on initial setup will likely be paid back over several years, after which significant time savings will accrue annually. Savings of class time should be realized immediately. If students are allowed to retake online tests, they will do it many more times than would be possible in class, resulting in dramatically improved test performance.

As I said above, the main disadvantage to online testing is that cheating is fairly easy. Nothing but honor prevents students from looking up answers. Teachers may counteract this by asking questions for which the answers cannot be looked up or by placing tight time limits on tests so students would not have time to look up answers. In addition, although access is customarily restricted by password, students could easily log on and then have someone else take the test for them. One solution to this is to require proctoring by someone in a position of authority. In an on-campus lab, this might be a lab monitor or a graduate assistant. If the test taker is far distant from campus, perhaps a local school official would serve. Another solution is to give quizzes both in class and online and compare the results. Students who perform much better online may be cheating. Alternatively, online tests may serve solely as practice for in-class tests, which may obviate the need for in-class review sessions.

There are several content-free applications designed to facilitate online testing. Some are stand-alone applications dedicated to testing (e.g., Perception), while others are part of a suite of course tools. In addition, some commercial drill-and-practice programs contain testing facilities (e.g., Benward and Kolosick 2000) limited to the content of their drill material. A few words of advice for instructors employing online tests: Always take tests yourself and try to cause them to break down, in order to catch problems before releasing them to students. Have contingency plans for potential problems beyond your control, such as network outages on test dates.

Record Keeping

Computer spreadsheets (e.g., Excel) offer many advantages over old-fashioned paper grade books. These offer (a) the ability to replicate formulas, making grade calculation an easy matter; (b) automatic recalculation, so that grades immediately reflect any new entries; and (c) the ability to sort records by any column. In addition to alphabetical order, sorting can also be done by grade, to identify groups based on test performance; and by student ID number, to post grades in an anonymous, scrambled order. With just a few extra steps, a spreadsheet can be posted on the class Web page. Spreadsheets can easily be printed out to carry to class. Course-management software customarily provides an automated grade book. These automatically record online quiz results and make students' grades available for them to view online. Unfortunately, some are very clumsy compared to stand-alone applications.

Online Courses

Online courses reach a wider audience and provide freedom of location for students and teachers. However, they are very time consuming to set up and run. Also, they require more work and greater motivation from students. The lack of regular class meetings leaves students with little incentive to work regularly. A plan to hold students accountable periodically, in order to curb procrastination, is absolutely necessary. I have reservations about placing music-theory courses entirely online. Interactive guidance from a teacher is helpful in all areas of theory and almost a requirement for the more sophisticated topics (counterpoint, part-writing, analysis). A combination of online and in-person instruction appears to work best. In a music appreciation course, Peterson (1998) found 85 percent online to be too much, even with honors students.

A fully online course is perhaps best delivered via course-management software (BlackBoard, WebCT, etc.). These products integrate several dozen useful tools into a single package. Most can support sophisticated, interactive courses but are no more difficult to learn than a web browser. WebCT advertises "fifteen minutes to an online course."[7] Course-management software can be equally as helpful when used piecemeal. If such software is available on campus, begin by picking one or two tools to integrate into your classes. More tools can easily be added later, since they are available within the same shell.

Most teachers find that employing computer technology does not save them time overall. Time saved on tasks that are sped up is offset by extra attention to quality and depth of work. Add to that the time required to learn the software, and using computers may result in a net loss, especially in the short term. But many believe that greater quality and depth are sufficient incentives to use computers.

SUPPLEMENTS TO CLASSROOM INSTRUCTION

In this section I will consider in some detail ways of delivering content, review, or drill outside the classroom. Teachers have always expected students to study on their own time. Some study activities, for instance, singing melodies at sight, are still best carried out in the traditional manner. However, computers have the potential to supplant and improve upon many old-fashioned study tools, such as flashcards, worksheets, and audio tape recordings. In addition, computers facilitate multimedia presentation of content on a level never possible before.[8] These capabilities permit a shift in the allocation of class time. Less time needs to be spent on presenting and drilling basic information and more may be spent on higher-order learning. Walls (1996) predicts that lecture time will decrease and small-group activities will increase.

Study and Review

No matter how brilliant a teacher's classroom presentation may be, students always need to study and review subject matter outside of class. Instructors with a modicum of technological savvy can easily place formerly print resources, including reading assignments, handouts, and lecture notes, on the World Wide Web. But the greatest advantage of technology devolves from the ability of computers to synchronize multiple media. Computers can convey all the richness of an in-class presentation and then some. For example, not only can they present an audio excerpt with the teacher's voice-over, but also they can simultaneously scroll both the score and a form diagram, highlighting the sounding portions. To approximate this without high technology, the student must juggle a score, an audio recording, and several printed resources, applying considerable perseverance to integrate corresponding locations in the diverse media. Most teachers will require considerable assistance to develop such multimedia instructional materials.

Drill and Practice

Most commercially available products for supplemental instruction fall under the rubric of drill-and-practice software (D&PS). This category is distinguished by its focus on exercises that have one right answer. In essence, D&PS feeds students questions or problems, scores their answers, and provides limited feedback, resembling automated flashcards. Some programs include cute reinforcement sounds (e.g., applause for correct answers, groans for wrong answers) and other features that make them seem like games, which may increase student satisfaction. Such low-level drill is fine for any body of information that is best memorized, working reasonably well for fundamentals (pitch and rhythm notation, scales, key signatures, intervals, and triads) and isolated ear-training items (scale degrees, intervals, and chord qualities).[9]

D&PS may also address longer exercises, such as dictation (melodic, harmonic, and rhythmic) and Roman-numeral analysis. For these, scoring and feedback must be more sophisticated to be useful. The program must recognize partially correct answers and also provide students clues as to what and where their errors are. The best results in this regard seem to be obtained when the programmer is also an experienced theory teacher. Some D&PS attempts to address more complex skills, such as part-writing and figured-bass realization, by isolating and limiting items so that there is only one correct answer. While this may prove helpful to some students, it does not address all of the necessary skills. Mastering voicing of isolated chords in an SATB texture will not in itself enable students to correctly part-write complete phrases.

When shopping for D&PS, Hofstetter's (1988) *Guidelines for Improving Music Software* (see pages 324–329) is a good guide to evaluating specific products. Several issues deserve elaboration here. One ubiquitous shortcoming of low-level D&PS is allowing unlimited time for answering. While self pacing is good in the initial stages of learning a topic, instant recall of flashcard-type information should be an objective. Students who need a full minute to figure out each key signature do not know them in any practical sense. They need ways to practice for fluency, which could very easily be provided by D&PS but unfortunately are not. A switchable, forced-pace feature would be a welcome addition to such software.

Quality of feedback is another important issue. Feedback should help students identify the faulty thinking that led to their errors. For example, if responses to a pitch-naming exercise in bass clef are a third too low, feedback should suggest that students check the clef. They are probably reading in treble clef instead. Quality feedback is uncommon in today's software, probably because of the content, knowledge, and time required to program it.

The method of generation is a concern for longer exercises. Randomly generated melodies and harmonies are inevitably unmusical. A pattern-recognition strategy, which many teachers propound, is fairly useless in dealing with such exercises. In contrast, examples from music literature are highly musical, but a short list of them can be memorized by students, limiting the amount of practice they can get. (It is not unheard of for a dedicated student to do literally thousands of items in D&PS.) Algorithmic generation produces fairly musical results by employing rules to join together short musical patterns. That method of generation or a very long fixed list are preferable to random generation. The method of sequencing exercises should also be considered. Random sequencing yields some odd results, such as the same item twice in a row. Pooled selection, which generates a pool of questions meeting certain criteria (e.g., all of the major key signatures without duplication) and then selects items randomly from this pool until all have been used, is a better approach. If the program's methods for generating and sequencing exercises are not obvious, work with it for fifteen minutes. If unmusical or duplicate items occur, suspect random generation.

Most D&PS keeps score in some manner. If it saves the right sort of information, it may be very helpful in facilitating performance-based instruction. Future practice (in class and out) can be made much more efficient by focusing on items the software reports as most frequently missed. Unfortunately, record-keeping facilities often do not provide the information that would be most useful. Common shortcomings include lumping too much data together, reporting either no time data or only gross time spent, and failing to collect all student data when work is done in several locations.

Many programs contain an automated curriculum, which advances students to the next level once they demonstrate mastery of the current level. A moderately sophisticated program will have various paths along which it guides the student. It may branch to supplementary material, either review or enrichment, or loop back through material not sufficiently mastered. This is great for independent study but may pose a problem as a supplement to traditional classes. First, the curriculum in the software may not match that of the course. If it cannot be shut off or modified, that conflict will lead to constant confusion. Second, a student may need to skip ahead to keep up with the class. Third, students may want or need to backtrack to review. Some auto-curriculums do not permit this. The best programs permit the auto-curriculum to be switched on and off. The better D&PS programs allow customization of many features. Students may control aspects of the presentation, including volume, tempo, and timbre of dictation exercises. Instructors may add questions or problems of their own and redo the pedagogical sequence.

Unfortunately, most of music theory and analysis does not deal in sole, correct answers. Analysis of form, stylistic composition, and melody harmonization (among many other activities) admit multiple answers or solutions with varying degrees of quality. To address these, more sophisticated software is necessary. In this regard, artificial intelligence (AI) holds some promise (Schaffer 1990, 1991).[10] In brief, an AI software tutor draws on a knowledge base containing rules distilled from experts' knowledge (both factual and procedural) to guide student work. For example, suppose in a melody-harmonization exercise that a student elects to begin with the mediant chord, which does in fact fit with the melody pitch. A D&PS program would probably respond "Wrong. Try again." An AI software tutor would likely provide the following, much more useful feedback: "At the beginning of a phrase, it is important to establish the tonic key." Sadly, no AI-based software tutors for music theory are commercially available as of this writing. Reasons include the difficulty of programming such software and the lack of financial incentive because the market is so small.

Supplemental instruction via technology must be well integrated into a course to be effective. One approach is to require a certain amount of time (say, an hour per week) of computer drill. This works best when deadlines are placed throughout the semester, thus preventing students from utilizing all of their practice hours the day before the final. There are two problems associated with a fixed time requirement: (1) Any given amount of time will only be right for a few students. The worst will need endless hours of practice, and the best will need none at all, with the remainder ranging in between. (2) Left to their own devices, some students seem unable to use their computer practice time wisely, working on topics they already know well rather than those on which they need to improve. A better approach is to make specific computer assignments. This solves problem 2, but a corollary of problem 1 remains: "One size fits all" does not work well for skill development.

Ideally, computer assignments should be tailored to individual needs. Software with an automated curriculum does that quite well, but its curriculum may not match that of the course. In small classes, teachers have time to work with each student individually and learn their strengths and weaknesses intimately, gleaning the necessary information for making up individualized assignments. It is more difficult but not impossible to individualize assignments with large classes. For that purpose, I have designed a performance-based system, which requires several days of planning beforehand but very little time weekly to operate. I plan lengthy, software-based assignments in advance, covering every aspect being studied (for example, for ear-training: melodic, harmonic, rhythmic, and two-voice dictation; melodic, harmonic, and rhythmic error detection; scale degrees; intervals; chord qualities and inversions). Then I excuse students from those aspects in which they have performed well so far. In grading the pretest and all quizzes, I give each item its own individual percentage score. Students are excused from those parts of the assignment on which they scored 80 percent or above the last time they were tested. I supply students with a grid on which to enter their test results, so they can see graphically what they need to practice (figure 9.1). The system is backward looking, which could result in students not practicing newly introduced difficulties, but I coach them to watch out for this. We have achieved good results with this system. Students take the assignments more seriously because they are individualized.

PRACTICE PLANNER FOR ET ASSIGNMENTS

Aural Skills I ET Quiz 2

(Applies to Weeks 10–13)

Everyone's practice time is limited. This sheet will help make your ET practice more efficient. Simply put an X on each line where your percentage score for items on the last quiz falls. If there was no such item on the last quiz, carry over your score from the quiz before that. If the X is to the left of the vertical line, you must do that portion of the assignment. If it is on the line or to the right of it, you are excused from that portion. This holds until you get your next ET quiz back. In addition, the two or three worse items (Xs furthest to the left) deserve extra practice beyond the minimum required by the assignment.

	Must Do This Portion .... Excused
Melodic Dictation	0 .... 25............. 50 ......60 ..... 70...... 80 ......90 100
Melodic Error Detection	0 .... 25............. 50 ......60 ..... 70...... 80 ......90 100
Pitch Pattern/ Scale Degrees	0 .... 25............. 50 ......60 ..... 70...... 80 ......90 100
Intervals	0 .... 25............. 50 ......60 ..... 70...... 80 ......90 100
4-Chord Progressions	0 .... 25............. 50 ......60 ..... 70...... 80 ......90 100
SBRN Chorale Dictation	0 .... 25............. 50 ......60 ..... 70...... 80 ......90 100
Chord Qualities and Inversions	0 .... 25............. 50 ......60 ..... 70...... 80 ......90 100
Rhythmic Dictation	0 .... 25............. 50 ......60 ..... 70...... 80 ......90 100

Figure 9.1   Example Grid for Individualizing Ear-Training Assignments

The best software for supplemental instruction mirrors the way an instructor teaches. Thus, as with textbooks, the best are those which instructors themselves write. As David Williams (1993) says, "The most effective music courseware is that which has been designed by the instructor, is contemporaneous with the course content, and reflects his or her pedagogical personality and biases." While tools for doing this are becoming easier to use and on-campus support resources are becoming more plentiful, it may still prove impractical to create custom software. In that case, the resources and advice supplied in this chapter should help in locating a suitable commercial product. Finally, to reap the maximum benefit of outside-of-class computer work, be sure to integrate it with in-class work (especially tests).

CONCLUSION

Ultimately, whether to employ technology in teaching is a personal decision. Most instructors already employ some sort of technology (perhaps not computers) in their teaching. Increasing one's use of technology is a good way to advance one's own teaching skills and to improve the educational environment offered to students. However, thoughtful planning is necessary for technology to have a positive effect on learning. Although computer technology leaves many human foibles untouched, such as procrastination and fear of failure, its positive effects are manifold. Goddard (1998) concluded that it (a) encourages greater depth of knowledge in present teaching and learning practices, (b) allows development of new teaching and learning practices that could not exist otherwise, (c) helps address different learning styles and ability levels, and (d) facilitates greater accuracy of information. These benefits make it worth the expense, time, and effort to employ computers in education.

RESOURCES FOR RESEARCHING SOFTWARE FOR MUSIC INSTRUCTION

Association for Technology in Music Instruction (ATMI) discussion list. Members are very willing to answer questions and offer opinions about specific software. To join, send e-mail to *majordomo@list.uiowa.edu* with the message "subscribe atmi" (include no subject and no signature).

Association for Technology in Music Instruction (ATMI). The *Technology Directory* (annual) is a benefit of membership. To find out current dues and where to send them, send a query to the discussion list above.

CTI Music. (Department of Music, Lancaster University, England). CTI Music: Downloadable Software <www.lancs.ac.uk/users/music/research/sware.html> provides brief descriptions and links to Web sites for dozens of free, shareware, or demonstration music software packages available for downloading.

Electronic Musician (5615 W. Cermak Road, Cicero, IL 60650). Contains reviews of software tools for professional musicians.

Murrow, Rodney C. (Northwestern Oklahoma State University). Resources for Music Theory Instruction (www.pldi.net/~murrows/tpsoft.html).

Music Educators National Conference (1902 Association Drive, Reston, VA 22091). *Music Educators Journal* contains reviews of software geared to K–12 instruction.

Queensland Conservatorium (Griffith University, Australia). Software Tools for Music Analysis (http://appollo.qcm.gu.edu.au/MA).

Schuler, Nico (Michigan State University). Computer-Assisted Music Analysis (www.msu.edu/user/schuler4/CAMA-Links.html) provides brief descriptions and links to Web sites for a few music-analysis programs. Because this is a student Web page, it may be gone before long.

Solomon, Dr. Larry. Solomon's Theory Resources (http://azstarnet.com/~solo/theory.html).

Spangler, Douglas (Michigan State University). Music Software for Ear Training (www.msu.edu/user/spangle9) catalogs and evaluates ear-training software. Because this is a student Web page, it may be gone before long.

SOFTWARE PRODUCTS

(If any of these site addresses do not work, try shortening them. Once you get to the corporate server, try links or search the site to find information on the specific product. If that doesn't work, try searching the entire Web with available tools.)

Benward & Kolosick (2000) software (see citations below)

Blackboard. Blackboard, Washington, D.C. www.blackboard.com

Chart Creator Digital Performer. Mark of the Unicorn, Cambridge, Mass. www.motu.com/english/software/dp/body.html

Director. Macromedia, San Francisco, Calif. www.macromedia.com/software/director/

Excel. Microsoft, Redmond, Wash. www.microsoft.com/office/excel/default.htm

Finale. Coda Music Technology, Eden Prairie, Minn. www.codamusic.com
Instant Messenger. America Online, Dulles, Va.www.aol.com/aim/home.
  html
Perception. Question Mark, Stamford, Conn. www.questionmark.com
PowerPoint. Microsoft, Redmond, Wash. www.microsoft.com/powerpoint/
  default.htm
QuickTime. Apple, Cupertino, Calif. www.apple.com/quicktime/
WebCT. WebCT, Peabody, Mass. www.webct.com

REFERENCES

Benward, Bruce, and Timothy Kolosick. 2000. *Ear Training: A Technique for Listening.* 6th ed. New York: McGraw-Hill.

Brown, David G. 2000. The Jury Is In!: Computer-Enhanced Instruction Works. *Syllabus* 14, no. 1:22.

———. 2000b. The Low-Hanging Fruit. *Syllabus* 14, no. 4:28.

Clarke, R. E. 1985. Confounding in Educational Computing Research. *Journal of Educational Computing Research* 1, no. 2:137–148.

Cohen, Steve, and Barbara McMullen. 2000. Shifts in Thinking: A Primer on the Foundations of Instructional Technology Assessment. *Syllabus* 13, no. 6:12–14.

Fortney, Pat. 1994. Annual meeting of the Association for Technology in Music Instruction, Savannah, Ga.

Goddard, 1998. Annual meeting of the Association for Technology in Music Instruction, Fajardo, Puerto Rico.

Hofstetter, Fred T. 1988. *Computer Literacy for Musicians.* Englewood Cliffs, N.J.: Prentice-Hall.

Kindred, Janis. 1993. Annual meeting of the Association for Technology in Music Instruction, Minneapolis, Minn.

Knowlton, Dave S., Heather M. Knowlton, and Camela Davis. 2000. The Whys and Hows of Online Discussion. *Syllabus* 13, no. 10: 54–58.

Kulik, James A. 1994. Meta-analytic Studies of Findings on Computer-Based Instruction. In *Technology Assessment in Education and Training,* edited by E. L. Baker and H. F. O'Neil, 9–33. Hillsdale, N.J.: Erlbaum.

Lake, William E. 1999. Online Class Discussion: Talk Around the Clock. Paper presented at the annual meeting of the Association for Technology in Music Instruction, Denver, Colo.

McGee, Deron. 1993. Annual meeting of the Association for Technology in Music Instruction, Minneapolis, Minn.

National Association of Schools of Music. 1999. *1999–2000 Handbook.* Reston, Va.: NASM.

Negrino, Tom. 2000. The MacWorld Web Searcher's Companion. *MacWorld*, May, 76–82.

Ottenhoff, John, and David Lawrence. 1999. Ten Paradoxical Truths about Conference Software in the Classroom. *Syllabus* 13, no. 3: 54–57.

Perelman, Lewis J. 1992. *School's Out: A Radical New Formula for the Revitalization of America's Education System*. New York: William Morrow.

Peterson, Larry. 1993. Annual meeting of the Association for Technology and Music Instruction, Minneapolis, Minn.

———. 1998. Annual meeting of the Association for Technology and Music Instruction, Fajardo, Puerto Rico.

Reese, Sam, Frederick Burrack, Jason Meltzer, and Richard Repp. 1998. Development and Evaluation of a Multi-Media Web Site to Support Professional Development in Music Education Technology. Paper presented at the national conference of the Association for Technology in Music Instruction, Fajardo, Puerto Rico.

Schaffer, John W. 1990. Intelligent Tutoring Systems: New Realms in CAI? *Music Theory Spectrum* 12, no. 2: 224–335.

———. 1991. A Harmony-Based Heuristic Model for Use in Intelligent Tutoring System. *Journal of Music Theory Pedagogy* 5, no. 1: 25–46.

Sullivan, Patricia. 1994. Computer Technology and Collaborative Learning. In *Collaborative Learning: Underlying Processes and Effective Techniques*, edited by K. Bosworth and S. J. Hamilton, 59–68. New Directions for Teaching and Learning no. 59. San Francisco: Jossey-Bass.

Taube, Heinrich. 1999. Automatic Tonal Analysis: Toward the Implementation of a Music Theory Workbench. *Computer Music Journal* 23, no. 4: 18–32.

Walls, Kimberly. 1996. Music Instruction Systems in the Year 2006. Paper presented at the national conference of the Association for Technology in Music Instruction, Atlanta, Ga.

Webster, Peter. 1993. Music Technology 101: Designing a Basic Course for the Undergraduate Music Curriculum. Paper presented at the national conference of the Association for Technology and Music Instruction, Minneapolis, Minn.

Williams, David. 1993. Finding the Shortest Distance between Music Content and Multi-Media Software Development. Paper presented at the national conference of the Association for Technology and Music Instruction, Minneapolis, Minn.

NOTES

This chapter is a guide to employing existing technology to enhance teaching and learning. It is not a guide to programming, to building a lab, or merely a collection of product reviews. Technology evolves very quickly. New hardware and software come out every year. Improvements to existing hardware and software occur every few months. Any recommendation of specific items for purchase would have to be updated at least annually. Although I do mention some specific software, my primary goal is to provide a framework for thinking about technology in music instruction and useful criteria for selecting among products. These concepts may then be applied to whatever is available at the time you are considering adopting a technology.

1. After all, math and science have their Unix systems, and graphic artists and designers have their SGI workstations. Why should music be denied its own specialty platform?

2. I have found that within a half hour I can teach students enough about Finale to enable them to note-process SATB chorales. No doubt the fact that the instruction is hands on improves retention. I also provide a handout for later reference.

3. It is instructive to realize that many fine music-software products (Music Printer Plus, NoteWriter, Vision, to name a few) have failed to survive the intense competition in the marketplace. They may have been easy to learn, reasonably sophisticated, and had loyal followings, but that was not enough. A similar fate could befall the current industry leaders.

4. Published by the Voyager Company, these are now out of print. The closest thing to them available nowadays are the CD-ROMs accompanying some music-appreciation texts. With a little ingenuity, these may be adapted for use in a theory class.

5. Help facilities built into software itself and/or independent training sites on the Web may supplement on-campus training, but will probably not suffice on their own. Two good Web sites for instruction on how to use a web browser are www.extension.umn.edu/media/module0 (that is a zero on the end) and www.learnthenet.com.

6. She was referring to music-appreciation classes, but I believe the point has broader application.

7. I tested this claim using the "course builder" wizard in version 3.0 to set up a syllabus, communication tools, grade book, and one content module. It actually took me twenty-two minutes. Many variables affect the time involved, so results may differ. If you want only one or two tools, the time could be cut to less than fifteen minutes. However, a completely online course is a massive undertaking. It might take five hundred hours for an expert to construct such a course.

8. To experience some excellent examples, visit Tim Smith's (University of Northern Arizona) online course materials (jau.ucc.nau.edu/~tas3).

9. D&PS should not be construed as satisfying the NASM (1999) technology recommendations. Good D&PS should not require students to read

manuals but should be intuitive to grasp, with what little written instructions it requires supplied onscreen. Students need to know only how to turn the computer on and how to use a mouse in order to operate it. Thus, they learn little about the computer as a tool for the professional musician when they are merely end users of D&PS.

10. Such programs are often referred to as "intelligent tutoring systems."

EPILOGUE

This book began with a discussion of the relevance of music theory to the undergraduate curriculum. It might well end on the same subject, for some part of the activities of the lower-division theory program touch virtually every aspect of a music major's undergraduate course work. In a broad sense the freshman and sophomore theory courses are the basic musicianship components of the curriculum. The word *theory*, however, remains the appropriate term for these courses. To use the term *musicianship* or *comprehensive musicianship* to describe theory courses, no matter how innovative the approach, implies that students will learn musicianship in these courses, if nowhere else.

Obviously, musicianship is of major concern in the applied-music studio, in the conducting class, and in all performing groups, as well as in theory, counterpoint, and composition. But no single component of the curriculum has exclusive rights to the word, for musicianship should be an integral part of much of our activity throughout the undergraduate program. Thus, music theory may and should enter into other parts of the curriculum. An organ or harpsichord teacher often deals with figured bass, for example, and music history and literature cannot be adequately comprehended without frequent reference to theoretical concepts.

The theory class, however, exists to impart those skills that can be called *basic* to musicianship. Sight-singing, ear-training, part-writing, analysis, and keyboard harmony are all prerequisites to fulfilling one's potential as a musician. The primal underlying principles of any art or craft can quite rightly be called its theory. Thus, *music theory* remains the proper term for these lower-division courses. Theory also continues to be studied at the graduate level, and not only by music theorists, for music theory is employed in some fashion in virtually all musicological studies.

Yet it is an almost impossibly broad term, this *music theory*. In the course of this book I have used it to encompass all of the elements of musical craft except pure performance technique, as well as the analytical and conceptual tools of the musical scholar. Can one really squeeze all of this into the two-year theory program? Perhaps not. It should be noted that my intention was to present a sort of universe of possibilities, many of which are essential in my eyes but of which some are no more than interesting options for inclusion. I am not sure, for example, that I would include accompaniment improvisation or popular arranging if I were designing a new theory program. This would depend upon the nature of the school, the orientation of the students, and my own special background. Yet these are possibilities that might prove to be quite significant in the appropriate curriculum.

Throughout this book I have tried to express my belief in the importance of *musicality* in the theory class—the idea that the theory teacher should be as much an example of fine musicianship as is the studio teacher or the conductor. This notion—along with the precepts and examples on how teaching and learning occur—that is what the book is about. If I have communicated this in such a way as to be helpful to present and future theory teachers, then I count the book a success. My ultimate objective, of course, is musical learning by the music students themselves, who I hope will find theory courses to be relevant, challenging, and musically rewarding.

To the readers of this book, most of whom will be graduate students of music theory pedagogy, I address my heartfelt encouragement to experiment with musical learning as their talents and inclinations lead them. Let the warmth of the musical experience and music making of every kind continue to be a joy in the theory classroom, as well as in the concert hall.

BIBLIOGRAPHY

Elkind, David. *Children and Adolescents: Interpretive Essays on Jean Piaget.* New York: Oxford University Press, 1970.

"Eulogy to Barney Childs." *Newsletter of the Society of Composers, Inc.*, winter 2000.

Forte, Allen. "A Theory of Set-Complexes for Music." *Journal of Music Theory* 8 (1964): 136–183.

Fuller, Ramon. "A Structuralist Approach to the Diatonic Scale." *Journal of Music Theory* 19, no. 2 (fall 1975): 182–210.

Fux, Johann Joseph. *Steps to Parnassus.* Translated by Alfred Mann. New York: Norton, 1943.

Goodman, Paul. *Growing Up Absurd.* New York: Knopf, 1960.

Hallahan, Daniel P., and William M. Cruikshank. *Psychoeducational Foundations of Learning Disabilities.* Englewood Cliffs, N.J.: Prentice Hall, 1973.

McHose, Allen Irvine. *The Contrapuntal and Harmonic Technique of the Eighteenth Century.* New York: Appleton-Century-Crofts, 1947.

Piaget, Jean. *Apprentisage et connaisance (premiére et seconde parties).* Paris: Presses Universitaires de France, 1959.

———. "Development and Learning." In *Piaget Rediscovered*, edited by R. E. Ripple and V. N. Rockcastle. Ithaca, N.Y.: School of Education, Cornell University, 1964.

———. *Structuralism.* Translated by Chanina Maschler. New York: Harper Torchbooks, 1971.

Read, Gardner. *Music Notation.* Boston: Crescendo, 1969.

Salzer, Felix, and Carl Schacter. *Counterpoint in Composition.* New York: McGraw-Hill, 1969.

Zarlino, Gioseffo. *The Art of Counterpoint.* Translated by Guy Marco and Claude Palisca. New Haven, Conn.: Yale University Press, 1968.

BIBLIOGRAPHY OF SELECTED
THEORY TEACHING MATERIALS

The annotations are designed to furnish some information regarding the contents of these texts, but to avoid value judgments or recommendations. Publications prior to 1970 are included only if they are out-of-print classics or have been revised or reproduced in recent subsequent editions. The reader must recognize that, since new publications are constantly proliferating, a bibliography such as this must be constantly updated and should be viewed only as a rough guide.

MATERIALS FOR SIGHT-SINGING
AND EAR-TRAINING

Benward, Bruce. *Sight Singing Complete*. Dubuque, Iowa: Brown, 1967. Unaccompanied melodies composed by the author and arranged according to degree of difficulty—all modes, fixed and movable do, letter names.

———. *Workbook in Advanced Ear-Training*. Dubuque, Iowa: Brown, 1974. Designed as a complete college ear-training course using such traditional materials as four-part harmonizations.

Berger, Melvin. *Elements of Choral Performance*. New York: Fox, 1975. A beginning approach to musical notation and sight-singing.

Berkowitz, Sol. *A New Approach to Sight-Singing*. First edition by Gabriel Frontier and Leo Kraft. New York: Norton, 1960. Subsequent editions exist. Unaccompanied melodies composed by the authors and arranged according to degree of difficulty. Chapter 2 contains modulations, and accompaniments are added in subsequent chapters.

Bowles, Richard W. *Sight-Singing Achievement Test*. Rockville Center, N.Y.: Belwin Mills, 1971. A short test consisting of sight-singing melodies in the key of C rapidly increasing in complexity (rhythmic and pitch) over two pages.

Brooks, Richard, and Gerald Warfield. *Layer Dictation*. New York: Longman,

1978. Bach-chorale approach to harmonic dictation in a programmed learning workbook. Time-proven method beginning with pure triads, gradually fleshing out texture until student progresses to complete Bach chorale (from background to foreground). Stems from same reductive principles as does Schenkerian analysis.

Delone, Richard. *Literature and Materials for Sight-Singing*. New York: Holt, 1981. A comprehensive sight-singing text using a wide variety of traditional, classical, folk, ethnic, and contemporary music by composers from the Middle Ages to the present. Arranged according to difficulty and including unaccompanied melodies, ensemble music, and accompanied melodies in different media.

Edlund, Lars. *Modus Vetus: Sight-Singing and Ear-Training in Major/Minor Tonality*. Translated and revised by Alan Stout. New York: Broude, 1974. Four sections: melody reading, rhythmic reading, figured bass, and keyboard harmony. Songs with Swedish texts.

Gottschalk, Arthur, and Phillip Kloeckner. *Functional Hearing*. New York: Ardsley House, 1997. Sight-singing and ear-training text in workbook format. Musical examples composed by the authors and examples from common practice literature. Uses movable Do. Instructor's manual available.

Hindemith, Paul. *Elementary Training for Musicians*. New York: Associated Music, 1949. Three parts: action in time, action in space, coordinated action. Approaches rhythm first, then harmony, then puts them together.

Kazez, Daniel. *Rhythm Reading*, 2d ed. New York: Norton, 1997. Innovative and comprehensive approach to rhythmic reading based in part upon the concept of "rhythmic cells" presented in *Guidelines for College Teaching of Music Theory* by John D. White (Metuchen, N.J.: Scarecrow, 1981).

Kodály, Zoltán. *Elementary Exercises in Sight-Singing*. Edited and annotated by Percy M. Young. New York: Boosey and Hawkes, 1963. Beginning sight-singing exercises composed by the author, arranged in order of difficulty.

Sherman, Robert W. *Aural Comprehension in Music*. New York: McGraw-Hill, 1972. A lower-division ear-training text that emphasizes aural understanding of music of the classical repertoire.

Trubitt, Allen R., and Robert S. Hines. *Ear-Training and Sight-Singing*. Books I and II. New York: Schirmer, 1980. An integrated approach combining workbook with text and with tape-recorded examples. Music from a variety of sources, primarily the classical repertoire. Includes ensemble music and innovative teaching approaches.

MATERIALS FOR KEYBOARD SKILLS

This section does not include the numerous texts designed for classroom-piano and functional-piano class.

Duckworth, Guy. *Keyboard Musicianship*. New York: Free Press, 1970. Emphasizes sight-reading, improvisation, transposition, and harmonization. Contains solo and duet music. For nonkeyboard music majors.

Foxley, William M., and Barbara R. Lowe. *Piano Study Guide and Workbook*. Provo, Utah: Brigham Young University, 1975. Beginning keyboard theory manual with worksheets for notation. Modulation, transposition, sight-reading, and piano repertoire at end of book.

Hunt, Reginald. *Harmony at the Keyboard*. London: Oxford University Press, 1970. Improvising melody harmonizations, realizing figured and unfigured bass, reading open score, and converting to piano style.

Lloyd, Ruth, and Norman Lloyd. *Creative Keyboard Musicianship*. New York: Dodd, Mead, 1975. Ear-training, transposition, and keyboard harmony including altered chords and secondary function. Emphasizes improvisation.

Melcher, Robert A., and Willard Warch. *Music for Score Reading*. Englewood Cliffs, N.J.: Prentice-Hall, 1971. Emphasizes reading of full orchestra score. Transposition and reading of seven clefs. Essentially an anthology of orchestral examples for score-reading practice. Subsequent second volume, *Advanced Music for Score Reading*.

MATERIALS FOR WRITING
SKILLS AND CONCEPTS

Aldwell, Edward, and Carl Schachter. *Harmony and Voice Leading*. 2 vols. New York: Harcourt Brace Jovanovich, 1979. Deals exclusively with eighteenth- and nineteenth-century music with emphasis upon the linear aspects of music (without using Schenkerian notation) as well as the vertical harmonic. Many musical examples and exercises based on materials composed by the authors.

Benjamin, Thomas, Michael Horvitt, and Robert Nelson. *Techniques and Materials of Tonal Music*. Boston: Houghton Mifflin, 1979. Rudiments in opening section followed by a common-practice approach with figured bass, part-writing, and so forth. Many assignments using materials composed by the authors, but also many eighteenth- and nineteenth-century musical examples. Final section on form and analysis.

Benward, Bruce. *Practical Beginning Theory*. Dubuque, Iowa: Brown, 1963. High school or freshman level, based on four-part choral texture with exercises composed by the author. Many subsequent editions.

Christ, William. *Materials and Structures of Music*. 2 vols. Englewood Cliffs, N.J.: Prentice Hall, 1966. A compositional and analytical approach to theory with many musical examples. Later editions.

Cooper, Paul. *Perspectives in Music Theory*. New York: Dodd, Mead, 1973. A historical-analytical approach spanning music from the Middle Ages to the twentieth century. Concepts and writing skills evolve from the study of music literature.

Duckworth, William. *Theoretical Foundations of Music.* Belmont, Calif.: Wadsworth, 1978. Four sections: Basic Parameters of Music, Tonal System, Extended Tonality, and Alternatives to Tonality. Nonintegrative, but with musical examples from the Middle Ages to the twentieth century. Uses term "parametric analysis."

Forte, Allen. *Tonal Harmony in Concept and Practice,* 3d ed. New York: Holt, Rinehart, 1978. Traditional approach based upon common practice. Emphasizes part-writing and figured bass. Many musical examples from the eighteenth and nineteenth centuries.

Harder, Paul. *Harmonic Materials in Tonal Music.* 2 vols. Boston: Allyn & Bacon, 1978. A programmed text that is essentially a workbook with commentary and guidance. Uses common-practice approach with conventional part-writing procedures. Contains musical examples.

Kohs, Ellis B. *Musical Composition, Projects in Ways and Means.* Metuchen, N.J.: Scarecrow, 1980. Step-by-step approach to composing in twentieth-century styles.

Kostka, Steven. *An Introduction to Tonal Harmony.* New York: Random House, 1981. A comprehensive survey of concepts and writing of the common practice period. Many musical examples. Separate workbook. Self-tests. Three-, four-, and five-part writings.

Kraft, Leo. *Gradus.* New York: Norton, 1976. Comprehensive theory text with emphasis on writing skills and analysis. Accompanying anthology in two volumes.

Lester, Joel. *Harmony in Tonal Music, Volume One: Diatonic Practices.* New York: Knopf, 1982. Modified Schenkerian approach to harmony and voice leading. Flexible stylistic approach, primarily related to eighteenth-century music in chorale and keyboard textures. Workbook included.

McHose, Allen Irvine. *Basic Principles of the Technique of 18th and 19th Century Composition.* New York: Appleton-Century-Crofts, 1951. Designed to develop the musical thought processes by correlating keyboard harmony, dictation, sight-singing, and part-writing. No subsequent editions. (Out of print.)

――――. *The Contrapuntal Harmonic Technique of the 18th Century.* New York: Appleton-Century-Crofts, 1947. A part-writing text with special emphasis upon the chorales of J. S. Bach. Although the book contains earlier and later music, the student learns to compose in a style distilled from that of Bach. No subsequent editions. (Out of print.)

Norden, Hugo. *Fundamental Harmony.* Boston: Crescendo, 1971. Concentrates on writing skills, especially part-writing.

Ottman, Robert W. *Elementary Harmony.* 2d ed. Englewood Cliffs, N.J.: Prentice Hall, 1970. Based on the theory of the common practice period with many part-writing exercises. Suggestions for ear-training in an integrated approach. Musical examples and additional sources suggested.

Persichetti, Vincent. *Twentieth Century Harmony*. New York: Norton, 1961. Survey of mid-twentieth-century compositional practice. Emphasizes creativity in various styles. Possible supplement to second-year theory text.

Piston, Walter. *Harmony*, 4th ed. Revised and expanded by Mark DeVoto. New York: Norton, 1976. Standard source for harmonic common practice. Numerous exercises and examples. Assumes integration of musical skills but does not include them.

Read, Gardner. *Music Notation*, 2d. ed. Boston: Crescendo, 1969. The classic guide to modern music notation—still valuable in spite of twenty-first-century music software.

Schoenberg, Arnold. *Theory of Harmony*. New York: Philosophical Library, 1948. A creative approach to traditional harmony. Contains no exercises. Students are expected to make their own, creating harmony as they learn it. Stimulates students to explore beyond author's views.

Sessions, Roger. *Harmonic Practice*. New York: Harcourt, Brace, 1951. Exercises composed by author in a unique approach to the study of harmony. Not a common-practice or even tonal-harmony textbook. Everything is perceived in terms of twentieth century.

Siegmeister, Elie. *Harmony and Melody*. Belmont, Calif.: Wadsworth, 1965. A workbook of rudiments based on exercises composed by the author.

White, John D. *Theories of Musical Texture in Western History*. New York: Garland, 1995. A study of major theoretical treatises from Pythagoras to the present.

MATERIALS FOR MUSIC ANALYSIS

Berry, Wallace. *Form in Music*. Englewood Cliffs, N.J.: Prentice Hall, 1966. A comprehensive survey of forms and analytical terminology primarily dealing with eighteenth- and nineteenth-century music. Many musical examples.

Crocker, Richard L. *A History of Musical Style*. New York: McGraw-Hill, 1966. A study of style from A.D. 700 to early twentieth century. Merges historical and theoretical concepts in an analytical approach.

Green, Douglass M. *Form in Tonal Music*. New York: Holt, Rinehart, 1965. Hierarchical approach to forms of the common practice period. Starts with motive and phrase and expands to sonata form, concerto, fugue, and unique forms. One chapter on analytical methodology.

Hutcheson, Jere T. *Musical Form and Analysis*. 2 vols. Boston: Allyn & Bacon,

1972. A programmed text in basic elements of musical form. Many musical examples.

Hutchings, Arthur. *The Baroque Concerto*. London: Faber and Faber, 1961. Historical/analytical approach to the development of Baroque concerto forms.

Larue, Jan. *Guidelines for Style Analysis*. New York: Norton, 1970. Unique approach to the study of style, purporting to merge the elements of music. So-called SHMRG approach.

Leichtentritt, Hugo. *Musical Form*. Cambridge, Mass.: Harvard University Press, 1965. Detailed explication of forms from Jewish and Gregorian chant to Schoenberg. Historical emphasis with hierarchical organization from phrase to sonata form.

Lester, Joel. *Analytic Approaches to Twentieth Century Music*. New York: Norton, 1989. Emphasis upon set-theoretical approaches and serial music. One concluding chapter on music since World War Two.

Nadeau, Roland, and William Tesson. *Form in Music: Process and Procedure*. Boston: Crescendo, 1974. Short book divided into two sections—polyphonic and homophonic. Many examples.

Salzer, Felix. *Structural Hearing, Tonal Coherence in Music*. 2 vols. New York: Boni, 1952. Standard English source for examples and explanation of Schenkerian analysis. Volume 2 presents examples of analyses, foreground on bottom in pyramidal approach.

Tovey, Donald Francis. *Essays in Musical Analysis*. 6 vols. London: Oxford University Press, 1935–1939. Explanations of forms and cut-and-dried analyses. A standard reference. I. Symphonies; II. Symphonies, Variations, and Orchestral, Polyphony; III. Concertos; IV. Illustrative Music; V. Vocal Music; VI. Supplemental Essays. Glossary of analytical terminology.

———. *The Forms of Music*. London: Oxford University Press, 1957. Articles on form from the *Encyclopaedia Britannica*.

Walton, Charles W. *Basic Forms in Music*. New York: Alfred, 1974. Straightforward format with many musical examples and recommended assignments.

White, John D. *The Analysis of Music*. Englewood Cliffs, N.J.: Prentice Hall, 1976. A textbook for analytical methodology combined with discussion of normative formal structures. Emphasizes the interdependence of the musical elements.

———. *Comprehensive Musical Analysis*, Metuchen, N.J.: Scarecrow, 1994. Analytical approach integrating all of the musical elements including timbre, texture, and dynamics.

MUSIC ANTHOLOGIES

Apel, Willi, and A. T. Davison. *Historical Anthology of Music*. 2 vols. Cambridge, Mass.: Harvard University Press, 1946–1949. Examples of Medieval and Renaissance music of Europe and Asia. Includes some oriental examples. A classic.

Arlin, Mary I., Charles Lord, Arthur Ostrander, and Marjorie Porterfield. *Music Sources*. Englewood Cliffs, N.J.: Prentice Hall, 1979. Includes excerpts and complete movements of Western music from the fifteenth to the twentieth centuries.

Benjamin, Thomas, Michael Horvitt, and Robert Nelson. *Music for Analysis*. Boston: Houghton Mifflin, 1978. Complete movements of music from the common practice period and the twentieth century. Variety of media.

Brandt, William, Arthur Corra, William Christ, Richard Delone, and Allen Winold. *The Comprehensive Study of Music*. New York: Harper's College Press, 1977. Five volumes of music in a variety of media from all periods. Primarily from Western cultures.

Burkhart, Charles. *Anthology for Musical Analysis*. New York: Holt, Rinehart, 1964. Still in print in many subsequent editions. A comprehensive selection of complete musical examples in a wide variety of media from the Middle Ages to the present.

Gleason, Harold. *Examples of Music Before 1400*. New York: Appleton-Century-Crofts, 1942. A classic collection of liturgical chant, organum, conductus, and other examples of pre-Renaissance music from Western culture.

Godwin, Jocelyn. *Schirmer Scores*. Cambridge, Mass.: Harvard University Press, 1975. Full scores of standard-repertoire orchestral works.

Kamien, Roger. *The Norton Scores*. New York: Norton, 1972. Two volumes of full scores of standard-repertoire works from all periods.

Kraft, Leo. *Gradus Music Anthology*. New York: Norton, 1976. Complete movements and excerpts in two volumes for use with theory text *Gradus*, by same author.

Palisca, Claude. *Norton Anthology of Western Music*. New York: Norton, 1980. Two volumes of complete examples from all periods conceived as a supplement to Grout's *A History of Western Music*.

Von Wasielewski, Wilhem Joseph. *Anthology of Instrumental Music from the End of the 16th Century to the End of the 17th Century*. New York: Da Capo, 1974. A small selection of seventeenth-century instrumental music.

Walton, Charles W. *Music Literature for Analysis and Study*. Belmont, Calif.: Wadsworth, 1973. Excerpts and examples from Baroque period to twentieth century.

Ward, William R. *Examples for the Study of Musical Style*. Dubuque, Iowa: Brown, 1970. A large selection of musical examples from all periods.

Wennerstron, Mary H. *Anthology of Twentieth Century Music*. Englewood Cliffs, N.J.: Prentice Hall, 1969. Works by selected twentieth-century composers of Europe and the United States. Biographical annotations and annotations of each work. All in original score form.

INDEX

223

About the Author

John D. White (born 1931) is professor emeritus of the University of Florida and lives in Evergreen, Colorado. Known best as a composer, his music is published by G. Schirmer, E. C. Schirmer, and other publishers and is widely performed. He is also the author of numerous scholarly books on music, the most recent of which is *Theories of Musical Texture in Western History* (Garland Press, 1995), which a reviewer for the library journal *Choice* described as a "milestone in the field" comparable to the *Geschichte der Musik Theorie* by Hugo Riemann. In 1996, White held a Fulbright Research Fellowship to Reykjavik, and in 1997 he was appointed Fellow of the American Scandinavian Foundation for his research on recent Nordic music. Scarecrow Press has also published his *Comprehensive Musical Analysis* (1994); and Pendragon Press will soon publish his *New Music of the Nordic Countries*, a collaborative book project with five authors from the Nordic countries.

White holds a Ph.D. and M.A. in composition and a Performers Certificate in cello from the Eastman School of Music. He received a B.A., magna cum laude, from the University of Minnesota. He has taught composition, theory, and cello at the University of Florida, Kent State University, and Whitman College; and he has served on the music faculties of the University of Michigan and (as visiting professor) at the University of Innsbruck and the University of Wisconsin. For twelve years in midcareer he served as department chair, associate dean, and dean at various institutions.